EntreLeadership

20 YEARS *of* PRACTICAL BUSINESS WISDOM
from the TRENCHES

Shepherd Well!
1 Peter 5:2

EntreLeadership.com

PRAISE FOR *EntreLeadership*

"Dave Ramsey is the real deal. His generosity, insight, and passion come through in every single thing he does."
—Seth Godin, author, Poke the Box

"Dave Ramsey's *EntreLeadership* speaks right to the heart of business leaders, showing not just the how-tos, but also the why-tos that apply to any size business, from a garage-based start-up to a powerhouse market leader. And by the way, I'm the biggest Dave Ramsey acolyte ever!"
—Dr. Arthur B. Laffer, economic advisor to President Ronald Reagan;
founder and chairman, Laffer Associates

"Like Dave, I believe that a business isn't good unless it also *does* good—for its employees, partners, and the community it serves. A business cannot have true success without also having a soul. In this book Dave shows us how to have both: great leaders who are also great people; great companies that are also great families. I plan on applying these lessons to my own small business—I only wish he'd written about them years ago. Entrepreneurs are needed in America now more than ever—but there's a big difference between starting a company and leading one. And there's an even bigger difference between a company that's valuable and one that *has values*. But Dave has figured out the recipe to being both things at once, and his lessons are invaluable. In fact, my only complaint is that if he'd published this a few years ago, he would've saved me a lot of sleepless nights trying to figure this stuff out on my own."
—Glenn Beck, #1 New York Times bestselling author

"Dave Ramsey has taken commonsense leadership principles and made them uncommonly practical, useful, and life changing. His straightforward and plain-talk approach is refreshing. Even more admirable is that his advice is not a bunch of leadership froufrou fluff, but it's solid and substantive. Millions listen to Dave Ramsey and are smarter and more free for doing it. Wouldn't it be great if we could get Congress on a steady diet of Dave Ramsey? Oh well, you can be smarter than Congress when you read this book!"
—Mike Huckabee, former governor, FOX News host

"Every entrepreneur is searching for the elusive formula that perfectly blends the creativity of the start-up with the leadership qualities to guide a growing team. Dave Ramsey reveals the ingredients in *EntreLeadership,* a guide for the complete business leader."

—S. Truett Cathy, founder and CEO, Chick-fil-A, Inc.

"Throughout my career, I've been blessed to spend time with millions of quality leaders at practically every level of every industry—and I haven't met one yet that could not benefit from the clear, practical business principles Dave lays out in *EntreLeadership!*"

—Dr. John C. Maxwell, *New York Times* bestselling author; www.johnmaxwell.com

"I have always said, 'Wisdom equals knowledge plus scars.' Having been an entrepreneur for almost thirty years, I have learned some things intuitively and others the proverbial hard way. In an effort to reduce the number of 'hard way' lessons, I began really listening to the wisdom of others who had been successful in the arenas I wanted to enter. Because success in any area of your life is not accidental—at least, not for long. I had a passion to be a good husband and father, so I picked the brains of couples with strong marriages and parents with children who were people of character. If it is your passion to be successful in business, it would be foolish not to listen to the wisdom of someone who has done so for decades. As I read, I kept thinking, *Yes! This is right on the money!* Great job, Dave!"

—Jeff Foxworthy, comedian, television and radio personality, author

"Dave Ramsey is a straight-shooting, no-nonsense, faith-anchored blessing to our world. Each time he speaks, millions of us listen up and learn. Now, we have an opportunity to learn even more. Dave leads one of America's most successful organizations. He has built it upon repeatable, godly principles. Learn from his commonsense counsel. You'll be glad you did."

—Max Lucado, *New York Times* bestselling author

"How do I know Dave Ramsey's *EntreLeadership* book can help every small business? Because my son, as CEO of our company, attended Dave's EntreLeadership ultimate business experience and applied the principles in our company with dramatic results. The

difference is bigger than black and white—the difference is between red and black!"
—Zig Ziglar, motivational speaker, *New York Times* bestselling author

"Over a thousand Hobby Lobby employees have proudly benefited from Financial Peace University for several years. Now I am excited to learn about *EntreLeadership,* which provides great insight on how to become a successful entrepreneur leader. Dave Ramsey's at it again using the same Bible-based, commonsense approach that has worked for *Financial Peace,* now in *EntreLeadership."*
—David Green, CEO and founder, Hobby Lobby, Inc.

"I love this book! One minute Dave sounds like a Harvard prof, and the next minute he is coming at you like an alley fighter! Either way you will wind up being a better leader."
—Bill Hybels, senior pastor, Willow Creek Community Church; chairman of the board, Willow Creek Association

"Dave Ramsey has become the most recognized master teacher of financial literacy of our generation, and he continues his remarkable influence with his latest book. *EntreLeadership* outlines a proven model for creating and sustaining a successful organization from the top, down. His willingness to share personal accounts of successes and failures and the lessons he has learned makes *EntreLeadership* a must-read for all leaders who aspire to make a significant positive change in our society."
—Dan T. Cathy, president and chief operating officer, Chick-fil-A, Inc.

"We absorb some books like coffee absorbs sugar; it is still coffee—just sweeter. But you will connect to *EntreLeadership* the way hydrogen connects to oxygen. Through a brilliant bonding process, two separate elements become one exciting new thing—water—that provides life and power. In *exactly* the same way, you and this book will together bond into something new—a passionate and powerful Dave Ramsey EntreLeader!"
—Rabbi Daniel Lapin, radio and television personality; author, *Thou Shall Prosper*

"With the skill of your favorite storyteller, Dave Ramsey has created an anointed blueprint for the kind of leader you and I want to be. *EntreLeadership* is the best book on this subject you'll ever read! *EntreLeadership* is a simple masterpiece of uncommon clarity. Dave Ramsey has created a pathway that you and I will be excited to follow for the rest of our lives. I'm getting started with these principles today!"

—Andy Andrews, *New York Times* bestselling author,
The Traveler's Gift

"From the first sentence of Dave's book, I was nodding my head in agreement. As somewhat of an entrepreneur myself, having started four different businesses, I identified with what Dave was saying. My first thought was that I sure wish I had had this book forty-two years ago when I started my first business. It would've saved me many mistakes and a lot of heartache. Dave is extraordinarily gifted as a communicator at all levels, and you will be inspired, challenged, and helped immeasurably by this book."

—Ron Blue, entrepreneur; founder, Ronald Blue & Co., LLC

"Dave combines his experience—good and bad—energy, and expertise to help those who want to improve their leadership, increase their reach, enlarge their impact, and to think beyond themselves. His humor, energy, and wisdom, combined with his excellent presentation, results in a proven product. I am confident if you apply 20 percent of what *EntreLeadership* offers, it will change your life."

—Dr. Michael Easley, former president, Moody Bible Institute;
lead pastor, Fellowship Bible Church, Nashville

"You know Dave Ramsey as the financial genius on television and radio who doles out those excruciatingly practical nuggets of wisdom. But there's way more to Dave than financial advice. Meet Dave Ramsey, the business pioneer and entrepreneur. Dave leads a world-class organization filled with some of the sharpest young leaders you will find anywhere. And in *EntreLeadership*, he tells us how he did it. Thanks, Dave!"

—Andy Stanley, founding pastor, North Point Community Church

EntreLeadership

*20 Years of Practical Business
Wisdom from the Trenches*

Dave Ramsey

HOWARD BOOKS
An Imprint of Simon & Schuster, Inc.
New York   Nashville   London   Toronto   Sydney   New Delhi

Howard Books
An Imprint of Simon & Schuster, Inc.
1230 Avenue of the Americas
New York, NY 10020

First Howard Books hardcover edition September 2011

HOWARD and colophon are registered trademarks of Simon & Schuster, Inc.

For information about special discounts for bulk purchases,
please contact Simon & Schuster Special Sales at 1-866-506-1949
or business@simonandschuster.com.

The Simon & Schuster Speakers Bureau can bring authors to your
live event. For more information or to book an event, contact the
Simon & Schuster Speakers Bureau at 1-866-248-3049 or visit our
website at www.simonspeakers.com.

Designed by Davina Mock-Maniscalco

Manufactured in the United States of America

20

Library of Congress Cataloging-in-Publication Data

Ramsey, Dave.
   Entreleadership : 20 years of practical business wisdom from the trenches /
Dave Ramsey.
     p.   cm.
1. Entrepreneurship. 2. Leadership. 3. Executive ability. 4. Success in business.
I. Title.
   HD57.7.R365 2011
   658.4'21—dc23   2011016820

ISBN 978-1-4516-1785-6
ISBN 978-1-4516-4601-6 (ebook)

*To the men and women of the Dave Ramsey Team.
Your dedication to "Work That Matters"
and doing that work with excellence while maintaining
love for each other inspires me every day.
Louis Falzetti, Matt Woodburn, and Bill Hampton,
my band of brothers, you have been true friends, comrades,
and warriors. Team, we have built something very rare
together; continue to breathe that "Rare Air."*

Acknowledgments

This book project has had so many hands lift it up that there is no possible way to create a proper list for a proper thank-you. But thank you to all who have pushed and lifted this project from the first day.

Simon & Schuster team:

Carolyn Reidy for believing we could do something big

Liz Perl, marketing genius

Jonathan Merkh, who would not take no for an answer

Becky Nesbitt, a fabulous editor who became a friend in the process

The Dave Ramsey team:

Sharon Ramsey, my first and only partner, advisor, friend, and wife

Bill Hampton, for spearheading this whole project

Allen Harris, a huge help with the writing and editing process

Jen Sievertsen, our marketing genius

Brian Williams, video extraordinaire

Daniel Bell, graphics/cover art

Blake Thompson, radio producer

Preston Cannon, project coordinator

Beth Tallent, publicity

Too many others to possibly mention

Note to the Reader

The stories, names, and circumstances in this book are from over twenty years in the trenches. The stories, names, and circumstances have been altered to protect anyone involved while staying true to the point or lesson learned. So if you think I was talking about you, as Carly Simon sang, "You're so vain . . ."

Contents

EntreLeadership

Introduction

And So It Begins

Have you ever been broke? I mean, can't pay your electricity so it gets cut off? I mean, have your home days from foreclosure? I mean, worrying about how to buy food for your children? I have.

Have you ever been *broken*? I mean, you set out to live your dream by opening a business and for a while everything goes great, then things start to happen? Bad things start to happen. No matter how hard you work or how smart you are, the dream turns into a nightmare. You invest every ounce of who you are emotionally, spiritually, intellectually, financially, and physically into your dream and it still hits the wall and disintegrates. Have you ever been broken like that? I have.

Over twenty years ago I set out to live the American dream of owning and operating my own business. As a young twenty-something go-getter, I grew my real estate investment business quickly. I started from nothing, and by the time I was twenty-six I had over four million dollars in real estate with over one million dollars' net worth. We owned and/or managed hundreds of rental units, ran three rehab crews, and quickly grew our little empire. However, I had built the business with too much debt and had managed and led poorly. Our primary lender was sold to another bank, and after looking at our situation, they made the fateful decision to limit their risk by calling all our notes—all at once. I spent the next two and a half years losing everything I owned. We were sued a gazillion times, foreclosed on multiple times, and finally went bankrupt. There I sat with a new baby, a toddler, and a marriage hanging by a thread, a broke and broken man. I was so scared and so scarred that I surrendered. Completely.

This is not a book about recovering from failure; although if you are going to lead and/or own a business, you will learn those lessons either in small ways or, sadly, in big ways. However, it is good for you to know the root, the DNA, of our tremendous success in every area of our business in the twenty-plus years following the crash. My total surrender following my failure is at the root of our tremendous success today.

Today we have hundreds of team members, millions of customers, and tens of millions of dollars in revenues. Our company started with very humble beginnings on a card table in my living room, after the total failure during my twenties.

This book is our playbook. I will show you the same methods we use to achieve unusual levels of not only financial success, but more important, tremendous satisfaction and joy from our business. The point is, you can win in business and have a blast doing it.

What you are about to read is not a business and leadership book that is *theory*. This is not a book with formulas based on research. This is a book with principles that were discovered by *experience*. If you look closely at these pages, you will see they are dotted with lots of blood, gallons of sweat, and many tears. This is the personal playbook of an ultra-successful EntreLeader. You are about to learn from me and my team of leaders what we have learned by DOING IT. We are practitioners. When I finish this chapter I will go into a marketing meeting, or a meeting with a problem team member, or a brainstorming session about making our customer service even more excellent. I actually do this "winning at business" thing every single day.

Surrender

So how does my surrender play into our success? I was so broke and broken, at the bottom of that valley, that my personal faith was deepened dramatically. As a Christian I made the decision to run every area of my life as consistently with the Bible as I could. Whoa, don't freak out on me. You are *not* about to enter the Christian theology of business zone. I promise not to pummel you with my faith in the coming pages. However, it is important to relate that once I started over and opened our new business, I decided that I would follow the spirit and the direction of Scripture to operate our business. I am convinced that those principles, woven into the coming pages, are the reason we win.

Even if you aren't a person of faith, you have to believe in hard work or you won't win. You have to believe in treating people like you want to be treated or you won't win. You will discover, as I unpack the principles we follow, they are very akin to common sense. There is very little that is mystical or weird about how we work, except that we win. Whether you are a person of faith or not, you will agree and nod as you read this book.

At the Start

We started our business of teaching people to handle their money on a card table in our living room. We started with one-on-one counseling and some speaking engagements. When all the hours of every day were filled, we decided to hire our first employee. I hired new employees, but I really didn't want employees. As far as I am concerned employees come to work late, leave early, and steal while they are there. None of them work as hard or care as much as I do. So I resisted a normal employee model and relationship. I am very entrepreneurial, so I wanted that spirit on my employees. I resist the standard employee mentality so much that I have quit using the word "employees." I call them team members, and I mean it. I make our leaders and our team use the phrase "team members." What's really weird is that we demand they actually act like team members—members of a team. We want givers in our organization, not takers. Takers leave our group really fast because they don't fit in.

So I hired my first team member, Russ Carroll, to help me with the financial counseling load. We moved our little bit of furniture out of my living room into a U-Haul truck and then to our first little office. I remember busting my knuckles on the door when I was carrying a desk to the truck. That desk is still in our building, and it probably still has somewhat of a bloodstain on it.

We hired a lady to be our secretary, bookkeeper, receptionist, and everything else that needed to be done. With long hours, lots of uncertainty, and passion, we slowly began to grow. We looked up a year or so later and had seven people on our team and had moved to a little better and bigger office. We were still very much pulling ourselves up by our bootstraps. It was at this point, with seven team members, I began to realize the need for developing other people to help me lead. That was a scary thought. Like most young entrepreneurs, I was very confident that I could get the job done and that I could motivate and lead people reporting to me to get the job done. But I was really unsure about letting go of enough control to let someone else lead. We formed our company into three departments (which later became divisions), and I began to pour hours and hours into the three men running those three departments. My goal was for them to be able to know what I would do at any given time in any given situation. The process of mentoring them into the young leaders we needed was slow and thorough. But my trust in those men has grown every day for twenty years, and today, as we have fought and bled together, they are some of my best friends and most trusted advisors.

As we continued to grow, it was time to grow more leaders. At that point we didn't have the luxury of time that my three EVPs and I had when we were growing, so we needed another plan. When in doubt a teacher . . . teaches. I am a teacher. Since I teach people every day how to handle their money, we decided the first thing we needed for growing leaders was a class. I started teaching a class on our operational and cultural playbook. I taught the class from five to six every Tuesday night. Since we close at five thirty, team members who wanted to learn how we run and grow our business could learn thirty minutes on my time and thirty minutes on their time. At first ten or twenty people came. Then my team started asking if spouses or pastors or friends or family members could attend because the content was, and is, so rich. Since we were just running the lessons through the copier and it was easy to add people, we said anyone was welcome. As I taught through the material a couple of times, we saw that we were growing confident and competent leaders. Before we knew it, there were close to a hundred people coming—and most of them didn't even work for us.

The Playbook Is Born

Sometimes I am not very smart, but I quickly realized that so many people yearn to learn how to lead well and to run their own business that we needed to expand the class. So we started teaching, and charging for, a weeklong cram course we now call *The EntreLeadership Master Series*. The response was huge and ultimately the reason for this book. Together in these chapters we are going to work our way through our playbook. The playbook that has caused unbelievable success, the playbook that was birthed in pain, and the playbook that was written one mistake at a time. Our championship team is no accident. We have intentionally built a culture, a value system, and operating principles that cause us to win. The vast majority of the plays in the playbook are from our mistakes. We screwed up, that screwup brought us pain, and we vowed to never get hit that way again.

Making mistakes and learning from them is crucial to winning. Learning from the mistakes of others is less painful. Henry Ford said, "Those who never make mistakes work for those of us who do."

It is this spirit that built America, and it is this spirit that has caused you to pick up this book. If you can relate or want to relate, stay with me and I will show you how to win.

1

EntreLeadership Defined

L ooking out the window of my personal office, I was watching the sun come up. I had come to the office extremely early because I couldn't sleep and I needed some answers. Our business was officially bigger than me and it was scaring the crud out of me. I was going to have to add more layers of leadership, which meant I was going to have to relinquish control or not grow. Sounds simple, but I am a control freak extraordinaire, so turning loose tasks and responsibilities is not easy.

Those of us who are small-business people have stacked our own boxes, answered our own phones, and served our own customers. So making sure business is done the way we would do it matters a *lot* to guys like me. No corporate training program that creates plastic scripts that mannequins spit out, where the customer leaves feeling like something fake just happened. Oh no, guys like me want everyone we come in contact with to feel our dream. We want and demand that customers have an experience. And many of us have had our corporate experience, and we didn't like it. We want something that is real for us, our team, and our customers. So turning loose is a really emotional thing . . . 'cause the person you task with that area really has to breathe air the way you do.

After having mentored and grown my first three key leaders over several years with one-on-one instruction, I was seeing the benefit of growing fellow believers in the cause. But this hand-to-hand method of growing leaders was way too slow and was holding back our business. I needed new leaders and I needed them faster than three years. In order to raise new leaders, my core team and I set out to teach a class that is our playbook on how to do business our way. We mentor, cuss, and discuss with our leaders daily—and in a very intentional way. But the EntreLeadership class is the foundation.

EntreLeader?

Tons of books have been written on growing leaders. There are famous leaders in all walks of life whose leadership principles I have learned from. As I sat that first morning trying to find a way to communicate to our next new leaders what we wanted them to do, I thought it might be as simple as teaching leadership.

What Is a Leader?

When I teach this course live, I ask the audience to picture the face of a wonderful leader. Then I ask them to write down the best one-word character qualities these great leaders have. What one word best describes the character of a great leader? When we do this we always get character qualities like:

• Integrity	• Passionate
• Servant	• Loyal
• Humble	• Listener
• Visionary	• Influential
• Decisive	• Driven
• Disciplined	• Charismatic

Taken together, this is a good definition of leadership. It's interesting to me that most of us can list what we want our leader to look like, but we don't apply it to ourselves. Have you ever asked yourself what kind of leader your team members want? If you want to lead, or you want to grow or hire leaders, they and you must have the above listed character qualities. We all have some of these qualities and we all have some we can work on. The big deal here is to remember that the very things you want from a leader are the very things the people you are leading expect from you. You must intentionally become more of each of these every day to grow yourself and your business. And to the extent you're not doing that, you're failing as a leader.

What Is in a Name?

As I sat in my office with the sun coming up writing the first lesson and thinking what to name our little leadership course, I hit a snag. I know that the title is supposed to give an indication of what is in the material (duh). When I thought about calling this material "leadership," I knew that wasn't right. Because there is so much more to business than simply leadership and leadership theory. I have sat in "management classes" and "leadership seminars," and for a practitioner, a doer, like me, they weren't enough. I learned something, I always do, but those classes were too much about concept for a guy who has stacked his own boxes and answered his own phone. I concluded that I didn't want to grow my business simply with leaders—that was a little too dry, a little too theoretical for an entrepreneur like me.

Entrepreneur

Maybe I was trying to grow entrepreneurs. Maybe I wanted a company full of little mini-mes. After all, when you think of an entrepreneur, what words come to mind to describe that animal?

- Risk taker
- Visionary
- Passionate
- Driven
- Work ethic
- Creative
- Out of the box
- Determined
- Courageous
- Motivated
- Learner
- Maverick

As I thought about what a pure entrepreneur is, I decided in three seconds I didn't want to grow a company full of us. Leading that group would be like herding cats or trying to nail Jell-O to a tree. I do want the spirit of the entrepreneur woven into our cultural DNA, but a whole building full of us would be a really bad plan.

So growing leaders was too refined and calm for me, but growing entrepreneurs was too wild and chaotic for me. So I decided we needed to grow a combination of the two . . . and thus the EntreLeader was born. I want EntreLeaders who can be

- Passionately serving
- Mavericks who have integrity
- Disciplined risk takers
- Courageous while humble
- Motivated visionaries
- Driven while loyal
- Influential learners

Are you getting the idea? We wanted the personal power of the entrepreneur polished and grown by a desire to be a quality leader. We wanted big leaders who have the passion and push of the entrepreneur. These character qualities are what we look for in potential leaders and what we intentionally build into our team every day to cause us to win.

Words matter. So when we call someone a "team member" at our place, that means something; it isn't some corporate HR program that tries to make slaves to jerks feel better by changing the words. It means you will be treated like and expected to act like you are on a team. When we call someone an EntreLeader it means something. It means you are more than a renegade lone ranger and it means you are more than a corporate bureaucrat who treats his people like units of production.

Defined

A leader, according to *Webster's Dictionary,* is "someone who rules, guides, and inspires others." The dictionary says an entrepreneur is "someone who organizes, operates, and assumes risk for a venture." The root of the word "entrepreneur" is a French word, *"entreprendre,"* meaning "one who takes a risk."

So for our purposes EntreLeadership is defined as "the process of leading to cause a venture to grow and prosper."

Once we had our title and definition, we had to determine the components of our playbook. We began to list what is essential for other new and growing EntreLeaders to know about starting, operating, and leading a business the way we do it. Because we are *practitioners* we ended up addressing mechanical things like accounting and contracts. Because we are very concerned about our *culture* as well, we needed to explain how a team is grown, motivated, compensated, and unified. Because we are also *marketers* we knew we needed to sell some stuff in order for all of us to eat. So our playbook has truly become "everything you want to know about building and running a business but didn't know who to ask."

EntreLeadership Basics

Let's start at the beginning: your mirror. John Maxwell has written a wonderful leadership book entitled *The 21 Irrefutable Laws of Leadership.* In this book John discusses one of his laws, the Law of the Lid. Basically he says that there is a lid on my organization and on my future, and that lid is *me.* I am the problem with my company and *you* are the problem with your company. Your education, character, capacity, ability, and vision are limiting your company. You want to know what is holding back your dreams from becoming a reality? Go look in your mirror.

When I first started leading in my early thirties, I was a horrible leader. My ambition and drive caused me to accomplish the task and pick up the pieces later. One cold winter morning when we had about fourteen people on our team, I became angry over people coming to work late. I don't get it—come to work early like I do. Don't come dragging your tail in twenty minutes late and mumble something about traffic. I have noticed there is less traffic before the sun comes up. Get to work on time. I am paying you, and when you don't come to work on time you are a thief.

We were at the beginning stages, and every sale meant our survival. Every customer was a big deal, and every person on the team had three jobs. I couldn't grasp how these people I hired didn't understand that if they slacked off, they would lose their jobs because we would go broke. Get with it. So I got angry. Sometimes it is good to be angry, but what you do with it can have lasting consequences. I am not proud of this, but on that Monday morning, for the staff meeting I moved fourteen chairs out on the sidewalk in sixteen-degree weather. I gave a talk that morning about showing up to work on time and said that if every one of us didn't do two people's work, we were all going to be "out in the cold."

I know those of you who lead and have experienced my frustration are smiling right now, but I will tell you that leading by fear and anger is not leading—it is bad parenting for two-year-olds. And if you "lead" like this, your company will perform like scared two-year-olds. I still to this day deliver the message to our team periodically about our expectations for work ethic, but that message is much more polished and pulls our team rather than pushes them.

So the problem with my company then and now is me. The problem with your company is not the economy, it is not the lack of opportunity, it is not your team. The problem is you. That is the bad news. The good news is, if you're the problem, you're also the solution. You're the one person you can change the easiest. You can decide to grow. Grow your abilities, your character, your education, and your capacity. You can decide who you want to be and get about the business of becoming that person.

I was teaching this lesson to a group of future EntreLeaders, and during the break George came to me to tell me I was wrong. George explained that he was in the drywall business and that there was no one in the workforce who was worth hiring. They were all slackers who didn't work, and when they did work, they did poor work. He stood there red faced explaining to me that the problem with his business was his horrible employees. This big tough construction guy's face got even redder when I told him his "turkey" employees were his fault. "How's that?" he asked with attitude. My answer was simple: he hired the turkeys in the first place, and worse than that, he kept them. His employees are his fault. George continued to argue that with what he pays he can't attract great people. That is your fault, George. Pay more, which means you may have to charge more, which you can do if you don't have to explain away the bad quality and constant drama brought on by having turkeys in your business. Your problems in business are your fault. That is the bad news and the good news.

Here's a great head-to-head comparison of what I'm talking about. Within the same week our team counseled two different guys in the landscape business, both in the same area of town. One was closing his business because he couldn't make a living, saying, "Nobody can make a living in this economy." And the other was having the best income year of his life. They were in the *same* business in the *same* end of town. What was the difference? You're catching on, right? It was the guy at the wheel. The person driving the ship was either a captain or he wasn't. You get to decide what you are. Starting now. Ready, set, go.

From the Top Down

To further motivate you as an EntreLeader you need to know that whatever is happening at the head of the organization will affect the entire body. The Bible says the anointing drops from the beard. In Old Testament days when someone was pronounced king, the Israelites had a tradition of pouring oil (lots of it) over that person's head. The oil symbolized God's spirit being poured over the leader. And the oil that was poured heavily over the head ran down the hair, the beard, onto the rest of the body, symbolizing that as goes the king, so goes the kingdom. That is a great picture for remembering that as the "king" of your business, your personal strengths will be your company's strengths and—you guessed it—your personal weaknesses will be your company's weaknesses.

I grew up in sales, so our company has always been great at marketing and selling. I am very entrepreneurial, so my company tends to be impulsive and too quick to act. We have had to counteract that by honoring and raising up team members who are more strategic in thought and practice. We have had to work with our natural strengths and against our natural weaknesses. And it is all my fault.

I spoke with the son of a billionaire who had been given his father's company. This intelligent and successful EntreLeader had taken his father's billion-dollar company to a three-billion-dollar company in just one decade. He had become more successful than his dad and yet was very respectful and grateful toward his father. He explained to me that the strengths of his father, who founded the company, could take the company only to a certain point, and then new approaches were required. The way he described the situation was, "The quirky brilliance of the founder could take us only so far."

EntreLeaders Are Powerful

To be a real EntreLeader you have to realize you have great power but seldom use it. Having great power and managing it as a tool is what real EntreLeaders do. When you hold the pen over the paycheck—the right to fire a team—you have power over their lives. That is positional power, the power given to you by your position. If you lead only with positional power, you are simply a boss. Any idiot can be Barney Fife. A "boss" is the kid at McDonald's who has been there a week longer than everyone else, so the manager gives him a twenty-five-cent-an-hour raise and promotes him to be in charge of fries. He then becomes the Fries Nazi—he has positional power and he uses it.

I actually *was* that guy for a few weeks once. When I was twenty-two years old I was selling real estate in a new subdivision for a large national home builder. I outsold everyone on the team, so they made the stupid decision to promote me to sales manager. I immediately became the Sales Manager Nazi, bossing everyone around, even those who didn't report to me. It didn't take them but about three weeks to take away my promotion and put me back where I belonged, in sales. I lost several friends and damaged relationships in my three-week tenure because I confused having a *position* with real leadership. Having children doesn't make you a good parent, it means you had sex. That's all.

EntreLeaders understand that ultimately the only power they can use to grow a quality team is the power of persuasion. Persuasion is *pulling* the rope and positional leadership is *pushing* the rope. And we all know you can't push a rope. If you want *employees,* then boss them around; if you want *team members,* explain *why* you do what you do. If they won't do what you ask, explain it again and again. Then, if they are simply contrary, they have to work somewhere else. But don't lead with threats and fear.

I have three wonderful children, and my wife and I have enjoyed all the ages of their lives. I have heard parents moan and groan about the teenage years, but we had fun with our teens and had good (not perfect) teens. Part of the reason for our success was a leadership decision. I discovered that fourteen-year-olds have multiple personality disorder. They have within their little growing bodies two people: a four-year-old and a thirty-four-year-old. The problem is, you as the parent never know which one is going to appear in a given exchange. Teens have a desperate desire to be treated like adults and oftentimes have an inability to act like adults. I decided to ask my teen with which person I am speaking: the four-year-old or the thirty-four-year-old? Because if I am speaking with the four-year-old, I will simply tell them what to do, and if they don't do it, there will be parental problems for them. As Bill Cosby says, "I can take you out and make another one that looks just like you." That is positional leadership, and if I resort to that with my teen or my team, I am not building to the future. I may get what I want right then, but I did not equip them to perform when my back is turned. If I am speaking with the thirty-four-year-old, I can explain why they can't stay out until two A.M., smoke a joint, and get pregnant: because it will destroy their life. I am older and wiser and will persuade them to perform within boundaries that accomplish all our goals. If I can persuade them, I have built into our future; we will both get to go places we could not have gone otherwise.

The weird thing is that while persuasional leadership takes longer and takes more restraint at the time, it is much more efficient over the long haul. When you teach team members or teens the *why,* they are more equipped to make the same decision next time without you. You don't have to watch their every move, you don't have to put in a time clock, and you don't have to implant a GPS chip in their hide when they learn how to think for themselves. Positional leadership doesn't take as long in the exchange, but you have to do it over and over and over and over. You never get to enjoy your team or your kids because they become a source of frustration rather than a source of pride.

Benjamin Zander has been the conductor of the Boston Philharmonic Orchestra since 1979. At age forty-five, something changed within him. He explains, "I'd been conducting for twenty years, and I suddenly had a realization. The conductor of an orchestra doesn't make a sound. [His power depends] on his ability to make *other people* powerful. And that changed everything for me. I realized my job was to awaken possibility in other people." He continues, "If their eyes are shining, you know you're doing it. If the eyes are *not* shining, you get to ask a question: who am I being that my players' eyes are not shining?"*

You Gotta Serve Someone

I remember attending a Christian leadership seminar where the guy up front said that great leaders are always servant leaders. My immediate reaction was, "You have got to be kidding. If I wanted to be a servant I would go to work for corporate America—no thanks." Often when I am teaching people to be EntreLeaders, I introduce the same idea—that a leader needs to have a servant mentality. And I get the same reaction from strong business own-

---

* Taken from Benjamin Zander's presentation at the TED conference. www.ted .com/index.php/talks/benjamin_zander_on_music_and_passion.html.

ers: "Servant? You have got to be kidding!" I think the reason they react that way is the same reason I reacted that way. I didn't hear "servant," I heard "subservient," as in, bow down to my team—or that somehow they would actually be in charge.

Once I understood that I am serving my team by leading them, just like I am serving my children by parenting them, I relaxed. I might serve a team member by reprimanding him or even by allowing him to work somewhere else. I might be serving the rest of the team by instantly firing someone who was sexually inappropriate with someone on the team. I am serving them by teaching and mentoring them. I am serving them to their good and the good of the organization.

Every summer we have a huge company picnic. Any time I am going into any situation, meeting, or event, my assistant gives me a tour book that has all the participants' bios (if I don't know them), maps to all the locations and a timeline of the event, and some facts and figures about what we are doing. On this particular summer day my wife, my teenage son, and I were on our way to the picnic. We have a very young team, with the average age under thirty, so we have lots of young families. As I glanced over my info for the day, I noticed that in attendance that day among six hundred people were ninety-seven children (of our team members) under the age of ten. So we had tons of kids' games—several giant blow-up bounce houses and slide type events. When we pulled up, parked, and began walking into the camp where the event was being held, it looked like a giant day care. Wow, kids everywhere. My wife immediately found team members and struck up a conversation. My teenage son and I began walking through this child-induced chaos toward the barbecue. He turned to me and said what any good teen would say: "Dad, how long do I have to stay?"

Right then it struck me that we had a teachable moment. I said, "Son, look across this field. What do you see?"

"Way too many little kids."

I laughed and agreed. "Actually there are ninety-seven kids here under age ten that are the children of our team members. Do you know what that means?"

"Nope, but I bet you are going to tell me."

"Yep, those kids' parents make a living, have a future, and those kids have a future partly because of how I act. If I misbehave in my personal life, if I fail in areas of integrity, if I screw up, it will mess up a ton of lives. As a servant leader, I understand that I am at least partially responsible for those little kids."

"Dad, that much responsibility is kind of heavy."

"I agree, son, but to whom much is given, much is expected. We as a family have all the financial and other blessings of having a successful business. What goes with that is we must take our responsibility as leaders very seriously. Son, even if *you* screw up, it will harm the future of some of those little kids. If you decide to get drunk, hit someone head-on, and kill them, we will get sued and all these people could lose their jobs. You have the blessing of being in this family and get to have and do all the things that success allows, but with that even you have a huge responsibility to make our family name one we are all proud to wear. Now let's get some barbecue."

Another example of this concept that brought tears to my eyes recently: I have a good friend who is CEO of a small manufacturing plant. He loves his team but is a very tough leader who demands excellence. The economy had a downturn and the plant's orders had dried up, causing him to temporarily lay off almost his entire production team—over 250 people. Some of those team members have been at his plant for decades, and they and their family are some of his best friends. The morning I called to check on him, I asked him how he was doing. His response was that he had just had a very long walk. He said that he had decided to park at the back of the parking lot every morning from that day until he could get the plant up and running again. Parking at the back meant a very long walk past 250 empty spots every morning, and that reminded him of what his job was—to get those team members back to work. That is a true EntreLeader.

So how do you begin to foster and live out this spirit of serving your team with strength? Avoid executive perks and ivory towers. Eat lunch with your team in the company lunchroom every day. Get your own coffee sometimes. No reserved parking spots. Look for the little actions you can take that say to your team that while you are in charge, and while you lead from strength, *you are all in this together.*

We do several large live events a year, which entails truckloads of equipment and product to sell. These days all that is prepackaged and loaded at the warehouse, but just a few years back we as a team had the opportunity to load and unload these trucks ourselves. With every able-bodied man present, including VPs, EVPs, CFOs, and the CEO, the work took only about thirty minutes. Yes, you read that right. I was in the truck helping unload and load. I never thought it was a big deal, but one day a new team member wrote me a long e-mail afterward, saying he had never worked in a place where the boss was a real leader. He had been with us less than two weeks and looked up in the truck and realized the guy handing him boxes was the owner and CEO. After having that experience, the guy will find it a little hard to cop an attitude about anything he is ever asked to do while he works on my team. The work I did that day took me just thirty minutes, but for years now it has had an impact on my relationship with my team.

Passion

Before we leave some leadership basics, let's talk about something that is really missing from a lot of organizations and their leadership: passion. You cannot lead without passion. Passion causes things to move, and passion creates a force multiplier. Passion actually covers a multitude of sins. Real EntreLeaders care deeply, and that is basically what passion is. Passion is not yelling or being wild; it is simply caring deeply. When you and your team really really care about what you are doing, the natural by-products are quality, excellence, impressed customers, employees who become team members, and ultimately a higher likelihood of profit. When you care deeply about the organization, lots of things start to happen naturally.

One thing that happens when you care deeply is a bent toward action. There is more energy in an organization with a passionate leader and team. Passivity is the opposite of leadership. The need and the ability to act are missing from failing organizations. It is the EntreLeader's job to insert passion and passionate people into the organization's processes and outcomes. There are lots of great leaders in America's companies today, but there are way too many large, publicly traded companies who hire leadership that is talented but not passionate. The results are like eating cardboard for dessert. Yuck. The customers, the stockholders, and the lawmakers see an entire company that is bland, tasteless, and self-absorbed. Why? Because their leader is. You must care deeply and it will run through the whole organization.

This bent-toward-action passion also increases productivity and excellence. People are naturally more productive when they care deeply about outcomes and the organization. They care more about the customer without even being trained to when they are passionate. When productivity and excellence are hallmarks of a company, you will almost always find team members, leadership, and even customers who are passionate about the brand and what it does.

Another surprising thing passion does is cause team members, leadership, and customers to be more forgiving of each other. If I am a customer and I believe you deeply care about delivering to me, I am more forgiving when there is a mistake. I know you care, so this mistake was not due to apathy or lack of excellence, nor was it something that happens very often, so I cut you some slack. As a customer, if I think you and your company really don't care, I will have you tarred and feathered for your mistake. As a customer I will actually defend your company to others if I know you and your team really care.

I am a PC, not a Mac. I have an iPod, my kids do, and there are several wonderful Apple products in my company, but I am a PC. Apple and iTunes are legendary for service that wows customers, and that is one of the ingredients of their success. They truly have built what Seth Godin calls a tribe, a deeply loyal and passionate following in their customers. Their customers will even defend them. I am so inept at computers that we have assigned an IT guy just to keep me going. So 99.9 percent of my mistakes are operator error. ID10T errors. So when I first signed up for iTunes it was no shock to anyone, including me, that I couldn't make stuff work. It may be intuitive for some of you, but not me. So I e-mailed iTunes, and they answered forty-two hours later, which was fine, and they did finally and patiently get me going (all my fault, not theirs). I casually mentioned in a conversation that the e-mail response had come back a couple of days after I sent it, and three Mac people (fellow customers) in the conversation passionately defended them as having world-renowned customer service, arguing that it must have been my fault. It *was* my fault, but I found it very interesting that these customers had become Apple evangelists at least partly because of the passion with which Apple operates. Good job.

This type of forgiveness or grace extension will work with your team as well. It even works between leadership and the team. As a leader, if I know you care deeply, then when you screw up, I will be quick to give you a second or third chance. However, I have a very low tolerance for your mistakes when you don't care. And in turn, when I mess up in my role as leader, team members are quick to forgive if they "know my heart," meaning they trust my intent even though I worded something wrong or even really messed up the whole event. Team members can have great unity among themselves only when it is a group of people who truly believe each member cares. Personality differences, cultural differences, and educational differences are all overlooked when they trust each other's passionate intent. We have a very diverse team, and outsiders often marvel at the way we truly love each other. One of the reasons is we hire and keep only people who are sold-out passionate about our cause. You cannot work on my team if you are simply looking for a J-O-B.

Passion is so key in leading and creating excellence that I will hire passion over education or talent every time. I prefer to have both, but given a choice I will take passion. La Rochefoucauld once said, "The most untutored person with passion is more persuasive than the most eloquent without."

These are some of the basics that foundationally prepare you and me to go through our championship playbook. As you continue through it, remember that we really do these things every day—this is not theory. Also remember that this is a "championship" playbook—we are winning. You are not learning from someone who has never actually met a payroll or been scared to death, or who has only graded tests; you are learning from a guy who straps on a helmet every day and hits someone, and has won a lot.

2

Start with a Dream, End with a Goal

*Living Your Dreams, Visions,
Mission Statements, and Goals*

In 1972 I was a hyper twelve-year-old on a long trip down the interstate with my parents and little sister. My parents were in the real estate business and were bent on torturing their children by listening to motivational tapes in the car on this long trip. They said it would be good for us to learn to dream, to think big, and to know that we could be anything we wanted to be. At twelve years old, all I wanted to be was somewhere else other than stuck in the backseat of that hot car, listening to Earl Nightingale's deep voice. He sounded like God himself, droning on about how "you become what you think about; this is the strangest secret." Or Zig Ziglar's Mississippi twang talking about how "you hit what you aim at, and if you aim at nothing you will hit it every time."

All these years later, it is interesting to look back and realize those messages by those wonderful men were inserted deeply into my soul. I also realize the gift my parents gave my sister and me, because I am convinced that a lot of my personal success in so many areas of my life can be traced back to being in the backseat of that Chevy Impala. As a captive audience, I learned that you have to dream and you have to do something about making those dreams happen. I have realized this with so much gratefulness that I have become friends with Zig and Jean Ziglar and their children. Zig is a national icon. Earl Nightingale has passed on, but I have on the bookshelf behind me an original LP record of *The Strangest Secret,* which was the first recording on motivation to ever sell a million copies. What a wonderful legacy these men, and people like them, have left us.

Dreamers

The movies, the poetry, and the seminars say to "dream big dreams." I think they are right—we should always be dreaming. Dreaming is a sign you have hope. Dreaming is a sign you still think you can win. Dreaming keeps you young. EntreLeaders are always dreaming about what can be and what is yet to come. We wake up in the morning and have two ideas over coffee, three more on our morning run, and six more dreams/ideas in the shower, and we haven't even gotten to work yet. Dreaming is the lifeblood of people and organizations that are alive and thriving. If you haven't been dreaming lately about something new, something huge, and something better, this is your reminder to start.

Dreaming also has a negative connotation as well. Some people dream and stop there. They never *do* anything about making their dreams come true. EntreLeaders like me get aggravated with people who don't move beyond dreaming. We call them dreamers, with a scowl on our face. A good friend who is a great EntreLeader told me over coffee recently that his daughter is dating a guy she described as a dreamer. My friend's response was, "Crud, they are going to live in our basement." When someone is called a dreamer, it's a put-down because it seems to indicate that person is all talk and no delivery. So you don't want to simply be a dreamer, but you do want to be someone with big dreams for the future. That makes a dad glad you are dating his daughter.

One of the lessons passed to me as a child is you can't just have dreams, you have to do something about making them happen. You must get up, leave the cave, hunt something down, kill it, drag it back to the cave, cook it, and then you get to eat. Roast duck does not fly in the window precooked. You must hunt the duck, kill the duck . . . you get the idea. I am amazed at the number of people I meet who think they get a pass—that they have found a formula for making roast duck fly, and fly into their window.

Nope, the process starts with waking up early one morning and dreaming of ducks and how great they taste. That is the dream. Then you have to go about making it happen.

I see dreams as essential to winning. However, the very nature of dreams is that they are not well defined. They are big and fuzzy, kind of in the clouds. As you begin to put some meat on the bones of your dreams and as they begin to take shape, some of the mist is blown away. As dreams start to morph and move toward reality, that is when I start calling those dreams *visions*. Vision is the next step of developing your dream into something. Visions are dreams with more clarity. Dreams become a reality only when you pull them gently from the clouds and convert them to visions.

Vision

Vision is the ability to see. When someone goes blind, we say he lost his vision, and that is true in life as well. Helen Keller said, "The most pathetic person in the world is someone who has sight but no vision." Being able to "see" is a skill that must be present or developed in an EntreLeader. People with no vision simply have jobs; they exist but aren't going anywhere because they aren't aware there is anywhere to go. In Proverbs the Bible says, "Where there is no vision the people perish." As a Christian I have heard lots of sermons and even seen entire books written on vision and how we must have it to win. So I always thought of this as "the vision scripture." But one day as I looked at it, I started seeing it through the eyes of a small-business man and I saw another word: "perish." With no vision in your organization, you perish . . . die . . . roadkill . . . dead chicken in the sun. Perish. You can't make payroll, your "team" becomes just "employees," morale goes down, turnover goes up, sales go down. "Perish" is a big word. I have watched lots of businesses fail for this reason only. They blamed other things that were all really just symptoms when the real problem was loss of, or lack of, vision.

Where there is no vision, your marriage will fail, your family will be dysfunctional, you will stumble in your spiritual walk, you will get fat and flabby, and your money will disappear. Vision affects every area of our lives. So this is a great chapter to share with your team and your family, because the extent to which they have little or no vision is the extent to which they are a deadweight in your life, holding you back. Grab some vision yourself and make sure to surround yourself with people of vision.

As the EntreLeader you have to share your vision with your team early and often. It is impossible to talk about it too much. Andy Stanley has a great book out called *Visioneering*. Andy says you have to discuss the vision of the organization twenty-one times before people start to hear it. He also says you have to restate your vision constantly so that as the organization grows and changes, it continuously reflects that vision.

Mission Statements

In the 1980s two of the big business buzzwords were "paradigm shift" and "mission statement." It seemed as though every other business book told us that we needed a new way of looking at things, a paradigm shift, and that we needed to clearly state our personal mission and the mission of our company for all to see. I tend to question everything, so I was very resistant to trying to quantify my personal mission on the planet in a couple of well-crafted sentences. I was even more sure we could not contain the entire future of my rapidly growing and changing organization with a few paragraphs—much less one or two sentences!

I have seen too many mission statements on company walls and in brochures that looked more like a wish list or a history lesson of how they used to be than the true mission of the company. In other words, they were not true or didn't ring true. Companies that have lost their soul, their real reason for being, cannot fix that by merely putting together some internal committees to develop a mission statement. So to me a mission statement was often too bogus to have credibility.

One morning in the early days of our company I was having coffee with a good friend, Dan Miller. Dan is a nationally recognized career coach and wrote a great book entitled *48 Days to the Work You Love*. In his book and his coaching, he always pushes for individuals and organizations to stop and decide what they are about before they get back to being about it. He reminded me that morning how big a goal setter I am; he said that without a really good mission statement you have the potential to get to the top of the ladder only to find it is leaning against the wrong building. The mission statement is further clarification and definition for your dreams and vision and assures you that your goals are aimed at the right target. So I halfheartedly entered the process of trying to do a personal mission statement and then began to think toward building one for our company.

Truthfully I hated doing it at first. To sit and put words to who we are and what that means was very hard. I guess some people like this stuff, but I felt like I had a term paper due. As I surrendered myself to a process that was stretching me, it became exciting. This idea of saying who we are out loud began to have some life-changing power as I worked on it. My personal mission statement to this day does not fit the formula. I have never been able to say enough in a few sentences to get me comfortable, so I broke the rules. I know that shocks you. I actually have about three personal mission statements dealing with business/ministry, family, and personal goals. I had to segment it to get my head around it.

Then my first team member and I began the process of deciding the future of our then little company by deciding what it might look like when we grew up. Since we are people of faith, we literally prayed and asked God to speak to our minds what He wanted from us. Then we worked on it and filled several wastebaskets with crumpled paper representing how frustrated we both were. It took over a month of prayer, work, and frustration to gradually form in our minds what we were going to be doing for the next several decades. The cool thing is that we still operate twenty-plus years later on the same mission statement. That says to us that we built a good one, and that we have stuck to our knitting, stayed true to our calling.

Our company mission statement: "The Lampo Group, Inc., is providing biblically based, commonsense education and empowerment which gives *HOPE* to everyone from the financially secure to the financially distressed."

We capitalize and italicize *HOPE* because that is the core goal of everything we do. When you are in shipping and ship one of my books, you did not ship a book, you shipped *HOPE* to a family wanting to get out of debt or become a future EntreLeader. When you sell an event ticket, you are not simply a ticket salesperson, you sold that person *HOPE*. You can see how I can work this idea into anything anyone with our team does, including the maintenance team and the hostess in the front lobby. We tie every team member and every activity back to this central premise. This establishes a real sense of unity, creates value in every position in the company, and keeps us all with our eye on the same ball. We are so crazy sold-out on this idea that we make you memorize and recite the mission statement in the first ninety days you work for us. This statement is who we are as a people, and you really need to know that if you are going to be one of us. Can you smell and feel the air in my organization? The mission statement is one way we create culture.

Our internal culture breathes this so much that the creatives (what we call our marketing/graphics/video team) held a poster contest for the best representation of the phrase "Articulate hope," because they know that, consistent with our mission statement, articulating hope is their job as marketers. When I walked into the creatives' department this morning, I saw ARTICULATE HOPE painted on the wall in large letters. Throughout the area are different posters showing some very cool ways to "articulate hope" to our customers. My team is getting it; my life is good.

One of the best business books of the last twenty years is *Good to Great* by my friend Jim Collins. Our mission statement helps us stay on track and concentrate on what we are good at. Jim calls this the flywheel principle.* Great companies figure out their strengths and calling and stick to them. Focus on the main thing, and keeping the main thing the main thing causes companies and individuals to be more likely to win. Developing your

---

* Jim Collins, *Good to Great*, HarperCollins (2001), p. 164.

mission statement forces you to decide in advance what you are and then by definition what you aren't.

Our mission statement has been valuable to us as a statement of what we are to ourselves and to others. But I think possibly the most valuable thing the mission statement has brought us is that it clearly says who we *aren't*. You need an out-of-bounds marker or the game is hard to play. One of the leading causes of small-business failure is success. When you become successful, several things happen that can cause you to become vulnerable. One of these things is tons of "opportunities" come your way. A while back this happened to a great small-business guy who came to me for counseling. He had a very successful residential real estate business. For many years he and his company had built a great brand in the market, had systematized their operation, and were making a lot of money. A friend of his who observed his success talked him into buying a restaurant that was failing and therefore a "great deal." Because our real estate guy had some money and "felt like he knew how to do business," he put a large investment of money into the restaurant. As the restaurant continued to fail, our real estate guy spent more and more time there trying to turn it around to protect his investment. The time away from his real estate company caused it to go down slowly at first and later rather rapidly. Thankfully he realized his mistake in time and closed the restaurant. And, you guessed it, as he applied himself back to his calling, real estate, his business began to improve and eventually prospered again.

His success gave him two things that almost caused his failure. First, it gave him money to play with outside his mission statement. Second, his success gave him the illusion that the same processes that made him a successful real estate broker were automatically transferable to the restaurant business. If he had had a mission statement, he would have realized the restaurant deal was out of bounds, the whistle would have blown, and he would have been protected from himself. Instead he lost several hundred thousand dollars in the restaurant and in lost real estate deals from lack of focus.

Because of my success and a little bit of media notoriety we get bombarded with "great ideas" that people just know I can help them with. Part of my personal assistant's job is to nicely refuse hundreds of requests to meet with me about ideas that are outside our mission. I am convinced that one reason for our success is not only knowing clearly what our flywheel is but sticking to that flywheel by turning down lots of "opportunities." Just because an idea is a good idea does *not* mean it is good for you or your company to take it on. Keep your eye on the ball.

So how do you build your personal and company mission statement? First, know this is not a one-meeting, two-hour event; you should commit some time to the process. Second, as your company changes and the marketplace moves, it is okay to deliberately but carefully make the decision to rewrite and change your mission statement.

Dan Miller says your mission statement should reflect your calling and should include:

1. *You or your company's skills and abilities.* This is the *what.* If you have been in manufacturing for twenty years, you likely should not have a mission statement that talks a lot about software development or marketing—that is not your thing. What is the thing you do, want to do, and can do?

2. *You or your company's personality traits.* This is the *how.* How do you and your team execute things? That is your personality. Are you very task oriented and project oriented, or are you very compassionate and people oriented? Maybe you are detail oriented. I am not sure I want an engineering firm to design an interstate overpass if they are more about compassion and people than details. Details matter there more.

3. *You or your company's values, dreams, and passions.* This is the *why.* This is why you are doing what you do. For a company mission statement, this is where you breathe real life into the lungs of your organization. The goals matter when this is articulated well.

In the bonus online resources for this book are a couple of worksheets to help guide you through the development of your personal mission statement. After you've done one for yourself, get to work on one for your company.

http://www.entreleadership.com/mission

Goals

Goals are visions and dreams with work clothes on. This is where we leave the theory and go to the practical. This is the stage where we leave the strategic and go to the tactical. Enough talking—it is time to kill something! Goals force practical steps into your life to make your dreams come true. We have dreamed the impossible dream, clarified it into a vision, and directed it with our mission statement, so now it is time to *do* something. Goals are the heavy lifting and cause the heavy lifting to occur.

Goals convert vision into energy. When you lay out exactly what you want to do in detail, you immediately start feeling the room move and the earth shake. You are pulled into your new life like some scene from a movie. Goals help make great men. J. C. Penney once said, "Give me a stock clerk with a goal, and I will give you a man who will make history. Give me a man without a goal and I will give you a stock clerk."

Don't Skip the Good Stuff

The information in this chapter is so elementary for some of you who have been successful and been quality leaders for years that you will tend to make one of two mistakes here if you aren't careful.

- You will miss the opportunity to read this chapter carefully to polish or fine-tune your already successful life.
- Or you could make the second mistake, which is worse: you don't take this reminder of how to win and share it with your team, your children, or others you should be mentoring.

I have made both mistakes. As I mentioned earlier, I first was drilled with the importance and process of goal setting at a very young age, so I tend to take it for granted. I thought everyone knew this material. I was teaching this lesson from our EntreLeadership course to my team one day when Jorge, a young man in his thirties, stopped me after class. He is a very sharp young man who has been on my team for some time, so it really surprised me to hear him say it was the first time in his life he had ever heard about the importance and the process of setting goals. He was so excited and pumped by this information—ideas I have known and lived for years—that his productivity went through the roof. He even opened his own business on the side. So make sure if you already know this stuff to take this chapter as a reminder for you to mentor those in your life—it might change their lives.

So much has been written and said about goals and goal setting that the mere mention of the concept is enough to turn some people off. People who aren't winning in their lives or business sneer at the mention of positive thinking or goal setting, and I tend to agree with their feelings. There have been too many books and seminars that seem to say if you just set goals and think positively you can do anything. Sorry, but that is bull. You can't fly. I don't care how many podcasts or CDs you listen to or how many goals you set or how positively you think . . . you can't fly. You can listen to messages while you sleep, putting them into your subconscious, and you still won't be able to fly. I am five foot ten and weigh just under two hundred pounds and I am over fifty years old; I will not be playing in the NBA or the NFL. No matter how much I dream, how hard I work, or what goals I set, I do not have what it takes to make it in those arenas, and me trying would be pitifully humorous. I can't fly.

For years I have seen Brian Tracy, Zig Ziglar, and others teach goal setting, and as they do, they always mention some form of what Zig calls "the wheel of life." The wheel has spokes that represent each area of our lives, and for our lives to be successful as a whole we must address each area. The spokes of goal setting are

1. Career
2. Financial
3. Spiritual
4. Physical
5. Intellectual
6. Family
7. Social

Those great teachers are correct: you have to set goals carefully and intentionally in every one of those areas. As you look at those areas you probably see two or three that you are naturally good at—they are easy for you. And you should see a couple of areas that you almost hate; you aren't naturally talented in those areas and may have never had great success with them. We all have this experience when we look at this list. What I have learned is that I still have to be intentional and put forth effort in every area. If you leave one side of the wheel flat, you have a flat tire. A flat tire will take more effort to roll your life forward, and just like a car with a flat tire, your life will have a lot more noise and unwanted heat.

The career and financial spokes have always come easy to me. I have always been able to make money. I have not always kept it—I went broke—but I have always been able to make money. I have an idea a minute to create or expand a business; it just comes easy to me. However, the one spoke I am the worst at is the social area. The weird thing is, I love people, and I don't mind big crowds of people. I am getting better because of goal setting, but I will confess that forced and concocted social events make me want to scream. As a young man I was so focused on my financial success and career that any kind of social gathering seemed like it was taking away time that I could be making

money or growing my business, so I hated it. As I have matured
and become successful I have enjoyed my friends and even some
of those parties more and more, but I will confess I have to be intentional about it. I am so bad in the social area, I am convinced
that without my wife, Sharon, I wouldn't have any friends, except
business friends. Years ago Sharon and I started the tradition of
setting goals at the beginning of the year. Not New Year's resolu-
tions, but real goals. Looking at these seven areas helped us be
purposeful in every area. You know those friends you run into
from time to time and lie to? The ones you say, "Let's get together
for dinner," to and you never call them. You lied. You didn't mean
to, but life gets busy and we just don't call. We decided to make
a list of those people and make dinner plans our personal goal.
I tend to have all those dinners in the first few months of the year
just to get them over with, because I am not social. I know that
is ridiculous and funny, but at least by having a goal in that area
I am getting some performance out of my life that I wouldn't otherwise. The more we have done this exercise, the more I have enjoyed the social life, and who knows, I may even end up good at it
someday.

Goals That Work

Goals that work have five components. You must address each of
these components to have a real goal that will work. Remember,
goals are not wishes, dreams, or even visions. Goals are bringing those things down to earth, and with our feet planted firmly
on the ground we begin to take actual action steps to make our
dreams come true. You really have to do all five of these things to
have an actual goal and actually accomplish those goals.

Goals Must Be Specific and Goals Must Be Measurable

Goals cannot be vague. Vague goals are not goals; they are dreams
and wishes, and you don't want to end up being one of those
dreamers who do nothing. You can't simply say I want to lose

weight; that is not specific enough. You can't say you want to be better educated; that is not measurable or specific. "I want to make more money" is a dream and won't happen, because while "more money" is measurable, it is not specific.

So you should set goals by saying things such as:

1. I want to lose thirty pounds.
2. I want a waist that is four inches smaller.
3. I want to make $100,000 per year.
4. I want a college degree in _____.
5. I want to have dinner with six couples.

Each of these goals is specific and measurable. One of the powers of goal setting is that it pulls you toward your goals because they are clearly set before you. Properly set goals can be put on the front of your refrigerator or on the whiteboard at the office, giving all who see them the ability to measure your progress. Measurable progress is called traction. When you can observe your movement toward your goals, it pumps you up.

Goals Must Have a Time Limit

Goals without a time limit are unable to be broken down into micro goals to measure your progress, to observe your traction. You might say, "I want to write a book." Great, when? In twenty years? In twenty months? If you don't put a deadline on the goal it will never happen and you will get to eat the bitter fruit of regret. You will say, "I always wanted to write a book, but I just never got around to it." I am not a very good writer in the literary sense, but a book like this is a great way to teach and convey ideas, so I write. As I sat down to write this book I had a December 1 deadline for a completed manuscript, so I did an outline of the chapters, which told me I needed to complete around four chapters a month, and that means one a week. So here I sit on Friday morning finishing this chapter to stay on pace to hit my goal. See how powerful goal setting is?

If you say you want to make $100,000, that is not good

enough. If you say you want to make $100,000 in this year, now we have something. I eat lunch in our lunchroom most every day because I would rather eat my wife's leftovers than restaurant food, because I can eat faster (I have never had a lunch *hour* in my life), and because I get to hang out with my team. We joke, talk football, and sometimes even discuss business. I was sitting with one of my young sales guys a while back and he decided to impress the boss by telling me he was going to make $100,000 this year. I have been in sales and managed salespeople my whole life, so I didn't believe him. I asked him how many calls a week he had to average to make $100,000, and he didn't know, so I told him he was full of it. This hurt his little feelings, so I pulled him into my office and gave him a lesson in goal setting. He is on 10 percent commission, so he needs to bring in a million a year in revenue to be paid $100,000. That is $83,000 per month, or about $21,000 per week. We know in his area what our average ticket sale is and how many actual quality relational contacts have to be made to result in one sale. So the math was easy, and my young talker now began to understand he had to make sixty-four quality contacts every week to make $21,000 in revenue, which when multiplied out end up making him $100,000 in income.

I watch our sales reports, which include activity by our reps, and I noticed for the next several weeks he was averaging well above sixty contacts, so he was going to hit his goal. I went by his work area and congratulated him. About six weeks later I noticed that his call volume had dropped to about thirty-five contacts per week, and I ran into him in the lunchroom again. I asked why he had abandoned his goal, and he replied that he hadn't. So we have another teachable moment. If you don't do the things to hit the goal within the time allocated, that goal will condemn you and call you a dreamer. Interestingly his call volume went back up, and he has gone on to be one of our better producers. The problem with hype is that you might even believe it. Winning is hard work—there are no substitutes.

I want to lose thirty pounds. Not good enough. When? I want to lose thirty pounds in three months. Now we have something we can build on. Are you already doing the math? That is ten pounds a month and therefore two and a half pounds a week. So we are going to exercise more and eat less to hit the two and a half pounds per week. If you hit the chocolate cake or the second helping, the scales will yell at you that you are off the mark for your goal.

http://www.entreleadership.com/goal

So if you want to be more social, lose weight, own your own business, increase revenues, write a book, or have a better marriage, your goals need to be specific and measurable and have a time limit.

The Goals Must Be *Your* Goals

"My wife wants me to lose thirty pounds." That will never happen. "My mother wanted me to be a doctor." I don't want to be your patient. "My father wanted me to be a preacher." I want a preacher called by *the* Father, not by his dad. If you don't own the goal and it doesn't come from your dream, then you won't have the toughness to persevere when the going gets tough. And I will promise you that the going will get tough. There is never an exception—everyone who wins must push through obstacles, lots of them. You simply will not get up at dawn for your three-mile run because your wife wants you thinner. Big goals require big backbone—wimps need not apply. You have to have courage and you can't import that; it comes from you caring deeply about the result. When you care about the end of the story, you will work your way through it.

Goals Must Be in Writing

For some reason this last component is the one where everyone drops the ball. It sounds good to put your goal in writing, but almost no one does. And the correlation is clear: almost no one wins. Winners are so strange that we admire them deeply. With very few exceptions winners have written goals. It is almost impossible to accomplish something big without a written blueprint.

One of my most prized possessions is a cheap faux-leather binder that contains my goal list and prayer list from fifteen to twenty years ago. On one of the pages from 1993 is the genesis of one of the biggest areas of our company. In doing one-on-one financial counseling I was becoming very frustrated. I would sit down with clients and begin to lay out their budget, showing them how they could pay their bills with the income they had and even begin working their way out of debt. I would get on the phone and stop their foreclosure, their repossessions, and negotiate a program that made the numbers fit within their income with their credit card companies. Problem solved; they were on their way. Then too many times they would file bankruptcy and fail six weeks later. This is the part where I yelled in frustration. It began to dawn on me that personal finance is not a math problem, it is a behavior problem. A budget and one meeting was not going to modify their behavior.

So one morning I was setting goals, brainstorming, and praying. I wrote down a simple goal: "Develop high-touch support group concept that is a seminar and counseling." Here is the power of writing down a dream, a vision, and then breaking it down into a goal; that simple statement became what we now call Financial Peace University. We have had millions of people go through that class, and it has literally changed millions of lives. Yes, there was a lot of hard work, many great ideas, and tons of frustrations and setbacks along the way, but two decades later I get misty-eyed looking at that old goal sheet, realizing that is where it all began.

http://www.entreleadership.com/marathon

The Bible says in Habakkuk 2:2, "Write the vision and make it plain." The written goal is the breakfast of champions. You just can't do big things without making your goals specific, measurable, yours, with a time limit, and in writing.

Leading with Goals

Remember this chapter has a dual purpose: to remind you of material you may have already seen, and maybe most important, to remind you to teach this basic success principle to your team. It is not unusual to have a leader who has become successful due partly to goal setting who then forgets to continue to set goals and, worse yet, starts demanding that his team set goals when he has none. *The moral of the story is, don't ask your team to set goals when you have none.*

With our company we come up with a big project or a big vision, then get everyone excited about it. Their excitement, their buy-in, causes them to automatically start seeing their part. So when you cast a big vision the team sees what part they play, and you are pulling people into goals instead of pushing them.

For instance, you can't go to your sales team and announce an arbitrary revenue goal for that department, which then dishes out sales quotas for each member of the sales team. Instead, talk about how important it is that we serve a greater number of clients and not only what that will do for each client, but what the increased income will allow us to do in the company, and better yet, what the team's personal income will look like. Then propose a revenue goal and ask each person to carefully craft what part of that goal he or she is going to contribute. Again, we are pulling instead of pushing. When leadership sets the goals by themselves they are not goals, they are quotas. And no one likes quotas.

One of the first management classes you attend will teach you MBO, management by objectives. MBO is simply getting your team to set their own goals as a part of the overall objective. From an accountability perspective it is emotionally and relationally much easier to hold team members' feet to the fire on a promise they made, a goal they set, than to try to boss them into accomplishing a goal they had no part in determining.

Shared Goals Create Communication

Most companies yearn for more and better communication. We have incredible communication in our organization, but that has not always been so. We work hard at communication, and we will take an entire chapter later to show you several practical things that can be done to make real communication part of your business culture. One of the big benefits of having very clearly stated and written goals is that doing so creates instinctive intuitive communication.

It could be as simple as football. Football has a very simple goal: put the ball into the end zone more than the other team. Everyone on the field knows this basic goal, whether they are linemen, quarterbacks, or placekickers. So when things go well we know the goal: put the ball over the line. When things blow up, we all still know the goal: put the ball over the line. So when there is a fumble, even one of the linemen, with hands taped into clubs and a body built like a Kia, knows his job just changed: pick the ball up and do something your body was not designed to do, run across the line. If we have a shared goal we do our specified job to hit the goal, but when the goal matters we can even do someone else's job to make sure the team hits the goal.

It is a normal event among our team to see a VP or EVP with sweat pouring off of them as we move boxes of books to make sure a table has books during a live event. A new team member spoke up in a staff meeting the other day and was blown away by the way our leaders are shoulder to shoulder with other team members to make sure the goal is hit. Yes, this has to do with setting the tone of servant leadership, but it also conveys the message to the rest of the team that we do whatever it takes to win. Can you even imagine a quarterback fumbling and a lineman not jumping on the ball and instead saying something stupid like "That isn't my job"? Companies all over America are failing because they have allowed a culture of leaders and teams who don't care about the goal, but just about themselves. When the team cares only about themselves, they are by definition no longer a team, they are just employees. As soon as that happens, the germ of failure has entered the organization. When failure occurs like that it is leadership and the team's fault. There was no clearly communicated shared goal that created buy-in from all parties. One of the things that will get you fired really fast from our company is saying something really stupid like "It's not my job." People who work for small businesses, even with hundreds of team members, have to wear multiple hats. There is too much work to do and too many different things to do for some ignoramus to have the idea that he is exempt from something outside his normal job description.

The communication created by shared goals lowers frustration because the right hand actually knows why the left hand is doing what it is doing. And this communication creates buy-in by all team members, keeping a selfish mentality out of the leadership and the team.

Shared Goals Create Unity

Most companies yearn for more unity, just like they do for communication. And just like communication, we are going to talk in depth about how to create the kind of unity we have on our team. Incredible unity, it sometimes seems, is a full-time job. Shared common goals are a big part of creating unity.

First, unity is created because it is easy to inspire other team members to victory and performance in their area. It's inspiring when you understand how linked their success is to your own success and the success of the whole organization. When you don't see how what the other guy does matters to you and the whole place winning, why would you be unified with him?

The horrible childish backbiting and interdivisional rivalry and hate in most organizations is honestly sickening. Selfish little children operating on the emotional level of four-year-olds actually wish failure upon other sections of the company. That is like your head hoping the neck that turns it quits working. This infighting proves again that most companies are their own worst enemy. We have never had that level of disdain internally. Why? Because you are allowed to disagree, even fight with each other, but only within the confines of how the argument is about the goal. The moment the argument descends into a childish territorial battle, you're on really thin ice in our company. To be plain, I will fire you for that kind of stupid selfish activity. Unity is created when everyone agrees on the goal and fights and claws together to get there. It is the team's job to act like grown-ups and keep their eye on the prize. It is leadership's job to continually shine a spotlight on the goal and remove any distractions, like team members who start acting like selfish "employees." After doing this for a couple of decades, my team is so strong they now will instruct a new member very directly on the proper way a member of a team works versus just being an employee. Our team doesn't have much tolerance for a bureaucrat in our midst, so positive peer pressure converts new people or runs them off. Frankly, either result is fine with me.

The second way to create unity is through shared personal goals. If you know the salesperson next to you is saving to buy his first home two years after he got married, you are his biggest cheerleader when he makes a sale. In short, this creates relationships. We have made the huge mistake in business of separating the task from the person and his life.

When leaders or team members can help other team members hit their personal goals, the Christmas tree of their mind and spirit is lit. One of my EVP's assistants is a wonderful team member and wonderful woman who has been with us for many years.

A couple of years ago I was reading through our team's business and personal goals that they turned in to me. Note: our team is encouraged to share personal goals they are comfortable sharing, but are not required. As trust increases, so does the depth of sharing.

> **I think there is something more important than believing: Action! The world is full of dreamers, there aren't enough who will move ahead and begin to take concrete steps to actualize their vision.**
> **—W. Clement Stone**

I noticed on this assistant's goals that she was about to be debt free, and one of the things she wanted to do some time after that was to purchase a Montblanc pen. Turns out she has a collection of writing pens. I had no idea and wouldn't have guessed that in a million years. I have several Montblancs and suddenly felt a tinge that I bought those without even thinking about it, and that was her big personal goal. So I ordered one and carried it up to her office the next day. She loved it, and I had even more fun catching her off guard and participating in her achieving one of her goals. Do you think unity in our organization increased as a result of that simple gesture? Well of course it did. So why don't we all have more of that kind of fun? Because we don't have shared goals. Shared goals help create unity.

Having a dream that moves to a vision, then to a mission statement, and then is broken down into goals is essential to winning personally but is certainly crucial for the EntreLeader. What is most interesting to me is how complicated and fun the synergy is that is created by a whole organization actually walking this out. Time for you to sit down right now and make some adjustments. Do it.

3

Flavor Your Day with Steak Sauce

Making the Most of Time Management and Organization

It is so unsatisfying to work my tail off all day and feel like nothing happened. How many of you have had this experience: you get up early and head down to the office, you have an entire day of fire after fire that needs to be put out, you can't remember what happened to lunch, and twelve hours later you arrive home completely exhausted, collapsing on the couch as your spouse says, "What did you do today?" And you shake your head thinking, *I have no idea.* Most of us who bust it, who are hard-driving go-getters, have had that experience. That experience is disgusting and unsatisfying; you feel like a stupid rat in a stupid wheel . . . run run run and get nowhere. To enjoy our work, our business, we must have a sense of traction.

Time management sounds to me like some cooked-up corporate training program by someone who has never really worked themselves. They have never faced an entire day of crisis after crisis. Yet when I apply these basic principles in my life I get a ton more done, and strangely I am more rested—or is it just more satisfied?

My friend John Maxwell says a budget (for your money) is telling your money where to go instead of wondering where it went. Managing time is the same; you will either tell your day what to do or you will wonder where it went. The weird thing is that the more efficient, on task, on goal you are with your time, the more energy you have. Working with no traction, or for that matter simply wasting away a day, does not relax you, it drains you. Have you ever taken a day off, slept late, wandered around with no plan or thought for the day, watched some stupid rerun of a bad movie as you surfed the TV, and at the end of your great day off found yourself absolutely exhausted? Strange as it may seem, when you work a daily plan in pursuit of your written goals that flow from your mission statement born of your vision for living your dreams, you are energized after a tough long day.

As a person of faith I always kind of viewed time management for the purpose of productivity to be a business kind of thing devoid of any spiritual or personal implications. I was teaching this lesson years ago, and one of my young leaders, who is very bright, came to me afterward and asked the leading question, "Dave, do you know where the concept of seconds and minutes was developed?" I said, "No, but I bet you are going to tell me." According to my young leader, who has a master's degree in divinity, prior to the 1300s man measured time only in hours using instruments like a sundial. Somewhere in the 1300s mathematicians who were monks were able to do the calculations that now allow us to break hours into minutes and minutes into seconds. The monks did this mathematical work in order to enable them to more precisely worship God. So managing money and time well and viewing them as precious commodities is a normal exercise for all of us, particularly people of faith.

The Urgent and the Important

All of us can spend time doing ridiculous things that are a complete waste of time simply to avoid going outside our comfort zone. Dr. Stephen Covey explains in his writing that all of our time is spent in one of four quadrants, things that are:

  I. Important and urgent
 II. Important but not urgent
III. Not important but urgent
IV. Not important and not urgent

Quadrant I items are easy. Most of us who lead or aspire to be a leader recognize and do the important and urgent things. In business it is things like paying payroll or the team will all quit this week. Or meeting a production deadline, otherwise we'll have unhappy clients. The type of things in quadrant I are the obvious tasks needed to stay in business. When you are just beginning in business, without a team to delegate to, you have to make the bank deposits, pay the payroll, turn on the lights in the morning—you wear every hat, or most of them. These tasks are necessities.

Quadrant IV items are almost as easy. Things that are not important and not urgent are an obvious waste of time. Most people reading this understand that. You may have some employees who, on their way to becoming team members, will have to be shown this, but generally very few leaders or productive people struggle here. Most watching of TV falls in this category, especially when done in excess like most folks do. Checking your personal Facebook or Twitter while you are supposed to be working qualifies as a waste of time. These are activities that people fall into and almost never intentionally set out to waste that time. The passive, unproductive moments and people all fall here.

Most people do not struggle with the first and last quadrants. It's the second and third quadrants we have to be very specific about in order to win at a higher level.

Quadrant III is "not important but urgent" items. This quadrant can be deceptive because the urgency of the item makes it seem important, when in reality it is a waste of time. While sitting here right now writing this chapter, an important task, I forgot to close my e-mail in-box. *Ding, ding;* I hear I have an e-mail, and like a moth drawn to a flame I have to stop my important train of thought and find an e-mail sent by a "friend" whose personal purpose on the planet is to forward every "funny" or political junk e-mail to me. Might be important or funny in another life, but I am so distracted I just did something urgent but not important instead of something not urgent and important. You do it too.

As you grow in responsibilities and go through different phases of life, what might be deemed important can change. When I was a small child we were trained, with great thoroughness, in proper telephone etiquette. Back in the 1960s the telephone was the lifeblood of real estate agents like my parents. My parents had a very low tolerance for some child answering the phone and costing them a lead or even a sale by handling it wrong. So as a very young child I could answer the phone like a professional receptionist. I remember clearly saying "Yes, ma'am" or "Yes, sir," taking the message, and repeating the phone number back to the caller with energy and a smile. Often upon returning the call my parents would get a compliment on how polite their teenager was, to which they would reply, "He is seven." Consequently, a ringing phone is drilled very deep into my emotions as something that is important. However, a few years ago, with teenage girls in the home, my social wife, and me relying on e-mail, I suddenly had a revelation: A ringing phone in my home is *never* for me. So why answer it? My childhood training causes me to jump when the phone rings, but given that it is never for me and we have a wonderful voice mail system, why would I want to take a message from one of the ladies my wife runs with every morning at the YMCA? So I quit answering the phone at my home. Completely. Sometimes it feels weird, but the call is *never* for me.

That is a great metaphor for spending time doing something that is urgent but not important. Ask yourself what you or some of your team members spend time on that is really not taking you to your goals. It may be that something is urgent and important enough to make sure it is done, but it's not important that *you* do it. The answering of my home phone has been delegated to a person who the caller might actually want to reach, or to a very capable voice mail system. As your business and responsibilities grow in size you have to pull back on the scope of what you personally do. You have to spend your time working on things *only* you can do. When a business first starts you are wearing hundreds of hats, and as you get more revenue and team members you begin handing off those hats. My personal assistant acting as a gatekeeper allows me to work on things I must personally do. When we first opened all those years ago I personally did one-on-one financial counseling. But for many years I have not counseled a soul. When my best friends or even family members need help, they will get better help and quicker help with great follow-up if I assign one of my counselors to help them. I would be doing people I love a disservice by counseling them today. And of course, as harsh as it sounds, that is something that I as a leader have to delegate. Do you still cut your own grass but hate it? You should set a financial goal to stop that very soon. What do you want to spend your life energy doing? Are you still answering the business phone personally, still doing the bookkeeping, still typing your own letters, still booking your own travel, or still vacuuming the office? I have done every one of these things and I am not too stuck up or proud to do them now, but I have learned that typing these pages, or speaking, or mentoring a young leader is something that only I can do, and I can't do it if my time is used up doing the urgent but not important.

Quadrant II is the important but not urgent. This may be the most important use of your time as an EntreLeader. The things that fall in this category impact the quality of your life and business possibly more than any other area. Examples of what falls into this area are exercise, strategic planning, goal setting, reading nonfiction leadership/business books, taking a class or three, relationship building, prayer, date night with your spouse, a day off devoted to brainstorming, doing your will/estate plan, saving money, and having the oil changed in your car. We can all agree that things that aren't urgent but are important may be the most important activities we engage in as we look back at our life. The problem is we live in a society where the urge to be in motion, frenetic motion, at all times seems to be the spirit of the age. There is something about a quad II activity that causes you to pause and let a breath out, sigh, then engage in it. Activities like the ones mentioned above are the building blocks of a high-quality life and business, and yet because they are not urgent they seem to be some of the things we avoid the most.

The interesting thing is that if you avoid quad II activities, eventually they will move to quad I and become urgent. If you don't exercise and eat right (because you just don't have time) you will have the opportunity for time off when you need triple-bypass heart surgery. If you don't have a date night and make sure relationship building is part of your month, you will get to take time for marriage counseling. If you don't change your oil, eventually you will get to buy a new engine. These not-so-urgent activities, when left undone, have a potentially large cost, so budget time to do only quad I and quad II activities, avoid quad IV as much as possible, and delegate or avoid quad III things.

Controlling Your Time with a To-Do List

When attending time management classes or seminars over the years, I have repeatedly heard the quote "If you spend fifteen minutes planning your day on paper every morning, you will add 20 percent to your productivity." If you are reading this book I doubt very seriously that you are wasting one-fifth of your day, but I would be willing to bet you have team members who do. So when you start properly managing time and teaching your team to do the same you will see a huge change in productivity and even more so in job satisfaction. Remember that traction equals satisfaction.

A very simple but time-honored method to manage your day before it begins is the prioritized to-do list. Each morning make a list of activities that need to be done today. Then look at the list and ask yourself which items must be done *today*. Put an "A" beside each one. Then look at the remaining activities and ask yourself what should be done very soon (and today would be nice). Put a "B" beside those. The remaining activities get a "C" and are great ideas that if not moved up to a B or A within a couple of weeks should be delegated or put in an idea file. Now look at all the A items and ask *what is the most important single item or activity that must be done today—and if that's all you get done, have you done the correct thing?* Put a "1" beside that, making that A1. Then ask yourself the same question about what is the next most important, which becomes A2, and so on through the A's, then the B's and C's. Of course we are now going to rewrite our list beginning at A1, down through the A's, then B1 and through the B's, and of course C1 through the C's.

You now have at the top of your page the most important single thing you need to do today, A1. I call this steak sauce in honor of A1 steak sauce. Put some sauce on your steak—your life—by spending your precious moments on this planet doing important work instead of reading junk e-mails. As you start your day with your prioritized to-do list, sometime in the first hour you will be given a test. You will look up, and leaning against your door with a coffee cup will be a coworker or team member with a "problem" or a distraction. You must train yourself to look at them and ask yourself, *Are they steak sauce?* Is their problem more important—not more urgent, but more important—than your A1? Usually not.

When our company was young and there were about ten of us, I had a young lady in sales who always showed up at my door when the copier jammed. It took a good while for me to train myself not to react to her frustration and run to fix the copier but instead get her to find someone else, anyone else, to handle it. On the other hand, a couple of years ago I was at my desk first thing one morning, having finished my little list, when my human resources director appeared at my door telling me an ambulance was on the way because one of the guys on another floor had passed out. Obviously this was more important than virtually any A1 I might have had on my list, so I went and stood by our guy, who had come to. Good news: even though they took him away in the ambulance, he was fine, just a sugar thing. Then it was, as Brian Tracy says, "back to the list."

When you have your day carefully planned, it gives you a plumb line, a guidance and measurement mechanism to evaluate interruptions and a place to come back to after the interruption if it was warranted.

As a young entrepreneur, before I became an EntreLeader, I often tried to manage results. I would do things like try to get sales revenues up or try to get team morale up or get profits up. I finally realized that results are generated by activities. If I manage my activities then the results I want occur. If my sales team makes more calls, has a better product, and serves customers better, the natural result is increased revenues. If we watch expenses like a hawk, creating a team culture that hates unnecessary expenses while we increase revenues, the natural result of those activities is increased profit. If I want team morale to be up I need to engage in activities like being very careful with how each team member's situation is handled, and the result is higher morale. Be careful in your management of your time and your team's time that the activities you engage in are the ones that cause the result you want. Don't work on the symptom; attack the problem that caused the symptom.

I have managed my time from the simple prioritized to-do list since I was in my teens. I was trained in this technique early, so I quickly lose patience with people who waste time. There is a time to relax with a good book and a time for recreation, which is good. But the person who walks the office with a coffee cup like a scene out of *Office Space* and whose sole reason for existence on the planet is to slow everyone else down will become very aggravating to you and your team once you increase your productivity and are aware of every precious minute.

Years ago I had a guy working on our team who was a great guy. Actually a hard worker, when there was work to do. But he is one of those people who must have human interaction, a lot of human interaction. So when he wasn't busy he would show up at my door and ask if I had a minute; thirty minutes later he still hadn't gotten to the point. I finally hired someone to keep him booked. He stayed busy doing a great job and left me alone. I am really not that antisocial, but like you I have a lot to do in a given day and people who are time wasters suck the lifeblood out of you and your company. Think about the financial implications: you are paying payroll for the time waster *and* for the person they are interrupting.

Some people are not quite such capital offenders against time and are more casual in their waste. These people can be repelled by your productivity. If your feet are moving, you are busy, your calendar is full, then the guy with the football story knows he has to wait. For purposes of communication we keep my calendar on Outlook, where my assistant can view it and change it, and my wife and several people in the company can view it on "Read Only" so they can find some time to connect with me on things we are working on. I keep a forty-two-inch flat-screen over my conference table in my office with the Outlook file open and my calendar on it. I am very busy so the calendar is full months ahead. This had an unintended consequence with a casual time waster. I don't now, but I used to budget some of my time to mentor young leaders in the community on a one-time basis, or some even a few times. I had a young leader wannabe request to meet with me to discuss how to grow his nonprofit ministry, so I agreed. My assistant is kind but very clear about meeting times and the fact that there is likely something happening on my schedule before and after, so the meeting will run on time. We had thirty minutes scheduled, so the young man sat down and for seventeen minutes discussed football. Then something interesting happened. He looked up at that flat-screen and saw my calendar. A lightbulb went on and he said, "Wow, you are very busy, we better get to the point." Which is what I had been thinking for the last seventeen minutes. Then we had a very productive thirteen-minute meeting. My productivity encouraged him to be more productive. That will work in your organization as well.

Do You Hate Meetings?

When your organization reaches the size where meetings are necessary in order to work on projects and to create quality communication, you will quickly learn to hate group meetings if you don't manage them very carefully. Have you ever been in a meeting with a few people where the reason for the meeting had been handled but everyone sat there and kept talking about nothing? When someone is not picking up the verbal cues that the meeting is over, you may have to resort to the stand-up technique. When the meeting is over but no one is admitting it, stand up. This is a little rude, but so is some goober sitting in your office burning daylight. When you stand up, you will see the meeting end and people will begin packing up their stuff and heading toward the door. If standing up doesn't do it then start walking toward the door; even the biggest clown will then get it and follow you out.

If you hate meetings because you think they are a waste, then something has to change. My friend Patrick Lencioni wrote a great book entitled *Death by Meeting* that has some great suggestions. Several of my leaders read this book and demanded we change some of our meeting processes. I currently have twenty-three people on what we call our Leadership Council. These are department VPs and other key leaders in the company. Once a month we come together to discuss anything and everything about our organization and where it is going. These people are a band of brothers and sisters. We have fought in the trenches together for an average of ten years—some for less time, some more time. We share a close camaraderie and bond. Often a Leadership Council meeting would turn into laughing, enjoying each other's company, and even telling old war stories. All of those things are good, but that was not the stated purpose of our gathering. As one of my EVPs pointed out, add up the pay in that room by the hour and then try to be excited about wasting an hour. Yuck, that will make your stomach turn. So now the only thing discussed at Leadership Council is what is on the agenda. Anyone on the council can put anything on the agenda up to an hour before the meeting, but we stick to the agenda. Last night we had a Leadership Council meeting that lasted only thirty-eight minutes, so we went home early to our families. Wow, I love a plan. I don't mind if those meetings run long as long as we are not just hanging out. Hanging out drives my leadership team crazy.

When scheduling a meeting, take time to prepare for the meeting. Too many times we go into a meeting and wing it. If you are going to invest valuable time and money by gathering people together, have an agenda and be prepared to present your ideas. It is almost as if each meeting needs its own mission statement; if nothing else, it certainly needs a stated goal. As solutions are reached assign the follow-up to a particular person by a particular time. It is very frustrating and demotivating to your team to participate in meetings where ideas are put forth and solutions proposed that are never acted on. It starts to feel like the meetings are a waste of time, because the meetings are a waste of time.

Try different styles of meetings. I have one VP who takes his key people on a ride in his pickup out in the country looking at farmland while they talk. He runs one of the most profitable departments in my company, so there may be something to this. We have a coffee shop in our lobby where I see a lot of team meetings happening. Certainly a quick run for some ice cream can encourage creativity to bust loose. If you are doing a leadership retreat or brainstorming session, do it off-site to cause new thoughts to enter the discussion. These things seem obvious but since I am a creature of habit I will sit in the same place having the same discussion and won't figure out why we get no new answers. Silly.

Technology

As I mentioned, my calendar is kept by my assistant on Outlook and readable by others. My e-mail, contacts, and calendar are accessible by computer and smart phone 24/7 on the road, at home, and at the office. I am never without this access unless I choose to be. This is really efficient, even when it comes to my wife planning a dinner party. She can look and see six months out what nights we have free.

In a small-business setting there are generally two types of technological failures. One type of failure is the person who resists technology and doesn't use the huge time-saving benefits of electronic calendars, e-mail, and great stuff like budgeting tools. I have a friend who is a custom home builder who runs all his estimating, budgeting, and scheduling on his smart phone. His office is the hood of his pickup. I know another builder whose idea of running a job budget is a small personal checking account in his back pocket for each job. I personally hate learning new technology. About the time I get used to my web browser with all my bookmarks in place and master how to use it, they want to update my software and I have to start over. Yuck. But every time I get a new and better phone or new and better software I increase my productivity after I get past the yuck. So don't lose several hours a week to your resistance to technology. I don't own a typewriter or a ten-key calculator anymore and there was a day that they were the staples of my business.

The second time-management failure due to technology is on the other end of the spectrum: focusing too much on technology to the point that all you do is play with your new toy and don't get any work done. The person who's prone to this tends to be younger and enamored with how cool the new gadget or software is. Yes, we need to understand all the wonderful things we can do with our toys, but we *do some work* as a result. It is almost as if a young gamer's addiction has just been transferred to a gadget addiction in the name of "business." So while we want to use technology to be more efficient, it is terribly inefficient to do nothing but learn about technology.

A Couple of Words on the Basics

Most of us are moving away from using paper. My to-do list used to be on a Word document on my computer; today mine has evolved to 90 percent contained in my e-mail in-box. I delegate, delete, file, and/or quickly answer my e-mails in order of priority. When you work on my team you will likely get a ton of one-word e-mails from me in a day. My e-mail might say, "No" "Cool" "k" "Yours." If you need me to expand you are going to drop down the priority list or we will call a quick meeting. Resist getting in e-mail fights where "Reply to All" is used to chew people out. I have fallen into that trap, and while it feels efficient at the time, it takes away from a quality connection with a team member that will allow you to further delegate later if you make this a teachable personal moment. Tim Sanders says to "stamp out 'Reply to All.'" I agree.

Since we are moving away from paper my personal assistant keeps all my files. I don't have anything in my desk but pencils. Delegate that type of time use. Your files should be on your computers and synced together so you can access them from anywhere at any time. I have on the corner of my desk a physical out-box where I lay anything I want my assistant to take and distribute. This would include things like receipts, signed letters, signed checks, or anything she put on my desk for me to deal with.

Your physical desktop represents the organizational condition of your mind and maybe even indicates the organizational condition of your whole company. I used to think stuff piled and stacked all over my desk meant I was busy and a hard worker. Then I found out it meant I didn't know how to organize and delegate work flow. The most glaring example of this was when I went to the office of a friend named Cecil. At the time I was a very young entrepreneur, and he offered to help me with some financial questions I had and wanted to encourage me through some hard times. Cecil owned a large financial planning operation with hundreds of team members and tons of money. When I went into his office, it was so clean and uncluttered I thought I had entered a surgical ward. He didn't even have a desk, just a library table with no drawers. He had a phone and a computer, and in the middle of his spotless desk was a yellow pad with nothing written on it and a pencil on top. This place looked like it was ready for a magazine photo shoot. Coming from my cluttered, stacked, and piled office it felt really sterile. He picked up the yellow pad and we had our meeting. At the end of the meeting I blurted out, "Where do you do all your work?" Like he had a secret messy office one room over and this was just for show. He laughed and said, "Right here." I couldn't grasp that, so I started asking questions like "Where is all your stuff? Don't you have a stapler? Don't you have files? It doesn't look like anyone works here!" He laughed again and began to explain to me that I would never have a business of size until I reached the point where someone else did the stapling and filing. He explained that his job was not to do that anymore; now his job was to set the vision of his company and lead well in all aspects, and the only "stuff" that took was brainpower and intentionality. So clean your filthy desk and office. No, you don't know which stack stuff is in, and no, you aren't artistic; you are simply disorganized. Clean it up, delegate it, or throw it out. File Thirteen, your trash can, might be one of the biggest time savers you can use.

Review

We've progressed from dreams, to visions, to a mission statement, to goals, and now to managing each of your hours and minutes to cause those to happen. Remember that even if this information seems very elementary and basic to you, as you teach it to your children and/or your team this information will seem revolutionary to them. I challenge you to bring fresh life to your new business by walking through this process. Try this time-management approach for ninety days without stopping. I can make you the promise that you will see a new level of traction and thereby a new level of satisfaction. Nothing is more unsatisfying than to work so hard and not move the needle.

4

"Spineless Leader" Is an Oxymoron

The Easier Way to Make Hard Decisions

A leader who won't, or can't, make decisions is never going to succeed and certainly will never become a full-fledged EntreLeader.

When you make the choice to call yourself a leader, or even better yet, aspire to be an EntreLeader, you have to declare that passivity is no longer an option. Leadership is not for the weak and the timid; it requires tremendous backbone, tremendous strength. The larger your dream, the larger the organization, the more complicated and emotionally draining your decisions. Big-time EntreLeadership is simply not for wimps.

> A *good* plan, violently executed now, is better than a *perfect* plan next week.
> —George S. Patton

Yet we have all faced decisions that cause us to freeze, to become indecisive. "Indecisive leader" is an oxymoron. Your business, your family, your team, and your future is paralyzed when you are. You put all you dream about in jeopardy when you are indecisive. Nothing gets killed by your gun when all you say is "Ready, aim, aim, aim, aim . . ." You drive your most talented people crazy by doing this and you will ultimately lose your best relationships by not pulling the trigger. Have you ever seen a great young woman dating a great young man who won't pop the question? Eventually he will lose her, because if she is a good one she isn't going to grow old waiting for him to grow a backbone.

The marketplace is begging for an adapted version of your service or product but you are stuck in the old method because you can't make a decision. If this is you then be assured a competitor is about to enter your life, just like the girl will find someone who will pop the question. And just like the guy who lost his girlfriend to indecision, you will lose your customer to indecision. The competitor entering the scene in either case is not the problem; it is the symptom. The problem is your lack of action. Had you taken action the competitor would have never had a foothold. You would have kept your customer and our young man would have won the hand of his fair maiden.

Indecision is something that happens to all of us. The challenge here is to systematically drive it from your life so you can win as an EntreLeader. To drive indecision from your life, you must first identify what causes it.

Fear

One thing that causes us to *not* make obvious decisions is fear. Fear is the ultimate cause of paralysis. We get that deer-in-the-headlights look and freeze right in the path of danger. The Bible says that a double-minded man is unstable in all his ways—in other words someone who can't make up their mind, make a decision, is unstable, unpredictable, and will bring ruin to their organization. I call that "squirrel theology" because it reminds me of the squirrel that runs in the road in front of your car. The fear of your car bearing down on the squirrel causes them to run one way, then another, and then another, all in the middle of the street, until you hear a *blump, blump.* Ouch. Indecision caused by fear will get you killed.

Once I discovered that fear was at the root of my indecisiveness and that indecisiveness would kill my dreams and ruin my life, I had to come up with a system to deal with it. One of the core values of our company is that we don't make decisions based on fear. Sometimes we are afraid. We might be afraid of losing a customer, or afraid of a lawsuit, or afraid of losing money. It is wise to recognize that those fears may be well founded and we should not ignore the potential consequences of our decision, but we will not allow the spirit of fear to drive us. Otherwise, every competitor who chooses to threaten us would make us run to the corner and suck our thumb. It is wise to recognize that the competitor may or may not pose a threat, but it is very unwise to let them paralyze you with their marketplace taunts. Les Brown, an old-time motivational speaker, says that too many of us are not living our dreams because we are living our fears. So in our group we intentionally say out loud that a situation or problem is making us afraid

We don't make decisions based on fear.

and then get about the business of making a decision without allowing that fear to be the driving factor in the decision. Dorothy Bernard says that courage is just fear that has said its prayers.

Criticism

You can count on criticism if you do anything of scale that matters. You can't be afraid of criticism. It comes with the territory. Yet I've met people who won't stand for justice and make a decision because someone somewhere might be upset. Instead you should just count on someone not liking the call you make. We will consider with wisdom who might not like something and work to build consensus on decisions, but at the end of the day, fear of gripes from do-nothing people or the opposition isn't going to keep the EntreLeader from making the call. Aristotle said, "There is only one way to avoid criticism: do nothing, say nothing, and be nothing." The more you do, the more someone will have something negative to say. As much media as I do and as large as our brand has become, we can bale our hate mail. It goes with the territory; don't let that keep you from making the call or living your dream.

Elements of Good Decision Making

Great EntreLeaders don't allow indecisiveness due to fear. We are afraid sometimes, but we make the call anyway and don't let fear be the driving force of the decision. Sometimes good decision making can mean deciding to be passively active. What? Deciding not to decide right now *is* a decision. That is different from being completely paralyzed by fear. Many times over the years we have decided not to decide today.

Early in our business our accounting department consisted of one lady who was our bookkeeper. I hated doing accounting and was happy to hand this job off. As a matter of fact I failed, because I handed the job of our books off so completely that I didn't even look at the process. It turns out she was not really doing our books at all, but every week she handed me a one-page report showing we were current on our payables and that all the receivables had been collected. According to what she told me, we didn't owe anyone money and no one owed us money. That's a good place to be.

But it was a lie. I was at Disney World with my family when a VP called to tell me the IRS was at the office ready to padlock the doors for unpaid payroll taxes. How could that be? I was sure I had seen reports otherwise. As my leaders dug into the situation they found that we were behind on several bills, and a lot of folks owed us money we hadn't collected. And worst of all, the IRS was right! The woman was a liar—with my money! There is now a ride named after me at Disney because I blew a couple of fuses and went into orbit. We pulled money from a personal account and paid the IRS, and when I got home we began a two-month process of collecting what was owed to us and paying what we owed. It was embarrassing and I was very angry. I made a decision not to decide this lady's fate while I was angry. I waited until my vacation was over, got home, and inspected the situation, and ultimately decided to fire her, but I waited until I had calmed down.

I decided not to decide while angry. Sometimes we decide not to decide until we have more information, or decide not to decide while we are tired or fearful. Deciding not to decide in the heat of the moment is different from indecision driven by fear. I am personally quick to make decisions and I have had to learn the art of slowing down and letting situations play out. That is simply the art of patience in decisions, again different from indecision.

Set a Deadline

Procrastination can be avoided by setting a self-imposed deadline or by recognizing the reality of an actual deadline. If your lease is up in August don't wait until July to begin shopping and/or renegotiating with your landlord. If your inventory burn rate has you out of stock by October, then for goodness sakes make sure you are shopping vendors or placing the reorder before then so you don't run out of widgets.

If there is not a reality-based deadline then set a self-imposed date for a decision to force yourself to deal with it. I am often asked on my radio show by a small-business owner when it is time to close a struggling business. A recent example was when Tim, a web designer, called my show to ask if he should "get a real job" and close his business. Big decision. Take time, but also set a self-imposed deadline. My suggestion to him was to think of three or four things to try to get his income up and give himself a date to measure the success of the new ideas. He was making only about $1,000 per month and felt he could get a job making $5,000 a month but wasn't ready to give up on his dream. As we talked I gave him a couple of simple marketing ideas and asked him to set a deadline to get his income to $5,000 per month. He said he thought he could do that in 120 days, so we put that on the calendar. If at that date his income was not up it was time to close. A weird thing happened . . . with the ax hanging over his dream he went to work marketing. Later he called me back to celebrate that he was making $7,000 per month and had saved his business. Remember that the ax hanging over his dream was installed by him. A self-imposed deadline to make the difficult decision to give up his dream caused him to get off his butt and get some customers.

A friend of mine who is a big, big income earner had left his big corporate job and opened a retail business with multiple locations. He called and asked if he and his wife could have coffee with my wife, Sharon, and me. The reason for our meeting was that his wife was in freak-out mode over the loss of the so-called security of the corporate job and thought this business was going to bankrupt them. His idea was that they would come to our home and I would set her straight. As we sat and looked at his start-up, I could see it was losing lots of money really fast. His burn rate was about $200,000 per month. He had about 1.6 million dollars to get the business moving but was going through that rather quickly, so his wife was freaking out. She was right and it was no wonder his marriage was messed up. Even a sixth-grade math student could tell that this millionaire was going to be broke in eight months at the current rate of loss. Of course anyone living their dream of owning their own business can be so blinded by optimism that they are in denial about the cold hard facts.

We talked through that for a while, and he agreed to set a deadline of four months, which would take the business through December, a really good month for retail. He admitted that if he couldn't make a profit in retail by December it would be time to call it quits. I wrote out a statement that said, "If we aren't profitable by December 20, I will close the business." That would leave him about $800,000, plus his retirement money and home, and he would do something else to earn a living. I made him sign that simple handwritten statement. When he did his wife began to sob. Not just cry, but sob. The relief on her face that her husband was not going to break them completely changed her attitude. My buddy now had a wife who was so transformed that instead of being his biggest critic she became his biggest cheerleader. She jumped in and started working in one of the stores to help him win. The next time I saw them they were smiling and holding hands. Wow. Weird thing happened . . . two months later (two months before the deadline) he called and said he closed the stores and got a job. The business failed, the marriage survived, and there was still money in the bank, all because of a simple self-imposed deadline to make a decision.

Take the Right Amount of Time

Another practice that causes us to make decisions and make good decisions is taking time proportionate to the size of the decision. Big decisions should take big time and little decisions should be done instantly. The more money involved the more you should slow down. The more time involved as a result of the decision, the more you should slow down. The more people are involved the more you should slow down. But for goodness sakes, when buying a pack of gum, just do it, and do it quickly—you are holding up the line!

As your business becomes larger the amount of money it takes to slow a decision gets larger. Over twelve years ago we purchased a phone system for about $7,600. That was a gigantic amount of money for our little company of seven or eight people. That represented a large percentage of profits or gross sales, so the purchase was a huge decision. We spent months getting bids and learning the details of the technology. We read reports and asked consultants. We were really really thorough and we made a great decision. Two of our criteria were that the system be scalable and use cutting-edge technology. It must have been both, because twelve-plus years later, with now hundreds of team members, we are still using the same system, although it has certainly been upgraded and added to. Today to make a $7,600 decision someone in a department will do the work to make sure we are being wise, but now that would represent such a comparatively small decision that it would be closer to buying a pack of gum.

Another way to look at this concept is to say the more important the decision to the health and future of the organization, the more time you should take on it. If you are signing a five- or ten-year lease, it is extremely important that you become a real estate guru. You should know values and really know how location is going to impact the future of your business. Picking the color of the sink in the restroom shouldn't take you long, though, so just decide.

Lots of Options

In high school way back in the day I had a "little black book." If you aren't old enough to know what that is, it means I had a small pocket-size phone book with the phone numbers of every girl I knew or met. That certainly doesn't mean all of them would go on a date with me or that I wanted to go on a date with all of them, but I collected their numbers. I had no plans to get married while attending high school, so dating was a really fun game. I learned really quickly that the best way to avoid a broken heart and/or avoid a dateless weekend was to have lots of options. The more options I had the less rejection mattered. I could even prioritize my options; after all, how would she know I called five others before her? The truth is that I was absolutely no teenage Casanova, quite the opposite, but I seldom sat home moping on Saturday night because I always kept lots of options when making decisions.

A powerful element of good decision making is to have lots and lots of options. Options are power and therefore options remove fear. If you have only one vendor that can supply you a key component to your business, you will and should have fear. Eventually you will be held up on price, quality, or delivery. They own you because you have no options. The more options you have and explore the better the quality of the decision you will make. When you are trapped, you feel trapped, because you are.

If you don't have any good options then you don't have enough options; search for more. A young leader was in my office last month convinced that if we didn't change a stand I had taken on principle that his department was doomed to failure. So his method of persuading me was to present me two options: 1) abandon a principle that we have built this business on for twenty years or 2) admit that his area was doomed. Neither one of these was a good option. He made two mistakes in his presentation to me: 1) he attempted to corner an old dog like me into doing what he wanted and 2) he didn't have enough options. After we spent a few minutes discussing this he left with the clear understanding that either he was going to find some more options, more ways to skin this cat, or I would be forced to find someone who could. It wasn't mean-spirited, it was a firm, fun teachable moment for him. He is a talented young man and will make a great EntreLeader. One thing he is learning on his way to becoming a great EntreLeader is that one reason people make bad decisions is they don't have a good decision as one of their options.

Early in our radio career we developed a great relationship with one particular company that owned a bunch of radio stations. They were our largest radio customer, meaning we were on more of their radio stations than any other company. In talk radio the typical financial arrangement is that the national show, us, gets a few commercial spots an hour that we sell to national clients to make money and the local radio station carrying our show gets the rest of the commercial spots to sell locally. They make their money from their local spots and we make our money from the national spots. We don't pay them and they don't have the overhead of having to pay on-air talent. A good arrangement.

Our large customer came to us and told us they had observed how many books I sell and how many other things our company sells at least partly because I am on the radio on their station. Their CEO's idea was that they should be making some of that money, so they decided to start charging us to be on their radio stations—millions of dollars a year. We were told if we were unwilling to pay that we would be taken off their stations, which represented major cities all over the U.S. They left us with two options: 1) lose millions of dollars in revenue due to losing the stations, or 2) lose millions of dollars in revenue because I "paid" that money to them. While we were in talks we began to explore the option of being on different radio stations.

We listed the cities in order of importance to us and our whole radio team, including me, began to look for, and create, new options. We were able to cover 80 percent of the potential loss before we notified our old customer that we would be leaving. We found other options, which gave us the power to walk away. An interesting thing happened in the process: in most of the major cities we landed on better-rated, more powerful stations. We lost a few cities completely that we have yet to recover, but our total listenership and revenue went up dramatically. There we were sitting perfectly happy until this problem popped up. We first thought this mess was going to ruin us, but by fighting through to find other options, what we thought was going to ruin us pushed us to do something we would not have done otherwise: get new and better outlets for the show. Wow.

What Is Your Worst-Case Scenario?

Another part of looking at your options is to consider the absolute worst-case scenario. I am amazed at how much power it gives me when I emotionally digest and accept the absolute worst-case scenario. Once I know that I am not going to die from making this call—even if I am wrong—it releases me to make the call. Obviously your worst-case scenario is unpleasant at best, but you seldom will die from it. Even if my worst-case scenario is the loss of money, or even the closing down of part of my business, or embarrassment in the market, I can move forward to make the call with a degree of confidence. But as long as "death" in some vague sense looms in the distance or in the future you will struggle to move forward.

We started a department years ago to broadcast our live events by satellite as a simulcast to multiple locations. The technology back then was very expensive and the locations were hard to come by. We, of course, started it thinking it would be huge and we paid cash, no debt, for the launch and operation of our great idea. Our worst-case scenario was that we would lose the money invested because we couldn't make the sales, we would be embarrassed by a failure, and the people hired would have to be absorbed into other areas of the company. Our dream became a nightmare. We lost $378,000 over two years, were mildly embarrassed (mainly internally), and we have those redistributed people working all over our company to this day. That certainly wasn't our plan, but we were able to make the call to move forward because the worst-case scenario was survivable. The risk was worth it to try to win a new way. It is fun, all these years later, to realize some of the people who joined our team as a result of this "failure" have made us much more than we lost on our little nightmare.

Later, when the technology changed and became affordable, we began to simulcast again and it has become a great department.

Information Is King

Ninety percent of making the right decision is the gathering of information. The bigger the decision, the more time you take, the more options you gather, and the more informed you should become. If you are a young broke college student the cell phone you buy is a big investment and it is your social umbilical cord, so this is a big decision. EntreLeaders should take a lesson from teenagers and the amount of research they do before they purchase a phone. They intuitively know how big a deal this is, so they do sampling (try other people's phones) and focus-group testing (they ask everyone in their world what the best phone is), and they generally purchase a phone that is exactly what they thought it was. Why do teens go into such detail on the information gathering? Because it is so important to them. Yet, I meet businesspeople who will lease a building, or buy a $20,000 computer system, or hire ten people, with no more thought and research than they would do before ordering dinner.

The art to making the call, a good decision, involves gathering information. Sometimes people think that the more information you have to wade through the harder the decision is. The opposite is true; the more information you have, the more obvious the correct decision is, and therefore it is an easier decision to make. Information removes fear. Titus said, "We fear things in proportion to our ignorance of them."

Teach Your Team

The easiest and most efficient decisions are the ones you never have to make. You don't have to make these decisions because you have equipped someone else with the art of making the call. Our goal as parents is to teach our children to make their own decisions, good ones. Why? Because it is inefficient and frustrating to have a forty-year-old living in your basement waiting for you to tell them what to do every day. Business is the same way, and in spite of how obvious it is we many times hand a pile of decisions to someone on our team without first making sure they are adept in the art of making the call.

We will discuss in detail the secrets of delegation later, but for now we have to talk through getting our team to make decisions. You can't make the leap from making all the decisions to having your team make all the decisions in one step. You have to teach your team the art of making the call, particularly your leaders or future leaders. The first mistake of a small business that has hired a few people is the team, and the owner, both make the mistake of giving the owner the title of "chief fireman." The owner's job is to put out all the fires by himself—to make all the decisions. This exhausts the owner and creates a work-flow bottleneck. When we first started I decided on the quality and price of paper we would put in the copier, the type of coffee we bought, and every other single detail. I was in charge all right, but very soon I was exhausted and the team had no power and no dignity. There was a line forming at my office to ask permission and direction on every single detail. This is a normal progression for the small-business person to grow past emotionally, but be quick to recognize this as a bad process and grow your people to make the call.

Steve Brown, a leadership teacher, talks about viewing this process with monkeys in mind. Once I did so it changed my perspective, even on parenting teens. This is how Steve describes it: When a team member walks into your office with a problem, a decision that needs to be made, visualize them with a monkey standing on their shoulder. When the team member makes the statement "We have a problem," you should visualize that monkey jumping from his shoulder onto the center of your desk (insert monkey noises here). So if your team drops by your office all day long and leaves you their monkeys, you will soon be running a zoo.

Your job as an EntreLeader is to make sure when your team member leaves your office they take their monkey with them. The first step is to give them some ideas for options and instruct them to come back with three good ways to solve the problem and a suggested course of action. The next step is to teach your team to come to your office with a problem only after they have found three or more possible solutions and a suggested course of action. That makes for some great discussions and teachable moments as you show them how you would make the call. After solving problems and making the call with your help several times, the best team members begin to see the pattern you use and can do what you do.

Now you are officially beginning to run a business instead of it running you.

The final step is very personally rewarding. The final step is when the team member sends an e-mail and tells you what the problem or opportunity was, what the possible solutions were, and finally how they already solved it. Now you are officially beginning to run a business instead of it running you.

Guiding Values Make Decisions Clearer

When you have a clear sense of ethics you can make decisions more easily and quickly. A simple principle we use is to ask if, when making this decision, the move causes you to lie or hide the truth (which is a type of lying). That seems so obvious but when there is a large stressful situation that can be made to go away by sweeping it under the rug it is tempting to do so, even for those among us with the most integrity.

Another example of a guiding value might be the Golden Rule—the real Golden Rule: "Do unto others as you would have them do unto you." Over the years of operating our company this rule has saved me a ton of heartache. We ask ourselves, if the tables were turned, if we were walking in the other guy's shoes, how would we want to be treated?

We had a very sharp young video editor apply to work with our team. The VP in that department had met the young man while we were editing a project using a vendor that does editing. They became friends with all the late hours poured into the deal, and it seemed natural for this sharp young editor to join our team. It was natural until we stopped and asked ourselves how we would feel if a customer of ours stole our talent. We put the brakes on and didn't conduct a formal interview. Our VP knew our rule, the Golden Rule, required him to go through this process a different way. We determined that if the shoe were on the other foot we would not mind a team member leaving to work with a vendor or a customer. However, having some class demanded that we ask permission to talk to their employee, and if it wasn't given we would pass on the team member. So with the editor's agreement my VP called the editor's boss to ask if we could interview him and hire him away. The owner of that company was shocked that we would first ask, was very appreciative, and granted permission. We hired the guy, he still works here, and we still do lots of business with his old boss. Everyone is happy.

The opposite effect happens when you don't follow the Golden Rule. We were buying almost a hundred thousand dollars a year from a local printing company on some small jobs. They hired two of our people without talking to us and in the process we learned they were speaking badly of our company. Of course we put that company on the list of companies we don't buy from. They asked why and we told them. They couldn't believe we would get our feelings hurt and used the stupid line "That is just business." They went broke eighteen months later, and we leased their space and bought a bunch of their equipment at a bankruptcy auction. I guess that is "just business."

http://www.entreleadership.com/goldenrule

Processes Change, Principles Don't

When you identify your values and state them clearly it helps ease decision making. I am talking about principles that we stand on. These principles are immovable. We will not change the fact that we do business by the Golden Rule. We don't change principles. People who change their values, their ethics, are not trustworthy and should be avoided. They have what we call situational ethics. Their ethics change to fit the situation.

Be careful to not confuse *processes* with *principles*. Process is simply a method or way of doing things. Sometimes as organizations grow they get confused and stick by the letter of the law rather than the spirit of the law. People who never change the process, who worship process, are called bureaucrats. If your team can't explain why you do something, you are filling your building full of bureaucrats and you have sown the beginning seeds of your destruction.

If we hear a sacred cow in the hallway mooing we try to have him shot. We do not allow the answer "Because we have always done it that way." That is never a reason to keep doing something. If we have always done it that way because it is in keeping with our values, then we need to explain that to our new team member so they know the next time what the call will be, but more important why we made that call.

Small Bites

Sometimes the decision you are making is just too large; it is overwhelming. The reason you are overwhelmed might be simple: the decision is too big based on the facts you have. We often figure out a way to make a series of smaller decisions to point us in the right direction of the overall decision.

If you have six options to your decision that may be too many; narrow it down to the three best. Many times we have considered launching a new product or service and we didn't have a comfort level. So we made a smaller decision and launched part of the product line, or launched it in just one city or one region. If it works there then we feel better about the risk on a national roll-out. Sometimes we will just focus-group or survey an idea. With social media like Facebook and Twitter you can ask your customers their opinion quickly, easily, and inexpensively. Or pay a few of your customers a small amount or feed them dinner to come and look at your idea and ask them to tear it to shreds. You may be surprised how brutal they become.

This idea for decision making is as simple as saying you should go on several dates over several months before deciding to marry. You will be statistically more likely to make a good decision.

Financial Questions

When making the call ask yourself and your team if you can handle the financial hit if your decision is completely wrong. When we launch an idea it has to meet at least two minimum financial criteria. One, we can't borrow money to fund the idea. Two, if it fails it can't be fatal, meaning if our decision is faulty it can't have the possible consequence of closing us down. In poker, you call this going "all in." Too many businesses have closed as a result of going all in on one decision that they just *knew* would be a success. I've spent twenty years building this business; I'm not going to risk the whole thing on any one decision, idea, or product line. We never go all in.

The rest of the number crunching on the decision is things like how profitable it will be if it works and when we can best afford the risk, the timing. Should we make this decision this month, or is six months from now a better launch date?

Ask Experts

As you gather options and information it is always good to ask the experts. When I do my estate plan I use an attorney who specializes in estate planning and a family business counselor who specializes in family business dynamics. When I am making tax decisions I use our CFO, our tax attorney, and our CPA. When all of their advice agrees and I understand it, I am very comfortable making decisions.

You may need a marketing expert or a production expert, or an engineer. The Bible says in Proverbs 11:14, "In the multitude of counsel there is safety." Gather wise counsel and experienced counsel. The experts can even be on your team. I have a floor full of web programmers and marketers. I really do not understand a thing about the details of programming, but I have a group of experts who can explain enough to me that we can make a quality decision about our web strategy.

Note: everyone who says they are an expert isn't necessarily wise. You knew that, didn't you? In some industries the word "consultant" simply means "unemployed." They didn't make it in their profession so now they run around charging by the hour for unproven, bad advice. So when selecting an expert, check references and make sure they have done something lately. There are business consulting firms that hire brand-new fresh MBAs straight out of grad school to teach people who are actually running a business what they are doing wrong. That is ridiculous. You can hire technical acumen from a fresh young face, but if you want seasoned business acumen I prefer talking to someone who has actually done something. Make sure your expert has actually lived his advice, not just read it somewhere.

Ask Your Spouse

We use the spouse decision-making principle in all important areas of our business. I absolutely, thoroughly learned the hard way how important this principle is. When I went broke in my twenties I never asked my wife about anything in business. Sharon was a stay-at-home mom with a home economics degree and I was the hard-charging entrepreneur with the finance and business degree, so why would I want her opinion? Wow, how many stupid things I have done without the wise counsel of my wife.

Proverbs 31 says, "Who can find a virtuous wife? For her worth is far above rubies. The heart of her husband safely trusts her, so he will have no lack of gain." Assuming you have a virtuous spouse who is not acting out some kind of dysfunction, their advice will give you "no lack of gain." We are from the South, and so when my wife gets one of those feeeeelings (insert southern drawl), we don't do the deal. Every time I go against her feeeeeling it costs me at least $10,000. So Sharon, while being a stay-at-home mom, gets involved in all major decisions. Even the Lone Ranger had Tonto.

A couple of times I have done network TV contracts for show development or for a series. That is a large commitment of time and associates our brand with a particular group of people. We had network executives down to spend the day with us and negotiate the final details of a very large deal. When lunch was served in my conference room my wife came to lunch and met each of the players. She was nice, social, and listened as we did business over lunch. I have often wondered if those big-time network guys had any idea that the entire deal was in the balance over lunch, that if one little southern lady had a bad "feeeeeling" they were toast. Because she can smell a crook a mile away.

This sounds so dramatic that you may be questioning whether I've lost my mind. I have not. I run my business; my wife does not. The reason her thermometer is so trusted is she almost never steps in and plays that card. She is never arrogant about it; as a matter of fact I often have to drag her to those meetings. Do you remember the part about being "virtuous"? "Virtuous" means that your spouse is not arrogant or flippant about the power associated with this decision-making tool. If that is the case it is easy to listen to them when they do speak about a deal.

The Six-Million-Dollar Woman

Our current office building was a spouse decision. We had out-grown the place we were renting so I shopped and shopped, becoming an expert on leasable space in the area. I narrowed the options down to three places. Two of the places were offering substantial free-rent packages and concessions, so they were my favorite. But I always like to have three choices, so we put a distant number three on the list.

Sharon and I spent the afternoon looking at the places and going over the lease numbers and terms. I was of course showing her how my two favorites were the best. When we got to number three she quietly said, "This is where our company needs to be." I was shocked and said, "But, honey, look at the numbers, this is not a big corporate landlord, just an individual, and he is asking way too much for this building and it will cost us a ton more. So why do you think we should be here?"

We were standing in the atrium lobby with glassed-in offices on each side, and she pointed out that we could someday put a bookstore on one side and build our radio studio on the other side so our fans could come into the lobby and watch the show. The building was the only freestanding building among our choices, and she pointed out that we could negotiate to rename the building, and since it was an individual owner we might even talk him into selling us the building someday if we could save the money. I really hated to admit it, but she was so right. It took an extra two months and tons of headaches to get the guy to recognize that he was way overpriced and to get him to offer us an option to purchase as part of the deal.

The option to purchase was for five years at around six million dollars, which was so much money we never dreamed that we would actually do it, but we had the option. Four and a half years into the five-year option we closed the deal for cash, and at that time the building was worth about ten million dollars. After remodeling and sprucing it up, we now own a signature building worth around twelve million—that we paid six million for. My point is that in this decision-making process, listening to my virtuous wife made me over six million dollars. She is truly the six-million-dollar woman.

Write a Report

Have you ever sat down with a friend to discuss a problem and by the time you finish describing the problem you know the answer and don't need his advice anymore? The reason is simple: when you force your thought process through another layer and verbalize your thoughts, you reach a higher level of understanding. This escalation of your thought process happens yet again when you write out your problem. Thoughts are one level, verbalization is another level, and by writing out a problem you have processed it once more.

So if you are really stuck on making a decision after you have done all the other things we have talked about, then write yourself a report on the decision. Write out clearly every element of the decision and you will most times have the decision appear with great clarity. You decide the format and length of your report, but the point is to simply commit the problem and possible solutions to writing. Doing so engages a different part of the brain.

Decisions Set You Free

Principled people, EntreLeaders, are forced to address evil, inequity, conflict, as well as matters of justice and mercy. Your progress as an EntreLeader will ultimately be tied to your ability to make the call. Work to develop *making the call* an art form, where you are literally painting a canvas of your life, your business, and your future with the colors of the decisions you've made.

Many of your decisions won't be right. You will make mistakes. President John F. Kennedy said, "There are costs and risks to a program of action, but they are far less than the long-range risks and costs of comfortable inaction."

You will find that decisions are liberating. The paradox is that some of the most stressed people on the planet are people who are frozen by indecision. There is a tremendous energy and peace that decision making brings. Your team is energized by a leader who can make the call as well. Can you even envision a scene in *Braveheart* where William Wallace would stand in front of his ragtag band of brothers and wring his hands indecisively, pacing back and forth, worried if he should attack or not? Can you imagine the fear that his troops would feel, and can you imagine them becoming afraid because their leader was indecisive?

The more you are able to make the call the more peace you will walk in. I am convinced that is one of the reasons I can be so extremely busy and yet energized. I try not to go home with decisions left undone. Even if I decide to wait until tomorrow to decide, that is still stress relieving.

So when making decisions, here is a great checklist:

- ❏ Make decisions in spite of fear.
- ❏ It is okay to be passively active; deciding to wait is a decision.
- ❏ Take time equal to the size of the decision; a big decision equals longer time.
- ❏ Set a self-imposed calendar deadline if a natural one doesn't exist.
- ❏ Gather options and more options.
- ❏ He with the most information makes the best decisions.
- ❏ Clearly state your values and make decisions that match.
- ❏ Break the decision into smaller bites.
- ❏ Determine the financial implications of the decision.
- ❏ Ask real experts with the heart of a teacher.
- ❏ Seek the counsel of your spouse.
- ❏ Write yourself a report if all else fails.

5

No Magic, No Mystery

The System, the Recipe, and the Truth
About Great Marketing

It used to be that if you were in the world of self-improvement and had a book to sell, you most wanted a call from Oprah. Publishers used to call it "the Oprah Effect." Entire publishing careers, bestsellers, and huge sales seemed to be based on the author's appearance on *The Oprah Winfrey Show*. Of course I dreamed about getting on *Oprah* so I could teach people about money and getting out of debt. If I could just get on *Oprah* my dreams would all come true. When I read now what I just wrote I chuckle at my stupid self.

Several times *Oprah*'s people called and teased us with the possibility of interviewing us. We got our hopes up. We would send out our best videos and press kits and then nothing. Couldn't even get a call returned. Such is the world of publicity. I appeared on every major show and media outlet but couldn't get the holy grail of appearances, *Oprah*. They teased us so many times that our joke became, we were the folks who had *almost* been on *Oprah* more than anyone.

At that point I had done appearances on *Good Morning America, The Early Show, The Today Show, Larry King, 20/20,* every show on Fox News, almost every show on CNN—most every daily talk show, radio show, and lots of local shows all over America, but *still* no Oprah.

I did an interview on National Public Radio's *This American Life* and a weird thing happened. Lesley Stahl with *60 Minutes* was listening on her car radio in New York and immediately called us to do a *60 Minutes* profile. An hour later Dan Rather, who was then still with *60 Minutes,* was listening in his car in Dallas and called with the same idea. CBS's rule was that the first journalist to post the contact on their log got the story. So we were blessed over the next several months to spend time with Leslie and her production crew. We had the same reaction you did when you thought of *60 Minutes:* "Great, they want to do a story on us . . . uh-oh, they want to do a story on us." That's because *60 Minutes* and Lesley have been known to fillet people on TV. The good news is that we didn't and still don't have any secrets. We just help people, so when they did dig into our company and our story they found almost all positive things.

Over the next months we became, and remain, friends with Lesley and her producer Karen. I have watched her take people apart on *60 Minutes* and I wouldn't want her after me, but we experienced wonderfully professional and kind people. Even still, we waited that November evening when our twelve-minute segment was set to air holding our breath and continuing to pray that these nice people hadn't hoodwinked us and done a mean segment.

We didn't invite a big crowd to the house for a viewing party because we were worried that we might be embarrassed. So my little family and I sat in the recreation room and watched, holding our breath. Twelve minutes later we were jumping and cheering because it was all nice, positive, and we could breathe again. Their producer had hinted that it was nice by warning us to get our website and other infrastructure ready for the "*60 Minutes* Effect." It turns out that they have as big or bigger impact—when they are nice—than Oprah.

Our brand and our sales on Amazon.com and the web shot way up for well over a week; it was awesome. Then it was over and we were back to work. A few months later Oprah's people called to tease us again, only this time they kept calling and actually booked me to do the *Oprah* show. So we spent a ton of time and effort working with their team, which is also very professional, getting ready for a taping in April. We taped the show, which was scheduled to air in May, and we loaded tons of books in the bookstores, beefed up the website again, and braced ourselves for our second big hit in six months. Then our *Oprah* producer called and said they had decided not to air the show in May. What!? How were we going to explain all these books to Barnes and Noble and all the other stores? Instead they promised to air our *Oprah* show the following September. Ouch.

A Star Is Born . . . Not Really

A cool thing happened on the way to the ball, though; *60 Minutes* had gotten great ratings on our particular show and chose to rerun it in August. So get this: I was going to be on *60 Minutes* and ten days later *Oprah*. We called Larry King just because we didn't want him to be left out! It was a publicity explosion!

Now the marketing lesson comes in. As I mentioned earlier, the team that was and is working for me is young, with an average age under thirty. They wear flip-flops and T-shirts, but they are brilliant and passionate. I began to hear rumblings in our organization that my young kids were thinking this *Oprah* and *60 Minutes* thing was so awesome, and yet they had the sense it was random. Random!? I saw a teachable moment for our team. Because although the actual timing of these airdates was somewhat random, we really hadn't been "discovered" by Lesley Stahl or Oprah. We were there working hard, helping people, doing media all along. The national media just happened to notice and I wanted our team to understand that this particular event in our company wasn't random. Instead it was more like we had worked our tails off for fifteen years and we were suddenly an overnight success.

I was afraid that our young team was not going to grasp the amount of work, sweat, and toil that had built our brand to get these airings. So I sat with my leaders and came up with a way to teach our team a life and a marketing lesson. We called it the Momentum Theorem.

The Momentum Theorem

Momentum is an interesting and somewhat elusive thing. When you have momentum in any area of your life you look better than you are. When your star is shining everyone thinks you are smarter and prettier than you really are. It seems like everything you touch turns to gold, all your ideas are great, and you can do little or no wrong. Things seem to go right, just because things are going right. When business, marriage, or life is like this you definitely look better than you actually are.

> **When business, marriage, or life is like this you definitely look better than you actually are. Conversely when you don't have momentum you are better than you look.**

Conversely when you don't have momentum you are better than you look. It seems that everything you touch turns to poop, not gold. Everything that can go wrong does. It feels like you are living in the middle of a bad country song. It is tough to come to work on time and every quote sounds like a cliché. When you don't have momentum you are definitely better than you look.

What we discovered is that momentum is not a random lightning strike, but on the contrary it is actually *created*. The formula to create momentum is what I decided to teach our team so they could grasp that this huge publicity break—when looked at over the scope of a business's life—was really not random. Unstoppable huge momentum is *created*, and here is the formula:

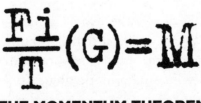

THE MOMENTUM THEOREM
FOCUSED INTENSITY OVER TIME MULTIPLIED
BY GOD EQUALS UNSTOPPABLE MOMENTUM

Focus

The F stands for "focus." Almost no one in our culture can stay focused. We can't watch a TV show through without surfing channels.

In business we can become so shortsighted that we jump erratically from idea to idea, from product to product. Companies whose stock is publically traded often fall victim to worrying about Q1 profits so much that they lose focus on the future. The whole culture has become afflicted with ADD, so much so that anyone or any business that can maintain its focus has an almost unfair advantage in the marketplace.

I was speaking to an NFL rookie camp and afterward got to talking to a veteran player, one of the league's best wide receivers. The actual physical intelligence of an NFL player is amazing. Those men can do things with their bodies and a football in a nanosecond that blows your mind. I never realized this fact watching them on TV, but standing on the sidelines and watching the game up close, it is amazingly fast and violent. What I didn't grasp was that if an NFL quarterback wanted to he could total your car with a football. His speed and accuracy is scary and he does all this while another man the size of a Kia is trying to kill him. So I asked this veteran wide receiver a facetious question: "How is it that you get paid ten million dollars a year to do one thing, catch a football, and then sometimes you drop it?" I smiled, hoping he would let me live. He smiled back and told me that if the ball is thrown correctly there is only one reason that the ball would not be caught: loss of focus.

He told me that players lose focus for a lot of reasons off the field, but in the moment of the game there are two primary reasons they lose their focus and drop the ball. The first reason they lose focus is fear. The same applies to you and me. Fear will cause you to lose focus every time because you are looking at all the potential for failure instead of concentrating on success. It was hard for me to imagine this specimen of a man before me being afraid of anything. He explained to me that when the announcer says, "He heard footsteps," that statement is not a metaphor. When a 310-pound man is chasing you with world-class speed, you literally hear footsteps that signal huge amounts of pain to follow. That signal of impending pain generates actual fear, which can cause you to lose focus and drop a ball, even if you are paid ten million dollars to do one thing: catch a football.

The second reason wide receivers, you, and I lose focus is greed. In the case of the football player he looks at the end zone and has scored in his mind before he has actually caught the ball, so when he turns back to catch it he is too late and misses. Football coaches teach the player to look the ball in, meaning to keep their focus until the catch is made, and then—and only then—turn their attention to the touchdown. When businesspeople get greedy they take their eye off the good of the customer and lose focus. Greed takes you out of the moment and into a sense of celebrating victories that have not yet been earned. Dancing before you get to the end zone makes you look foolish.

Intensity

Intensity is an interesting thing. Some people don't think of themselves as intense until they find something they care deeply about. Oftentimes we can be intense about the wrong things. I can get really intense when someone cuts me off in traffic; what a waste. We should be intentional about our intensity. Our intensity must purposefully be directed at things that really matter and purposefully not directed at things that don't.

Since we are talking football I will admit to being a season ticket holder to my Tennessee Volunteers and my Tennessee Titans. I was at a Titans game recently and the temperature was somewhere way below freezing, which for a southern boy is totally unacceptable. I looked down about ten rows in front of me and I saw this big-bellied fiftysomething-year-old guy with his shirt off and painted completely blue. I get doing that as a college student but I had to wonder about this guy.

He is obviously intense about his Titans and I am sure CBS and the players think that is awesome, but I couldn't help thinking, *Is this guy that intense about his career, about his marriage, about his kids, or even about his health?* I made the judgment call that he probably was suffering from misplaced intensity.

My suggestion is that you metaphorically paint yourself blue, because passion and intensity are two of the hallmarks of the EntreLeader.

But don't be intense about the wrong things. I want to make sure I am intense and focused when working on things that matter. If I am willing to lose my voice yelling for someone else to be successful on the football field, I should also be serving in my leadership role with great intensity. I should be engaged in conversation with my wife of thirty years with even more intensity than when we were dating. I should pursue friendships and my spiritual walk with fervor. I should be passionate about work that matters.

Time

Most people can focus if they concentrate. And most people can be intense for a while. Focused intensity at some level can be achieved by most people if and when they care enough about a certain outcome. However, few people can add the next element of the formula for very long—time. Focused intensity over time. A child can have focused intensity in the grocery store for five minutes when they see a cookie they want. Some adults can have focused intensity for a week or a month, and when they do we usually applaud them and notice the movement in their lives.

When you can find an individual who can stay focused with intensity on a certain task or subject for a whole year, you have a very unusual person and they will create such synergy in their lives that they likely can coast off the momentum for a while. Writing and publishing a book is about a year of focused intensity. I wrote my first book, *Financial Peace,* in 1992, and that is still selling thousands of copies a year. A year of intense exercise and watching what you eat will likely change the trajectory of your life physically. You will melt away fat, tone up muscle, feel better, and change your habits, likely for life. But only ten days of that exercise program won't move the needle on the scale. To create big-time success you have to stay focused and stay intense over an extended period of time.

If you can find someone who can stay on mission, on task, with focused intensity for an entire decade, I will show you someone who is world-class in their chosen area of endeavor. They are likely a national brand, or will be. In his great book *Outliers,* Malcolm Gladwell writes that one of the keys to unusual heights of success is spending ten thousand hours of practice at your chosen craft. The Beatles spent countless hours playing at summer festivals before you ever heard of them; Peyton Manning, widely regarded as one of the best quarterbacks to ever play football, has been known for his work ethic since he was a child. I just won my first Marconi Award, which is essentially the Academy Award for radio, and afterward counted up that I have been on the air over ten thousand hours. Remember, you work your tail off for fifteen years and you are suddenly an overnight success.

One of my beliefs is that you should study, interview, and when possible hang around with people who are better than you in an area you want to win in. If you want to get in shape don't spend a bunch of time with couch potatoes. If you want to be rich, interview and hang around millionaires. I started doing that many years ago after I went broke. Once I became a millionaire I started interviewing and in some cases becoming friends with billionaires. That is one thousand million dollars. Wow, that is a lot. There is plenty to learn from these people. I was blessed to have lunch with one such gentleman. He is not only a billionaire but a great man of faith, a great businessperson, a great husband, and a great dad and even granddad. He is the whole package, so with my blank yellow pad in front of me I asked him how I could be him when I grow up. In other words, I asked what advice he'd have for someone like me.

He said that there are at least two things I should do. One, always be generous. Generous in business, generous at home, and generous in the marketplace. Secondly, he said that there was a book I should buy and read. Since I am a book junkie, I loved that answer. I think books contain most of the answers, and reading them will get you where you want to go. At this point in the conversation I was dying to know the title of the book this billionaire was recommending. He continued by saying this book was vastly important in almost every area of life, and so much so that he read this book to his children and even now to his grandchildren. Well, I sat poised for the big answer with pen over paper, ready to write.

So this billionaire looked at me and said, "Have you ever read the book *The Tortoise and the Hare*?"

"Funny, that is what you have for me?" I said. "That is your pearl of wisdom, an Aesop fable?"

He laughed at me and continued: "Every time I read the book, the tortoise wins!" We live in a culture full of hares, people who can't keep their eye on the ball, who can't be focused or intense for very long at all; they can't even keep their eye on the goal long enough to win the race. Slow and steady wins the race. Slow and steady wins the race.

Businesses and entrepreneurs have become experts at microwaving rather than Crock-Potting their business plan. They are so worried about the moment, Q1 or Q2, that they lose their vision and their soul. They trade real, rich, abiding, deep success for the momentary win and then are constantly having to start over. Have a long-term vision and execute it. As the billionaire advised me, slow and steady wins the race.

God

I am a really focused person and I am very intense. Some people who are world-class have focused intensity over long periods of time. However, I am finite. My skills, abilities, and talents have a limit, and so do yours. So as a person of faith, I am convinced that my limited effort should be multiplied by the infinite God. So when the step of faith is added to my comparatively puny effort, the cause in question can literally explode. If you are trying to get momentum in marketing, business, marriage, your physical condition, or your parenting, take your best focused intensity over time and multiply it by God for unstoppable momentum.

I covered an abbreviated discussion of my Momentum Theorem in a writing project with other writers that my friend Seth

Godin put together. The next day after it was published a friend of mine who is an atheist couldn't resist poking good-natured fun at me. He said in his e-mail to me that as a fellow math nerd I should know that since there is no God that multiplying my formula times zero would result in zero momentum. Funny, I like people who can think and maintain their sense of humor. Well, if there was no God then he would be right, or if God is a really small "one" then we break even in the multiplication, but my personal experience is that my business and many others operated by people of faith have had a level of success that is simply unexplainable by looking in the mirror for the sole source of that success. You can do this Momentum Theory thing however you want and we will still be friends, if you think and maintain your sense of humor.

Marketing 101

A lot of beginners in business think of marketing merely as selling. When you first start your marketing plan may consist of simply making sure sales are made so you make payroll and pay the rent. That is what you should do, but I want you to see a bigger picture of marketing while selling that I didn't see when we first started. I had marketing classes in college and they were some of my favorite, but survival demanded I make a sale, not sit and strategize.

Marketing is really the overall plan that gets the product or service to the customer. Marketing is much more than just personal selling and an advertising plan. The selling and advertising are the micro that touch the customer directly. These smaller decisions flow from the overall big plan, known as the macro, just like your dreams and visions direct your mission statement, your goals, and even your time management. So instead of plowing the field we are flying over it at several thousand feet to get a real view of the whole field, and that allows our plowing to be more efficient and profitable.

Timing

When we dream up some great new idea inside our company, or when you dream up a great new idea that is going to become your company, one of the first things you have to determine is your timing in the marketplace. A great idea timed poorly can die a thousand painful deaths. If you are going to open a retail store you would want to consider Christmas. Most retailers make the majority of their entire year's income between Thanksgiving and New Year's Eve. So starting a new retail store in February might not be bad, but you would need to have the money to survive until sales kick in. You would want to be very careful opening a gym or starting a landscape company in November, because it is going to be several months before you have any customers. The gym will likely have its best month in January, and the landscaper will obviously start to do most of his business in the spring. This is a painfully simple and obvious observation, but there are a number of beginning small-business people and even supposedly sophisticated corporate marketers who overlook timing because they get so excited about the whole project that they plow without first flying over their field.

Timing is of course more than just which month you launch, it is also about your timing in the marketplace in a broader sense. Where are the competitors and what is the economy like? A real estate developer who gets so excited about his cool condo architecture and location and fails to realize he is in the middle of a recession will likely go bankrupt. If the market is flooded with competition you must be much more careful about your timing as well. What is in vogue, in fashion? I have a book out that sold several million copies titled *The Total Money Makeover*. The book was first published in 2003, when everything and everyone was getting a "makeover." Today you and I would not launch a new "makeover" project because that is "so ten years ago."

Timing includes the geopolitical climate as well. Wars and rumors of wars affect when you should go to market. After the 9/11 attacks we Americans were sure we were going to war. The only question was exactly when. How would you have liked to have your grand opening the night we were all glued to the TV watching the night sky light up over the desert? So you have to time product releases according to things outside your control like seasonality, the economy, competitors, and the geopolitical environment.

Timing is largely common sense, but it does require some research and understanding of the mind-set of your customer. In our business of helping people with their money we know January is a big "get out of debt and get my money straight" month. Money, weight loss, and quitting smoking are the three perennial New Year's goals people set, so January is always a big month for us. What we didn't find until later is that September and October are almost as big for self-improvement. Apparently after summer vacations are over and the kids go back to school people tend to want to restart positive things in their lives—as much or more than in January.

Talk radio gets its biggest ratings in the fall because the restarting effect, football, and politics are all at their apex in the fall. Summer ratings are the worst in talk radio. People are at the lake or the beach, and Dave Ramsey or Glenn Beck is not as appealing as a good Brad Paisley song. Consider timing when launching a new product or service, otherwise you may have a long dry spell that might not be survived.

The more experienced you are in a particular field, the more timing becomes almost second nature. You should go with your instincts, but the more experienced you are the better your instincts will be. Years of nonfatal failures will create a fabulous gut instinct that is born of experience. There once was an old man known for his great wisdom and a young man asked him how he became so wise. The old man said, "I have good judgment." The young man said, "How did you get good judgment?" The old man replied, "I have experience." Of course the young man asked, "How did you get experience?" The old man answered, "Bad judgment."

Also, for a person of faith your instincts are enhanced and directed by prayer. As scary as business can be, it has caused me to get better and better at prayer, as I am often reminded to pray about decisions.

Prototype

One of the first lessons you learn when you actually get into business is the truth of economies of scale. "Economies of scale" simply means the idea that the more widgets you order the cheaper each widget is, so when you buy in bulk you get a better deal. Not really. It is only a better deal if you sell all your widgets. If you sell half your order, then throw the rest away due to version 2.0, you will lose money because you over-ordered. In the early days of our business we thankfully didn't have the money to over-order. But I meet plenty of beginners and some supposedly educated people who are naive about their first launch, and in their excitement they over-order.

No matter how much research you do and how great your instincts, there are still some prototypes that never even make it to market in their original form. And the first version of your new product or service is almost never the version that becomes successful, so don't order in bulk.

Entrepreneurs all have ego involvement in the launch of their baby. I have seen some really ugly babies but never met a mom who thought they were ugly. You are emotionally blinded by your pride in your creation, and if you aren't really careful you will lose tons of money thinking your first version will be your hit.

In March of 1994 I launched what was to be the class that would change the way Americans handle their money. I was on one little radio station that was in bankruptcy, so they weren't even operating at full power. I made my big announcement about the new class and how the first night was free, so come one, come all. I set the chairs in the meeting room for 135 people and positioned the overhead projector to change the world. I didn't have enough money or I would have ordered a thousand workbooks to get ready for the huge turnout. I had the graphics done and made color copies of the workbook cover. I took a paper cutter and trimmed the copies to insert the cover and spine in a three-ring binder from the office supply store. Six people came the first night. Ouch. The class was called Life After Debt and was designed to help people who were struggling financially avoid bankruptcy. Six months and about a hundred customers later we had completely changed half the lessons to reflect that most people coming weren't bankrupt but just wanted to learn about money. We also changed the name to Financial Peace University, which in its many evolving versions has now had millions of people attend. Humble beginnings, but also lessons learned that your prototype, your first version, and maybe even your fourth version may not be where you find success. Allow your idea to die and be reborn repeatedly; it will get better each time.

Focus Groups

If you have gazillions of dollars you can hire marketing research firms to survey and interview groups of people you will target your marketing to. They are called focus groups. Sometimes that works, but the environment in which the potential customer is sitting is artificial, so you can possibly get bad information. Kind of like watching lethargic animals in a zoo versus being with them live on a photo safari; the animal behaves different in an artificial situation.

Most of the time you won't have the luxury of formal research or focus groups because you may not have the money to spend. However, that doesn't mean you can't survey existing customers and learn a lot about what they like. The book I wrote in 1992, *Financial Peace,* is still selling and has been revised, revisited, and redone, and now it's on version 4.2. The last time we did a big national relaunch we had the publisher develop their best cover and our graphics team develop our best cover, among the attempts, with a third choice that neither really liked. We put the three covers up on a board in Financial Peace classes in several cities around the country for people to vote on anonymously. You guessed it: they picked the cover that the "professionals" liked the least, so that's the cover we used. That is an example of an inexpensive, somewhat unsophisticated focus group.

Two years ago we alternated three different types of graphics on our website to sell live event tickets. The one that I hated sold the most. So we dropped the other two and went with what worked. So your ego and your best guess may be proven to be as pitiful as mine was. Target your idea, test it, measure your results, then change it. And don't think you are the exception; in all your brilliance, you may just have an ugly baby.

Product Life Cycle

As you are flying over your field before, during, and after plowing you always want to be aware of where your product or service fits in what marketers call the product life cycle. Almost no product lasts forever, so be aware of how long yours lasts and where it is in the cycle. There are four stages to the product life cycle and they have four distinct personalities and attributes.

Introduction Stage

The introduction stage is when you are just launching your product. This stage is characterized by a high cost of goods sold because you are placing small orders, causing your widgets to be more expensive per widget for all the reasons we just covered. You will have very high promotional costs because you are trying to get the word to the market that you exist and let people know what you do. You're just trying to get off the ground at this stage, and remember, a jet expends most of its fuel for a trip on the takeoff. Things level off once you're flying high, but takeoff can be expensive. You will have low sales and revenues because you aren't selling a lot right out of the gate. Since you have high expenses and low revenues, the introduction stage is characterized by low to no profits.

Growth Stage

As the product takes off and sales begin to grow you can slightly lower your promotion costs. Since you are ordering more widgets your cost of goods sold will go down some. You will start to realize that this is going to work. Your profits increase as sales increase and your order sizes increase, which lowers per-unit costs.

This is a fun stage because profits are up and energy is everywhere. Experiencing some wins gives the whole process momentum. Since we spent a ton of fuel getting the plane off the ground successfully, now we can let off on the gas a bit and enjoy the flight.

Maturity Stage

Once the product matures in the marketplace, your advertising schedule can be reduced to a maintenance program. Needing only minimal advertising to let your customers know about you lowers promotion costs considerably. This stage is also characterized by the lowest cost of goods sold, because you have been, and are, ordering in bulk. Plus you have found the best prices on all your materials and are much more streamlined in production. Because you have developed a track record in the marketplace your sales will be very predictable. With low costs and high sales, this is usually the most profitable stage. This stage is honestly the least stressful, with one exception: competitors have taken notice of your great success and typically enter the market at this stage.

Declining Stage

This stage is where you realize the mortality of your product; nothing lasts forever. Sales begin their decline, and while the cost of goods can be very low you will have leftover inventory. The cost of goods can be very high as reordering in small quantities drives up per-unit cost. Advertising and promotion should be limited and low, keeping costs down. Overall profits begin to decline as sales decline. This is the time to make sure you are suggesting add-on sales to your customer base by adding another product to the order as an up sale. And this is the time to begin thinking about reinventing your product.

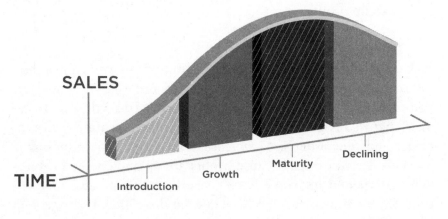

You Are Here

The product life cycle can be very, very short or very, very long with a particular product. An interesting exercise is to think about where in the cycle the individual product is, where your company is, and where your industry is. This will give you really good insight as to how you should move through your marketing plan and the message you should be sending your customer.

I will illustrate with one industry I am in, publishing. The industry of creating books is a very old industry. The product life cycle of the whole industry is centuries old and is probably in the maturity stage. A book published by me on leadership has concepts that are timeless and so hopefully will have a five-to-ten-year life cycle. Other books last a year or two in the fiction category before tapering off, and books by my friends who write on politics dealing with the problem of the moment often have about a ninety-day life cycle. The vast majority of sales for the typical book are in the first 120 days. There are exceptions, like business books such as *Good to Great* and the Bible, which is a perennial bestseller. But since most books are in the 120-day cycle, most bookstores think 120 days at a time and are not geared to house long-lasting books.

When we launch a new book it is at the introduction stage, while the industry as a whole is at the maturity stage and my company is in the growth stage. We have to consider all the layers and what that means to the marketing plan. First, the industry is mature, so we don't have to tell people about this whole new way of getting information and explain how it works; we all "get" books. However, there are lots of new ways books are purchased in the e-world, so we have to make sure we are there. Our company has a nationally known brand and we are growing, but how do we take that momentum and point it all at a book? Lastly the book is brand-new, so lots of education and promotion will have to be done to take it through the introduction stage. Sometimes all these viewpoints feel like common sense, and when you take the time to fly over your field you will see them fairly easily and quickly. The problem is so many businesspeople spend so much time in the field that they miss these easy observations and they make mistakes like pouring unnecessary advertising on a mature product.

If you are behind the plow you don't always see the end coming and therefore don't stop to reinvent yourself. As the product matures, do you reinvent yourself or let it die and go on to the next product? Some products are created with a knowledge that they will die. A book attacking the presidency of Bill

People don't want to be "marketed to," they want to be "communicated with."

—Flint McLaughlin

Clinton might have sold well during his impeachment hearings, but that book would be seriously dated today. But a book like Stephen Covey's *The 7 Habits of Highly Effective People* has a long life and can be reinvented with a new cover and some "updates." My first book, *Financial Peace,* has been "revised," "updated," and even "revisited." Each time we reinvented the book with some new chapters, updated statistics, and a new cover. This reinvention restarts the product life cycle, but not from the same low point as the beginning. Overlay a new life cycle with the introduction overlapping the old cycle way into the declining stage. You will never look at "new and improved" the same again.

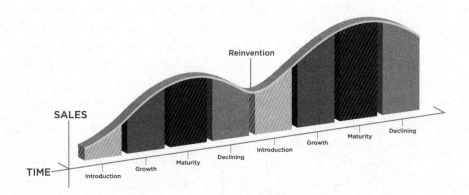

Pour Your Customer Through a Funnel

When you first start your business you normally start with just one product or service. We all have that great idea that strikes us like lightning and we take off running into the marketplace. That passion and energy is great, and it is how great companies are born. As you get your first product working you should be very strategic and thoughtful about the further development of other product lines. A great way to build a loyal and continuously grow-ing customer base is to build a line of products and services using the funnel approach.

The funnel approach is simply having some inexpensive or free and quick ways to interact with your company. The quicker and cheaper the product or service, the more people you will draw. This can be as simple as having lots of quality content that the customer can get for free on your website. Then you develop a product that has a little more cost and might take more time. You should continue this down the funnel until you get to your most expensive and time-intensive product. The more money and time you ask of your customers, the fewer will follow you down the funnel. But remember, the greater the number that enter at the top, the more will come out the bottom. If ten people visit your website to read content for free and four end up buying a $59 product, and then one of them purchases a $3,500 product, you have accomplished your goal. Your next goal would be to have a hundred people start at the top instead of just ten. So while mil-lions of people may buy and read this book for less than $30, the number of people who will shell out $6,000 to go to a week-long class taught by me on leadership in a resort location is much smaller.

When I taught this lesson at our EntreLeadership Master Se-ries a guy who owns a heating and air company thought this was worth trying. He thought he just did HVAC repair and replace-ment, but by flying over his "field" this way he saw something new. He went home and changed his website to reflect the funnel. He first offered free downloadable reports on how to make your furnace, air-conditioning, and hot water heater last longer with some simple free maintenance tips. The most popular free report was "Ten Things Anyone Can Do to Lower Their Utility Costs." He asked for an e-mail address to get the free reports and offered his e-mail newsletter to continue the free education. Oh, and by the way, did you know that replacing a ten-year-old or older, inefficient HVAC system with a new one can cut your utility bills in half?

Next down the funnel he offered a $59 HVAC tune-up, which included a fourteen-point checkup and cleaning to make the system run better in the hot summer or cold winter and make sure the unit is safe. Of course sometimes the tune-up led to the discovery that the system was on its last legs and it would have to be replaced. So the funnel started with a free report and ended for some folks with a $3,500–$5,000 purchase. Not to mention duct cleaning, allergy filter systems, and other products. He sent me a note to say that simply viewing his product offerings through the funnel had opened up a ton of new business for him. Again, this is kind of common sense, but when you are fighting to make payroll and dealing with the day-to-day fires that running your business entails, sometimes you forget to step away from the plow and fly over your field.

Marketing Stew

The mystery of marketing is not really a mystery. There are just so few people in business who do all the parts intentionally. The marketplace's reaction to our best ideas can be mysterious, but how to build a plan to let people know how we can serve them is not mysterious. Just like making a great pot of stew on a cold winter's day, there is truly a recipe.

If you have worked through the prototype and fully developed the product, and if you have studied with a focus group how your customer will react, you are getting close to launch. Of course you consider the timing of your product, where your company and industry are in the product life cycle, and even consider what the funnel approach is telling you about pricing. Most of all you really want to make sure your product quality is as perfect as you can make it.

Mike Hyatt, a friend of mine and CEO of a major company, has a great saying: "A great marketing plan helps a bad product fail faster."

So in other words, never have your grand opening on your restaurant until all the recipes are proven and beyond yummy. You can draw a huge crowd to your business, but if they have a bad experience they'll spread the negative word about you. So make really sure your very best is ready before you go to market. If you are ready, then it is time to make sure you have all the ingredients for marketing stew.

Ingredient One: Passion

In my early twenties I was involved in network marketing, or multi-level marketing, for about three months. I learned a lot of things to never do in business, but I also took away a lot of good lessons as well. One of the things I learned is that passion sells. One superstar of this multi-level was a guy named Dee Pinkard. He used to say, "There is no energy in logic, only in emotion." I agree, and marketing has to have energy. Logic, while factual, is flat and moves no one to action.

You will only sacrifice when you passionately believe in the outcome.

If you are selling one-on-one, marketing, or leading, passion makes the sale. Passion will cover a multitude of errors and misunderstandings. Passion will overcome a lot of ignorance, when you don't know what you don't know. François VI, duc de La Rochefoucauld, said, "The most untutored person with passion is more persuasive than the most eloquent without." I agree; I have seen very academic, intellectual, and sophisticated marketing plans that had no spark and flopped. There needs to be a champion or a building full of champions willing to fight all enemies of success, because the outcome matters deeply to everyone involved. If you and your team can't get shouting-excited about the thing you are doing, then don't do it. Marketing requires a catalyst, and that is almost always a person or group of people who will fight to the death to win because they believe so deeply in what they are doing. So many marketing plans lack this deep soul-based emotion and I am convinced that is one of the reasons so many marketing plans fail.

When you and your team have passion, when there is a sense you are on a crusade, you become willing to sacrifice to make something bigger than you happen. There is always a price paid in energy, time, money, and pain to succeed. You will only sacrifice when you passionately believe in the outcome.

Ingredient Two: Activity

I got my real estate license three weeks after I turned eighteen years old and worked forty to sixty hours a week selling real estate while I went through four years of college. I was a crummy salesperson, an immature kid, but a working maniac. I made cold calls, knocked on doors, and sat in open houses with an unmatched enthusiasm. So even though I wasn't very polished I sold houses in a 17-percent-interest-rate environment. Why was I able to overcome all those personal and marketplace obstacles? Activity. I outworked almost everyone. My broker (boss) during those times was a kind man who would just shake his head in amazement that I even survived. One day he said, "Ramsey, your success is amazing; I guess even a blind hog can find an acorn if he wanders enough." Since I am not from the farm I am not exactly sure what he meant, but I took that to mean a hog eats acorns and even a blind one that keeps moving won't go hungry.

Marketing dreams that come true equal an absolute explosion in the marketplace. Your sales and success soar. This kind of explosion almost never occurs randomly; it requires tremendous amounts of activity: lots of promotion, advertising, sales teams, and whatever else it takes to inject an energy into your market to create the potential for an explosion. Another principle for taking your activity and causing an explosion is to compress your activity in a shorter time frame. When you do a year's worth of work in ninety days, you are forcing a huge amount of activity into a small time frame, which will often give you critical mass and make the explosion occur. A diesel engine runs on this same principle. There are no spark plugs to electrically ignite the fuel in the combustion chamber, so the injectors mist the fuel into the chamber and as the same amount of molecules are forced into a smaller and smaller area by the piston driving up, an explosion occurs, driving the piston back down. So cram a ton of activity in a small space of time and your marketing engine will run.

More activity is insurance against failure. Simply, if you make a hundred sales calls you are more likely to make a sale than if you make ten sales calls. That is such a ridiculously simple concept that I am really confused why entire companies die from lack of activity in their approach to marketing. More activity gives you more options to make a sale, and just like the art of making the call can be enhanced by options, so can your marketing.

Increases in activity should be based on a certain boldness. Timidity and passivity don't work in capitalism, so you must make the bold proclamation that you and your company have arrived and the market should stand up and take notice. When you pour out yourself and your company in the marketplace you will begin to win, and as you win, expect criticism and complaints. You can't lead, market, and/ or run a company successfully without drawing fire from people who don't understand. So as you win prepare to be misunderstood and lied about.

> **The only people who never fail are those who never try.**
> **—Ilka Chase**

Activity and success make rejection and nonfatal failure easier to work through emotionally. When there are a ton of customers, one that is mean to you doesn't matter as much. I remember when I wrote my very first book, *Financial Peace,* and had some at the back table to sell after a little keynote speech for twenty-five people at a lunch. A guy came to the table to argue with me about my comments and about what my book said about money. He was angry about what I taught and it took me several days to recover from that confrontation. Now that I have sold over two million copies of that particular book I almost find it humorous when a guy like that sends hate mail or tries to corner me at a party. The success and numbers, due to activity, take the power away from detractors, because they are obviously wrong. But when I just had one baby and someone called it ugly, it was devastating. Activity gives you a different perception or viewpoint on the trash that comes with success.

Ingredient Three: Scarcity

Everyone wants a table at a restaurant that is full, everyone wants to join a country club that is hard to get into, and everyone wants the latest electronic game or gadget so badly they will stand in a mile-long line to get it. When you can create the perception that your product is scarce or rare you have added tremendous marketing energy to your plan. I would never suggest that you do this without integrity. However, what we are trying to do with a huge prelaunch strategy is make so much fuss in the market that people will stand in line. Some camp in line around the block to buy an iPhone that in three weeks can be bought just by walking in the store. Apple does a great job creating this fervor to be the first to own something rare and precious; it is part of their marketing genius.

Toy marketers create the same level of frenzy by scarcity, usually around Christmas. Certain dolls or computer games reach such a level of fervor that people buy them and mark them up ten to twenty times and sell them on eBay. If someone were to wait simply thirty to sixty days, the same item would be on sale for half off. Wouldn't it be great if your product had so much marketing energy around it that people would stand in line and get in fights over their place in line for the opportunity to give you their money? Wow.

Sometimes scarcity is the reality of limited production, but sometimes it is based on huge amounts of quality or talent. There are people who cut hair, and then there are the people who develop such a reputation at cutting hair that it is a privilege to be on their calendar to have them cut your hair and charge you triple. As someone with no hair, I truly don't get it, but I have to stand back and admire that they created such a mystique around themselves and their service that they are in such great demand due to perceived scarcity.

Ingredient Four: Urgency

A cousin of scarcity is urgency. If your product or service is scarce it immediately conveys urgency to the customer to "act now— there is a limited number at this price!" Jim Rohn says, "Without a sense of urgency, desire loses its value." Think about the concert with a performer who is so hot that tens of thousands of tickets sell out in minutes. Why does that happen? Urgency. The concertgoer believes, accurately so, that if he isn't on the website at the perfect time to purchase tickets, he will miss his favorite star. When we are doing huge live events in arenas and we are down to our last few hundred

> If you make a product good enough, even though you live in the depths of the forest, the public will make a path to your door, says the philosopher. But if you want the public in sufficient numbers, you better construct a highway.
> —William Randolph Hearst

tickets to sell, and I go on my radio show and announce accurately that we are almost sold out, the last few tickets sell in minutes, when just a week before we didn't sell that many all week.

Ingredient Five: The Momentum Theorem

Of course we go back to the start of this chapter and remember the Momentum Theorem: focused intensity over time multiplied by God equals unstoppable momentum. As you approach your product or brand strategy, make sure you use this to stir your marketing stew.

You are focused, you are intense, and you look at scarcity, urgency, activity, and passion to apply all of your efforts to make the stew. However, like the farmer, after you have planted the crop with your hard work and intelligence, you will still have to count on God to send the rain. If your outcomes are limited to the result of your best efforts then your outcomes are too limited.

Tastes Great

Most businesses large and small, primitive and sophisticated, seldom are intentional about making sure all these ingredients are in their stew. Most business also never take the time to think about how to plow their field by first flying over it. We are in such a hurry to get to market that marketing as a strategy and a thoroughly designed plan is seldom done. I have cost myself so much money with false starts and mistakes that it makes me sick to think about it. But with as much regret as I have for those, I take even more pride in the times we did things right. It is immensely satisfying to create a multilayered, multifaceted plan, execute it, and win as a result. Slow down and do this marketing stuff right.

The natural result of marketing stew created by all these ingredients and you being more thoughtful about your approach to your customer is that you are then given the opportunity to serve them with your product or service.

6

Don't Flop Whoppers

A Practical Guide to Launching Your Dream

Standing in his garage, full of uncertainty and a healthy dose of desperation, in 1972 was an energetic young EntreLeader-to-be. The garage wasn't anything special and if it weren't for his wife's passion for cleanliness it would have been dusty or even dirty. They made precut picture frames that you could assemble yourself in those days, and they still do. He and his wife worked at night, as did their kids as they got older. A background in retail made our young entrepreneur dream and know that this company of his could be big. Starting with only $600 and a dream, this thirtysomething-year-old began to build a company that eventually became wildly successful. My friend David Green built Hobby Lobby, with over twelve thousand employees and billions of dollars in revenue, starting in his garage.

In 1946 there was a little nondescript grill in South Atlanta. World War II had just ended and an extremely energetic young man decided to get in the restaurant business even though the economy wasn't that great. He purchased, cleaned, and dove into a little place called the Dwarf Grill. Later the little grill became known as the Dwarf House and is where my friend Truett Cathy says he invented the chicken sandwich. Dan and Bubba, his sons, will tell you stories of being paid to work, doing things like cleaning gum from under the tables, when they were eight or nine years old. They opened the first Chick-fil-A in 1967 and now have billions of dollars in revenue and employ tens of thousands. They have the most unique operator-partners business model in the industry, which has made many of their hardworking operators wealthy as well. Eat More Chicken.

In 1972, the same year Hobby Lobby started, times were tough. We were in the middle of Vietnam, inflation was rampant, and lines at gas stations were about to become normal. That same year an inventor had a weird idea. George Ballas discovered that really thick fishing line twirling quickly would cut grass. The Weed Eater was born, and sales reached eighty million dollars in just five years, by 1977. Today the Weed Eater brand has so much penetration in our culture that the name is used interchangeably for all weed whackers. Just like all tissues are Kleenex and all petroleum jelly is Vaseline.

A few years ago I met a man named Jay Steinfeld from Houston, Texas. Jay started a drapery business in a little one-thousand-square-foot shop in 1987. In 1993 he paid $1,500 to build his first website, and a couple of years later spent another $3,000 to upgrade it to have an e-commerce element where he could actually sell window blinds online. By 2001 the website run from their garage had exploded, so they sold the little drapery store. Jay has been wise and worked really hard transitioning his company to a web-based seller of window blinds. From those humble beginnings Blinds.com now is the largest seller of window blinds online in the world; more than half the blinds in the world sold online are sold on his site. He and his 115 team members will this year sell more than eighty-five million dollars in window blinds and associated products at Blinds.com.

In the middle of high inflation and an energy crisis a young computer genius started the whole personal computer revolution in his garage and dorm room in 1975. No doubt you know that was Bill Gates; he was twenty years old. A few years later in 1984, probably inspired by Gates, Michael Dell started Dell computers in his dorm room at nineteen years old. Note that our economy was still reeling from a deep recessionary mess in 1982.

Great oaks are grown from humble beginnings as small acorns. Small-business start-ups bootstrapped from nothing are a part of our American story. Many of you reading this book need to know that the company you work for likely deserves your respect because of the heritage it represents. Maybe you are thinking about becoming one of those stories or are in the midst of making your dream become a reality.

I want to encourage you in your start-up to keep it humble. You don't need to go $100,000 in debt on an SBA loan against your home so you can open with an executive office lined in walnut. Start small and be proud. Start humble and be proud. My business started on a card table in my living room. These businesses that start from home are often called microbusinesses, or cottage industries, or home-based businesses. Accurate statistics about these businesses are very hard to find, because the very nature of this type of person is they don't want to be on the radar of the government. These people like their freedom; that is why they went into business. However, each of the vastly successful businesses above started in some form or another in the garage, the living room, or the dorm room—no fancy office, no huge manufacturing plant, no team of MBA executives, and no idea if they were going to make it.

I am convinced the backbone of our economy is the small-business entrepreneur. Currently 64 percent of Americans work for a company that has less than five hundred employees. The Census Bureau says that 98.3 percent of the companies in the U.S. have less than a hundred employees. Right now, somewhere in America, maybe reading this book, is the next Bill Gates, Truett Cathy, or David Green. The right and the ability to take nothing and make something from it is inherently American. So don't be ashamed or afraid to start small.

Part-Time

Also, some businesses start part-time and even remain part-time, which is a good thing. Sometimes a fireman who works forty-eight hours on and then has a few days off will start a landscaping or painting company. He has no intention of quitting the fire department but his unique schedule frees him up to pursue all kinds of small-business ideas.

The best part-time job is very possibly a small-business idea.

I have nothing against Burger King, but why flop Whoppers at minimum wage when there are a million small-business ideas you could start with today? There is no point in remaining unemployed "looking for work." Work isn't really hard to find if you look at the needs people have and how you might serve them.

A microbusiness begun on a part-time basis may or may not become a big deal, but again, there is no shame in starting small. Matt knocked on our door one morning and took a step back on the porch, so as not to be threatening as my wife answered the door. He explained to her that he had opened a business for the summer to pay his college tuition in the coming fall. He'd purchased a pressure washer and was at our home to offer to pressure-wash and seal our driveway, because he and his friend were going to be working in our neighborhood that week. Eleven hundred dollars and ten hours later he was on his way. If I do my math right little Matt is making more than some attorneys. But some college students working on a marketing degree can't find summer work because the economy is bad according to the newscaster. Shut up.

One winter break my college roommate and I knocked on the doors of homes with chimneys and made the same pitch as Matt, only we wanted to sell them firewood. In a very quick and cold month we sold, cut, and delivered seventy-eight ricks of wood, which paid for our tuition for the next semester. Meanwhile we had friends flopping Whoppers at minimum wage taking out student loans. I wish I was smarter and would have been Michael Dell or Bill Gates instead of Paul Bunyan swinging an ax, but you work with what you have.

Certainly all the cottage industry ideas aren't manual labor either. I love stories of people who work smarter, not just harder, like this golf fan:

> Golf was once just a hobby for Jason Droege. Now it's his livelihood. One day, while playing golf with a friend, Droege was struck with a vision: Lying in the garages around our nation were thousands of discarded golf clubs. Droege knew that one person's trash is often another person's treasure, so in 2002, he launched his business, the Back 9 Golf Co.

Jason would go to garage sales and other sources where individuals wanted to sell used clubs and buy them cheap. He cleaned them up and put them on eBay for sale. He kept growing his idea, made some connections with major, national golf retailers, and within four years he had $2 million in sales on eBay. . . .*

In January of 2004 Cain Bond at nineteen years old decided to do the same concept of buying used, then re-selling, but he did so with used baby strollers. A short five months later in June of 2004 he moved $30,000 of product on eBay. He continued to grow and a year later opened a bicycle store and by 2006 did over $1 million in sales at twenty-one years old.†

These are both stories from *Entrepreneur's eBay Startup Guide*. There are hundreds of thousands of stories like this with lesser numbers. So whether it is e-tailing, dog walking, data entry, or swinging an ax, you always have opportunity out there.

Often on my radio show people are calling me for advice about how to get out of debt or get themselves out of some kind of money pinch they are in. Sometimes they can cut spending, but often they simply need to make more money, and a part-time job is a great temporary answer to that. The part-time small business is a great part-time job, but you can also simply look at your part-time job as your business.

I am known for telling people to go deliver pizzas or throw papers for some quick extra money. I had an energetic and analytical young man working for our team during the day, but he wanted some more money so he decided to deliver pizzas. Anyone can just walk up to the door and hand someone a pizza. But John was not content with doing just the basic process because his best money came from tips, so he began experimenting with several variables that caused his tips to increase. He built a spreadsheet so he could

---

* *Entrepreneur's eBay Startup Guide*, a publication of *Entrepreneur* magazine, June 2006, p. 28.

† *Entrepreneur's eBay Startup Guide*, p. 80.

graph the results of each of his ideas. First he found that given the territory of his pizza shop, if he left with more than three deliveries in his car at a time, by the time he got to the fourth one he was running late in the customer's mind, and the proof was that often the pizza was cold. Two deliveries was inefficient and four was too many. He discovered that after ringing the doorbell he needed to take at least three steps back so the person answering the door was not intimidated by his height and presence.

He also found that when he could he should park his car in sight of the room where the TV likely was, so that someone would see him arrive and announce throughout the house, "Pizza is here!" After parking where people could see him in advance, he found he should jog slightly as he went to the door, showing he cared. He tried whistling while he ran and while he waited for the door to be opened. He even tracked whether one tune he whistled was better than another. He became very intentional about smiling and reminding them that the pizza was piping hot and delicious.

Other than calculating the proper number of deliveries to take at one time, thus making sure he delivered hot pizza, what he did to increase his tips the most was genius. John noticed that a large percentage of the time a dog greeted him with the family member ready to pay. Being a dog lover, he realized how it helped his tips if he would pet the family dog and make conversation about it. That is when he had his breakthrough: he went to the building supply store and bought a nail apron that tied around front with two pockets in it. He then put dog biscuits in the nail apron so he could give Fido a treat right in front of Fido's master. Brilliant!

So your pizza delivery guy parks so everyone sees him coming, jumps out of the car jogging with service energy to the front door, whistles and smiles, steps back until the door is opened, gives your dog a treat, and hands you a piping-hot pizza as he is reminding you verbally that it is hot and delicious. If you don't tip this guy lavishly you are a troll! Transpose that with the guy who pulled up in front of my house one time and sat in his car honking the horn until we walked out to the car, where he handed us the pizza through the car window and snarled how much we owed. See? Everyone is ultimately self-employed, aren't they?

Want to hear something really stupid? John quit delivering pizzas for that company because the store manager, a real boss, became jealous of his tip income and demanded he start carrying more pizzas per run, thus messing up the whole formula. Leadership is required to win in business.

Time to Jump

So when is it time to quit your day job so you can devote all your energies to your new small business? Most people get so excited that they tend to want to quit too soon. I suggest you wait until the boat pulls up to the dock before you jump in. What I mean is if you quit your day job before you get your small-business net income up high enough, you will miss the boat and become all wet.

So I look at two things when helping an EntreLeader decide when it is time to make the jump to full-time. One, how much are you making as a percentage of your day job? A young EntreLeader named Tim called to ask me if he should or could quit his full-time job and make the jump. Last year he made $6,000 at his part-time graphic arts business. He works as a graphic artist for a big company, making $70,000 a year. When we hear that, you and I instantly know that is too far to jump and he will put his family in jeopardy if he does. So I prescribed that he increase his efforts and hours dramatically, working like a crazy man to get his income up. It is hard to work your day job and spend a ton of hours on your business, but it is harder to make a mistake and lose your home in foreclosure because you jumped before the boat was close enough to the dock. I recommended that he have one year of making at least $45,000 from his side job, then make the jump. This does two things: one, we know

It is hard to work your day job and spend a ton of hours on your business, but it is harder to make a mistake and lose your home in foreclosure because you jumped before the boat was close enough to the dock.

that he can actually make a living as a small-business person, and two, with making $70,000 at the day job plus $45,000 from his business, he should be able to build up a nice cushion in his savings, making the jump more likely to work. He won't starve out.

The second factor when deciding if you are ready to jump is to consider how the income is trending from your small business. In the case of our graphic artist, Tim, if he has shown a steady and predictable increase in income he might make the jump sooner rather than waiting a whole year. Last year he made $6,000, which is $500 per month. So what if next month he makes $1,000, and the next month $2,000, and the next month $3,000, and the next month $8,000, and the next month $9,000? Then he has shown that the business grows based on his increased effort, so dropping the day job that is now paying less per month is not as tough a decision. But apply common sense to this analysis; if all this income is coming from one client, you aren't ready to jump. If this increased income is proof that a well-diversified client base and an excited marketplace exists, then you can make the jump after a good six-month trend.

Time to Expand Your Company?

One of the scariest decisions is when to hire that first team member. Really every hire is scary up until you have ten to fifteen team members. As I teach small-business people I am often asked how to decide if you are ready to expand. The answer? Use the same thought process that we just discussed for deciding to go full-time. You should be putting in ridiculous hours that are all creating extra income for several months to ensure that you really need help. Just being overworked isn't enough; you need to have income created by that work to pay people. Seems obvious, but a lot of people go from a microbusiness to hiring just because they are tired, not because they are profitable. Small business is not for wimps; suck it up until you make a profit, then you can expand. Until you are making a profit you don't have anything you want more of anyway.

Higher Calling?

At its most basic level there are two reasons to work. We work for money to provide food, shelter, and so on, and we work as a higher calling. I often suggest part-time work or a part-time small business just to make money to get a family through a rough spot, and there is great honor in that. Working only for money should only be a temporary arrangement while you clean up a mess, hit a goal, and/or move toward your passion, but there is great honor in doing what it takes to save your family or to hit a short-term goal. Don't sit unemployed for two years with your home going into foreclosure because you haven't been able to work in your passion; that is irresponsible.

Don't sit unemployed for two years with your home going into foreclosure because you haven't been able to work in your passion; that is irresponsible.

While you are working only for money, make sure you do that job with passionate excellence, as if it were your life's calling. You never know who is watching. As a teenager I went with my family to a wonderful steak house for dinner. Our waitress, who was probably not working in her life's calling, was on fire. She was there at the table taking the order and bringing the food with a smile and an energy that every restaurant manager dreams of. My dad hired her the next week to sell real estate for our family real estate company. The first year, this twentysomething young lady sold a million dollars' worth of real estate, which in today's dollars would be about ten million. You never know who is watching when you are working for money, so do it with excellence.

Matt didn't consider sealing driveways his life's calling and passion; he wanted money for tuition. I certainly didn't consider cutting firewood my life's calling or passion; I wanted money for tuition. John wasn't delivering pizza with excellence because it was his life's calling or passion; he was doing that for money to pay off debt. There is great honor in working for money with excellence to hit a short-term goal, but don't lay out a life plan or business plan for the long term that is just for money.

Passion Matters, Calling Matters

Seth Godin says, "Instead of wondering when your next vacation is, maybe you should set up a life you don't need to escape from." Business is way too hard to work at something just for money. Winning at business at times requires that you exhaust every ounce of spiritual, emotional, and physical energy you have. You won't put that effort in day in and day out, year in and year out, just for money. Money is great, but it is ultimately an empty goal. Bigger homes, bigger cars, and even more giving is just not a big enough goal to keep you creative and energized throughout your life. You have to have a passion, a higher calling, to what you engage in. Malcolm Gladwell says, "Hard work is a prison cell only if the work has no meaning."

So only the spiritually and emotionally immature person picks a business to go into simply because they think they can make a lot of money. Find something you love doing so much that on the tough days you have a reason to fight on. The "why" of your business has to be so big that it keeps you on fire and even bleeds over to your team and ignites them.

Simon Sinek does a great TED talk (TED is an online motivational series) about people and companies who win because they get the *why* of their calling. He calls it "the Golden Circle." Picture three rings making a bull's-eye. In the center ring, you have *why*; in the middle ring, you have *how;* and in the outer ring, you have *what*. As Sinek explains it, every company knows *what* they do (their product or service). Most companies know *how* they do it (their process or work flow). But very few companies know *why* they do it at all. The companies that really get the *why* of their business—their purpose, their reason for existing—are the ones that win big-time. They operate from the inside out, pushing their *why* out through their *how* and *what*. That way, everything they do—from products to processes—is centered on the very core, the heart, of their mission.

The bottom line for businesses, according to Sinek, is that "people don't buy *what* you do, they buy *why* you do it. The goal is not to do business with everybody who needs what you have (the what). The goal is to do business with the people who believe what you believe (the why)."

This isn't just about products either; it's about people. He explains that if you hire somebody just because they need a job (the what), they'll work for your money. But if you hire someone who believes what you believe (the why), they'll give you their blood, sweat, and tears.

Sinek nails this point using the Wright brothers as an example. The race for manned flight was on at the turn of the twentieth century. Several people had gotten close, and many people began to believe for the first time that it might actually be possible for man to fly.

Two brothers, Orville and Wilbur Wright, had a dream of flying. They knew in their hearts it was possible. They had no money, no backing, no support, and not even a college education between them, but they were motivated by a passion to fly. They had a *why,* and they were determined to drive that *why* into a *what*—man's first airplane.

They weren't deterred by failures or crashes. In fact, they took five sets of parts with them every day when they went out, because they knew they'd crash at least five times before the end of the day. But they kept trying. And then, on December 17, 1903, the Wright brothers' powered glider took off and landed successfully for the first time, literally changing the world with a single 120-foot-long flight that lasted only 12 seconds.

But the big takeaway from this story is that another man, Samuel Pierpont Langley, was the big flight dog of the day. He was considered the one most likely to crack the code of powered manned flight. The government gave him a grant of $50,000, so money was no object. He taught at Harvard, worked with the Smithsonian, and interacted daily with the best minds in the country. In fact, *The New York Times* followed him around and wrote several stories about him, and the whole world was practically waiting on Langley to launch man's first airplane.

What he didn't have was a passion, a higher calling. He didn't have the *why.* The best minds, the most money, and all the other reasons to win didn't produce a winner because there was no passion. He just wanted to get rich, and he thought he could do that by flying.

And not only did Langley not win, he became a sore—and stupid—loser. As proof of that, Langley stopped all research and closed up shop as soon as the Wright brothers won the race. If he was passionate about flight, he could have taken his talent, all the money, and the best minds and built upon their success, even applauded their success; instead, he simply quit. He basically took his toys and went home. He quit because he was only in it for the money and had no passion. Langley didn't have a *why*; he only had a *what*. That's why you've never heard of him.

Selecting a Business

The moral of this section of the story is that you can and should make money, lots of it. But for the long term, select something that causes a chill to run down your spine. Whether you are selecting a business for the long term or for a short-term financial goal, there is seldom a need for you to make a huge lurching change in the direction of your life.

If you are trying to make some extra cash and you are a graphic artist, don't go try to get an accounting degree. Just open up your laptop and design yourself some great graphic artist business cards. If you are a bookkeeper or accountant, you don't have to get a PhD in art appreciation to make some extra money; just start doing books for some small-business people who need your help.

Career coach Dan Miller, whom I mentioned earlier, wrote a bestseller called *48 Days to the Work You Love*. Dan says that you should always begin building your life bouquet from those flowers that are within reach. He further says that your career choice, or small-business choice, should be a reflection of three main areas:

1. *Skills and Abilities*. What have you been trained for and what are your natural talents? I am very good at

math; it is a natural and a trained talent. So finance is a place I feel very comfortable.

2. *Personality Traits.* I am a people person and very task oriented, but not good at details, so even though I am good at math and could make a lot of money, being a tax accountant would make me want to shoot myself every day.

3. *Values, Dreams, and Passions.* I don't believe in debt, so it would be inconsistent with my values for me to sell something every day, all day, that involved the customer going into debt; I would be miserable.

So on its most primitive level gathering flowers within reach for a part-time business just to make money simply means you should do something you know and have the tools to do. If you have a lawn mower, you can cut grass. If you have a car, you can deliver pizzas. If you know accounting and have a computer, you can keep books. Simple. However, at its deeper level gathering this bouquet means really growing and searching out the life mystery of why you were put on the planet. Only select a business to be in as a career choice that meets the above three principles.

So if you have always loved working on things and you love motorcycles, maybe you'll start the next Orange County Choppers. But don't be like Chris, someone I met with who was suicidal, literally. He is a great sales guy, a lover of people, and hates details. His brother-in-law talked him into opening a franchised tax-preparation business and it worked. He became very successful, making a lot of money over the next ten years, and hated to go to work every day. His team was miserable because their boss was miserable. His wife was miserable, and these rich people's lives were falling apart. I recommended he sell his franchise, which he did for a ton of money. He took the money and has built another successful business, this time as a marketing consultant. He is actually making more money now, but more importantly he, his family, and his team are having fun; they are happy. That passion and happiness could be the reason he is even more successful. I personally don't care that he made more money; I am more thrilled that he found his calling. You won't get to the end of your life and wish you had made more money.

A Calling Gives You a Path

Your business will change. It will change early and often and you need a well-defined path to follow. This is not the narrow path, but a general direction and philosophy that guides your growth and change. The Bureau of Labor Statistics found that the average worker will have ten different jobs by age forty. If there is that much change and movement in the marketplace, you need to make sure your business direction incorporates that. The whole marketplace can move under your feet very quickly, and your passion and calling can keep you at the cutting edge of change. If your business is simply a set of mechanics that produces profit, you will never see the change coming, you will never embrace the change, and you will never ever lead the charge.

My grandfather was one of my heroes. He was very bright and started in accounting at Alcoa, an aluminum company, as a very young man during the Great Depression. He worked there diligently for thirty-eight years, eventually becoming one of their head cost accountants. Those days are simply gone. The days of a young person taking a job and staying with the same company for forty years at a "steady job" are over. Those days are over because people view careers differently, but those days are mainly over because the rate of change in the marketplace is much greater. Entire companies or their product lines cease to exist almost instantaneously in today's market. The only way you survive that as a business owner or leader is to be passionate and have a higher calling for what you do.

Passion Trumps Obstacles and Age

I have often heard from people thinking of living their dream through the opening of a business who are concerned that they might be too old. The interesting thing that I have observed is that while the corporate world seems to have a tendency to throw away a talented fifty-three-year-old, that same fifty-three-year-old likely is in for the best income decade of his or her life. It has been my observation as a financial counselor over twenty years that the decade of your fifties is likely to be the greatest income decade of your life if you don't quit dreaming and looking for your passion. If you have been discarded by the corporate world you should approach the next chapter of your life like they did you a favor.

Age, your current position, and even your current level of education are not obstacles to those who find their calling. Sylvester Stallone worked behind a deli counter and as a movie theater usher when he was thirty. What if that were your son, or he wanted to date your daughter? He wrote the screenplay for *Rocky* in his thirties and started his acting career with an Academy Award for Best Picture, and all of that having had a disability from birth. Martha Stewart was a stockbroker at thirty years old. She found her passion and her gift in the restoration of her own farmhouse, and the rest, as they say, is history. Rodney Dangerfield sold aluminum siding in his thirties and didn't get serious about his comedy—no pun intended—until he was well into his forties.

Colonel Sanders had mainly the wrong jobs just for money most of his life. He was a steamboat pilot, insurance salesman, farmer, and railroad fireman before he ever started frying his famous recipe at sixty-seven years old. My family visited the Sistine Chapel in the Vatican a few years ago as a part of seeing Rome. The tour guide pointed to the back wall of the famous chapel, with a huge masterpiece the size of a billboard painted on it of the return of Christ at the end of time. This masterpiece, according to our guide, was painted by a seventy-eight-year-old Michelangelo.

You are never too old. You are never the wrong color. You are never too disabled. You are never the wrong political party. There is never a big enough obstacle to keep a person with passion operating in a higher calling from winning. Is it tougher for a five-foot-something Pistol Pete Maravich to play in the NBA than a really tall guy? Sure. But he practiced and dreamed so hard that he did it. I hope this little personal pep rally reminds you how important it is for you to select a business that you are passionate about. If you choose well, the way you spend most of your life, your vocation, will truly be a vacation.

Warning: Work-at-Home Scams

USA Today reports that work-at-home scams are one of the fastest-growing categories of complaints with the Federal Trade Commission. I would recommend never buying a kit or signing up for training or a program that allows you to work from home or start your own business. Most of these "business in a box" programs are either complete scams or at the very least are considerably overhyped.

It seems to be human nature to try to find the easy way to get rich, but the number of people who have paid $100 to $5,000 to buy a system or get training to open a particular business and found it to be a complete rip-off is staggering. I have actually talked to several people who paid $49 or so to buy a kit to begin licking and sealing envelopes at home. You have to be kidding! Do you not know there are machines that can auto-seal envelopes by the thousands an hour? There are people who honestly thought they could make some extra money at home licking envelopes! There are tons of people who have no accounting background, have no medical background, and hate details who have paid thousands of dollars to learn to do medical billing from home. It is as if they have no idea that doctors have had practice management systems in place to do their billing and accounting for decades. Yes, sometimes, some doctors outsource their billing, but it is never outsourced to little Sally Smith with an eighth-grade education to do in her living room while her five kids are napping. Oh, brother!

There is an easy way to avoid being ripped off by work-at-home scams. Don't buy one. Instead follow the process and discussion above, where I told you to find a work-at-home idea from something you already know and love. If you love and play with guns like my friend Tony, then start doing some gunsmithing for some friends from home and charge them. Tony started that a few years ago and now owns a gun shop.

Another way to avoid being ripped off is to remember two of Grandma's old sayings. One: there is no shortcut to any place worth going. In other words if someone has already put the business idea in a box for sale, you are too late; try something else. Two: if it sounds too good to be true, it is too good to be true. If this great idea is fail-safe and guaranteed to make you rich easy and quick, you are being ripped off.

The funniest thing about these scams is the worst ones will actually have a disclaimer that says "100 percent scam free." Please run as hard as you can in the other direction when you see this. When an offer says that, it's the same as the girl you dated in college who told you on the first date that she isn't crazy. You of course found out that means 100 percent of the time she is *crazy*. Or it should remind you of the salesman who told you three times in the first five minutes of a conversation that you could trust him. You of course found out later that means 100 percent of the time you can't trust him; he is a crook. Run.

Mompreneurs

I don't know for sure if the book by Patricia Cobe and Ellen Parlapiano was where the Mompreneur name was started, but it has surely caught on as a category of small business. Most Mompreneurs, as you might guess, are moms who work from home so they can be with their kids. Sometimes the business starts there and becomes the business that ate the garage. Or sometimes the kids grow up and so does the business, and it can become huge. And sometimes the business is simply a way for a mom to make an economic impact on the household by adding some income while being at home with her kids. Whatever the result, this movement has really caught on.

I have taken hundreds of calls on my radio show over the years from very talented and educated ladies who had made the decision to stay at home with their kids but still loved the thrill of the marketplace and/or really needed/wanted to add to the household income.

Some of these moms are very well educated and have highly sophisticated business plans and businesses from home. And some of these moms have very simple but very profitable ideas that they execute. The interesting thing about these ladies is they are seldom out to impress anyone with their sophistication or their walnut office; they just want to make some money, to put another paddle in the water.

Rick left his corporate job to open his own insurance office. He was fighting and struggling to get the business moving while Lindy, his wife, was busy at home with the kids. In a desperate discussion one night Rick told Lindy that he was paddling as hard as he could but with just one person in the canoe, he felt like the harder he paddled the more they spun in circles. So Lindy decided to be a Mompreneur and put another paddle in the water. The weird thing is that Lindy isn't making that much, but the little she is making helped Rick and helped them paddle straight. Sometimes you just need another paddle in the water until the momentum is built.

Several years ago Crystal Paine started blogging about being a wife and a mother of three. A post about couponing received so much feedback that she wrote a whole blog series on couponing, followed by an e-book, and now an e-course on the topic. But her readers asked for more, so she started a blog devoted exclusively to couponing. Moneysavingmom.com now has sixty to eighty-five thousand visitors per day and more than 2.5 million views per month. Talk about making a bouquet with the flowers that were within reach!

Lisa always had a great eye for arranging flowers. She would often get comments from friends visiting her home that she was gifted in putting baskets together. Visiting a friend in the hospital who had just had a baby, she noticed a cool gift basket. A relative from the friend's hometown had sent a gift basket chock-full of not only flowers but of items from that particular town. Jellies, candies, hot sauce, barbecue sauce, postcards, and souvenirs were all there to remind her of home. Lightning struck in Lisa's mind:

she realized companies that had visitors from out of town might like that same basket to remind them of their visit to Lisa's city. She made up ten such baskets and called on corporate executive assistants, leaving the basket as a gift and sample of what her work would look like. Within weeks the orders started pouring in. The orders came in so quickly that her entire garage and most of her house became a warehouse for the components of her baskets, and her husband told me he was up until two A.M. helping get the orders out.

E-Mealz

Jane DeLaney of Birmingham, Alabama, found a crumpled five-dollar bill in her pocket in 2003. She says that was the inspiration for starting her company, and she optimistically opened a business account with that five dollars. Jane and her sister Jenny began to build an online tool to help a family plan and budget their meals a week at a time. The planning takes stress away from the family and stretches the dollars spent considerably. They charge a whole $1.25 per week, or, you guessed it, five dollars per month. By 2006 Jane and Jenny had over a thousand subscribers and came to us to advertise on *The Dave Ramsey Show*. Our national ads are way too expensive for a company grossing $100,000 per year and we didn't want to sink them, so we offered to sell some of our Internet-only ads at a bargain rate.

That little bit of web advertising and Judith, their third sister, joining the company to create a marketing strategy caused an explosion. As they grew they were able to become national advertisers on our show. Now they have over sixty thousand subscribers—that is almost $4 million a year they are grossing. Jane, her sisters, and their husbands can't quit smiling. They are helping families remove stress, spend more time together, and save money. And they are getting paid very handsomely for providing this wonderful service.

To Franchise or Not

Let's start this discussion with a disclaimer: I am the entrepreneur's entrepreneur and I am cheap. I would prefer to make some mistakes and even take more risk than to have someone telling me what color to paint the walls in my business, so a franchise is not for me. However, just because I am a hardhead doesn't mean that franchises are bad; as a matter of fact, they are not bad. So let's look at this subject objectively.

Choosing to open your business by buying a franchise can be a great way to go. A franchise can offer you a built-in national brand. You are more likely to attract customers to a Subway than you are to Dave's Sub Shop. That is very valuable. Also franchises offer you a proven system for operating the business. They can assist you with determining the location, the hiring, the production process, the equipping of the business, the marketing of the business, and even the ongoing operations. Franchisors often have made many, many mistakes over the years that they have learned from and developed processes and systems to avoid those mistakes. This proven path through the forest can be very valuable.

If I am going to open Dave's Sub Shop I will have to make a lot of those mistakes on my own, and one of those mistakes could very well be fatal. I have to honestly tell you that franchising can be a great way to go for some people.

Dangers/Warnings

First off, franchises do fail. They fail every day, and honestly the percentages are not impressive at all. CNN Money rated the ten most popular franchises in the U.S. The top five were Subway, Quiznos, the UPS Store, Cold Stone Creamery, and Dairy Queen. The survey found that the average failure rate is 16.6 percent among the top five. To be fair, some do better and some do worse, but the point here is that in spite of the fact that these are all household brand names, almost one out of every five people who try to live their dream running one of these fails. Failing is bad enough, but the standard way to buy and open a franchise is to take a Small Business Administration loan out with your home pledged as collateral. Translation: one out of every five tries among the five most popular franchises ends up bankrupting the guy trying to live his dream. They do fail, and it is often financially fatal to the family involved.

The second issue is that you could just be buying a job. If your territory is limited, and it almost always is, then you may simply own your job. If you can never develop the business to the point that you work *on* your business, not just *in* your business, then you may simply own your job. You work there every day and make a good living, but you have to be there and you are stuck; you're paying someone else for limiting factors that may mean you simply own your job. That is different from owning a business.

Third, don't become enamored with their passion; it has to be your passion. Sometimes people become so desperate to "work for themselves" that they are just looking for a way to make money and be their own boss. This will lead to disaster. I have said it before and will again: business is too hard to work only for money. There must be meaning and you must have passion about it. I had a client years ago who had spent twenty years managing large retail department stores and thoroughly enjoyed it. When his store closed he bought a transmission repair franchise! What? How do you get from one of these to the other? He of course ended up miserable, ran the store into a ditch, and sold it cheap, almost completely losing twenty years of savings.

Finally, franchisors and franchisees have a love-hate relationship. Typically the franchisee opens the new store and gets lots of attention from the franchisor until things are up and running, as it should be. One year after opening, the franchisee starts to realize that no matter how good the franchisor is, no matter how much support they provide, and no matter what good ideas they have, the success of the business will ultimately be on the shoulders of the owner, the franchisee. So after pouring in years of blood, sweat, and tears, the franchisee often begins to resent paying royalties monthly on their sales because they know they are the key to success and tend to forget the jump start that buying a franchise gave them. If the business doesn't go well the franchisee often wants to blame the franchisor, when it might not be the franchisor's fault; it may be that they aren't good at running a business. I almost feel sorry for the franchisor, because they lose either way. But they do get paid well, so not so many tears.

Points to Consider Before You Leap

Number one: is this your passion? As I mentioned, don't buy someone else's passion. If you are just looking to make money you will eventually be very disappointed with a franchise.

Second, don't borrow to open a business, particularly a franchise. We will discuss this concept at length later, but when considering a franchise my suggestion is that if you have to borrow—and oftentimes pledge your home, and bet against bankruptcy—that tells me you can't afford to do this deal. I had a friend who left a six-figure career and violated every one of these warnings. He sold manufacturing equipment for decades and decided to borrow against his home with an SBA loan to open a toner cartridge recharging franchise. Disaster. Nothing in the whole deal worked. He ended up selling the franchise and the business and keeping most of the debt from the start-up. He was forced to sell his home and went through a couple of years hanging by his fingernails to avoid bankruptcy. He will tell you borrowing is a really dumb idea.

Next, ask yourself how you will feel in ten years. After you have run this business for a decade, will you still feel okay about paying the franchisor a monthly fee for the national brand, for the limited support, and as a tribute to the fact that they helped you get started? I will tell you from personal experience that it is hard to remind yourself that was the deal you cut. I had a great literary agent land me my first book deal. She got me more money than I had ever seen and put me in a deal I would have never been able to do by myself. For that service she gets a cut of my royalties from the sale of that book, and she should. I have to admit that while my intellect understands that and I know that she earned it, my emotions struggle sometimes with her still getting a check fifteen years after she last lifted her finger in this deal. She has done nothing wrong; she did what she was supposed to—I am the problem. Face that demon inside you before you buy a franchise.

Next, decide whether the national brand matters in the business you are looking at. For instance, I might go to a chain restaurant because of the brand, but I really don't care if I recognize the brand of my dry cleaner.

You should also consider whether the franchise has a unique process or proprietary equipment that will give you a huge competitive advantage. Sometimes a franchise is built around a unique product or equipment that has been invented, and the only way you can enter that business intelligently is to have that competitive advantage. Usually, though, you can figure out a way to duplicate what the franchisor considers essential. Also, if technology is involved in this uniqueness, remember that the technology will be obsolete in a few years.

My family had close ties to ERA Real Estate franchising back in the late seventies and early eighties. We owned a franchise, my dad sold the franchises, and when I went off to college I chose the local ERA broker to work for as a real estate agent. ERA stands for Electronic Realty Associates. They have grown and morphed over the years and continue to be a legitimate franchisor. When they started in 1972 they had cutting-edge technology; you could go to an ERA agent and they could get black and white pictures and descriptions of homes from another city you might be moving to with this really cool machine called a "fax machine." It was called the Moving Machine because it helped families move. So if you listed your home in Dallas with an ERA broker a family moving from Seattle could see a picture and information about your home before they ever visited Dallas. *Wow.* Telling stories like that makes me feel old, but what if you had purchased that franchise mainly because of that fabulous technology? That seems almost funny now, and what is cutting-edge today will be very funny in just five years, so be careful.

Lastly, before you leap, check their references. No, don't just check the references that the franchisor gives you. Find some other franchisees in cities and neighborhoods like you are considering and call them. Find someone who will talk badly about the company, because there is someone. Talk to the most successful franchisees and ask them how much of their success is due to the franchise. Talk to the struggling franchisees and ask how much of their struggles is due to the franchise. If you are going to drop hundreds of thousands of dollars in franchise fees and start-up costs, for goodness sakes, do tons of homework. Make lots of phone calls and buy a few plane tickets to visit some of the winners and some of the losers.

Multi-Level Marketing

Multi-level marketing, network marketing, and direct sales are the names used by those in that type of company to describe how their business models work. Their detractors call what they do "one of those pyramid schemes" with a snarl. These companies are not pyramid schemes; they are a legitimate method for some people to make some side money and sometimes to literally build their own business.

A pyramid scheme is illegal and is where no product or service is sold; the business exists just to bring in recruiting fees. These still pop up from time to time and are an illegal cousin to the Ponzi or Madoff scheme because of the last-man rule. The last-man rule is, if you were to extend the company's success until the last man on earth joined the business, would it be over because they only make money from recruiting and never the sale of a product or service? If it would, this is illegal.

The most famous among the legitimate MLMs is Amway and thousands have entered that market since their beginnings in Grand Rapids, Michigan. A network marketing company makes money by a member selling products/services and sometimes recruiting someone to join their network. They utilize the natural trust your friends and relatives have in you and their belief that you won't steer them wrong. Network marketing is by most estimates a fifty-billion-dollar-a-year business. Names like Mary Kay, Pampered Chef, Avon, Primerica, Arbonne, and hundreds of others dot the landscape.

The Good
The good of an MLM is that you can find something you are passionate about and make money sharing it with friends. Another good thing is you usually can get in the business for a small amount of money. Sometimes this can be a decent part-time job as a small business. Many people who join MLMs do so to "live the dream" of becoming wealthy by being your own boss. I have at least five or six friends who come to mind at this writing who have become millionaires and who make several hundred thousand dollars a year in several different MLMs. Sometimes it does happen.

The Bad
Most of the bad of network marketing falls under two headings: hype and greed. When an MLM or a hierarchy within an MLM goes bad, it often has hyped itself and its people into a cult-like frenzy. This causes several problems. One problem the hype causes is that hyped-up people tend to exaggerate to the point of lying about how hard it is to make really serious money in an MLM. To make really big money you will have to work really hard and be really smart for a long period of time, just like anywhere else. So avoid the get-rich-quick feel of an MLM.

Second, the hype causes people to get so excited that they violate some standard best practices of business. An example of that is very excited people who fill a garage with inventory that would take two years to sell. Your inventory should be based on what you have actually sold, not your hyped goals, and not your dream—your actual sales. Keeping low to no inventory is a great goal as you get started.

Third, the hype causes people to suggest and be involved in all kinds of integrity breakdowns. I actually heard one hierarchy leader suggest that a room full of women buy tons of inventory on their credit cards and not tell their husbands—*shhhhhh*. Wow, unbelievable! If the MLM you are looking at is suggesting you lie to your spouse, you should *run* away. If they or their leader is suggesting any kind of integrity shaving, then get away. If their opportunity is legitimate it won't require you to go into debt to fill your garage with inventory or to lie about it.

If you get involved in the hype you will lose your friends. Most of us have that friend who has been in every MLM out there and we hate to see him coming across the church lobby to say hi. We have all had the calls from old friends or long-lost relatives who want to show us a "business opportunity." Remember, if you have to pressure and push your friends or relatives about any business, you are over the top; stop it. Some of us don't want to join and we are still going to heaven. Stop it.

The greed and the hype run together to cause these problems, but often the greed causes someone to get in a business just because they think they can become wealthy. Once again, money is not a good enough reason; you must actually care about your business passionately.

Lastly, you should have a realistic expectation of the business you are choosing. If you want to make a lot of money and build a career in network marketing, you need to remember what business you are in. You are in the business of recruiting, training, motivating, and leading a high-turnover sales force. Your best recruits will be people of influence who have credibility in several areas of life so they can sell to and recruit their natural market. So recruiting an eighteen-year-old high school dropout will seldom lead you to success. If you think you are getting in the business of helping ladies with their makeup or in the business of selling some cool pots and pans, you will have a short career with what may be a bad part-time job. But if you have always wanted to build and run a large sales force with high turnover, you might be very successful over time.

So all in all MLMs are a legitimate business and can be right for some people. If you are going to get in one, follow these warnings and you might have the ride of your life. But if you are going to do so, please, for the sake of the rest of us, have some class.

Conclusion

So this is the chapter where businesses are born. If you are already in business or you are leading within someone else's company, it is good for you to ingest this information so you remember or you know what is in the DNA of your company. Your mighty oak was once a very scared little acorn. Your big train was once the little engine that could. You need to remember that the things covered in this chapter are what drive our economy and keep that sense of healthy desperation, that sense of entrepreneurship, and that thrill of stepping out to create where no man has gone before. The exciting unknown is the essence of business, and in that sense all business is small business.

7

Business Is Easy . . .
Until People Get Involved

Hiring, Firing, and Personality Styles

Jean had to be let go. Fired. Her big personality, her big mouth, her openly belligerent disrespect for me, and her gossip spreading through our little office left me no choice. There were only about twelve of us in those days and so one bad apple represented almost 10 percent of my entire staff. She was our only salesperson and she was doing well with sales, which made her get confused as to the level of power she had in our little company. I wasn't scared of her, but I let the trash go on so long that I began to fear what would happen when I let her go. Would I lose clients? Would some of the other team members leave angrily because they were more loyal to her than to me? By being too nice and extending too much grace I had let several layers of misbehavior go on six months too long, and now I was actually having some fear about my business—because of an employee. Ridiculous.

The morning I fired her I got to the office early to pray and rehearse my speech. I had warned her, I had reprimanded her, and I had let this go on way too long. As I sat there watching the early commuters fight traffic outside my office window I wondered to myself how I had let this mess happen and get so out of hand. From that morning meeting with Jean, complete with her attitude, and the process of letting people go in the early days of my business I quickly began to form a philosophy regarding adding and subtracting from my team. I will tell you that when that woman left our company our customers and our team rejoiced. I felt like Dorothy in *The Wizard of Oz* after she accidentally killed the

Wicked Witch. To my surprise all the players celebrated. I started realizing that I was making mistakes in hiring, and even in firing, because I didn't know what I was doing.

Most businesses are horrible at hiring and firing. Now, years later and hundreds of team members later in my leadership growth, I have become very good at both hiring and, very rarely, firing. I am so good at it that I am convinced this may be one of the most important chapters in this book. Our team is so central to our success that our interaction with them as they come in the door and even as they go out the door is vital, fluid, and very intentional.

Turnover Is Bad for Business

Proper hiring creates a good team, and a good team lowers turnover. Turnover is very expensive, particularly in a small business. When you lose a team member, not only is *their* job not getting done, but oftentimes *your* job isn't getting done because you have to stop what you are doing and begin the interview process again. Plus, new team members have to be trained. That takes time away from other tasks, and the new team members take a while to become good at their task, costing you even more productivity. Using the philosophies and process covered here we have lowered our turnover to about 4 percent per year. We measure two kinds of turnover: The first is turnover due to life events like having a baby, getting married, or moving to another city to follow a spouse's new job. Since I have a young crew, a bunch of whom are in their twenties, we lose people mainly to life change. The second, turnover of people we fire, or who quit for a "better job," is less than 4 percent. Our overall turnover rate runs about 9 percent per year.

Turnover is not only expensive due to lost productivity but also causes morale problems. When your team likes and respects each other and someone leaves, it actually hurts emotionally. People are sad when "family" moves on. Also, a self-fulfilling prophecy can begin to unfold when your team starts to wonder if something is wrong, something they don't know about, and is causing all the people they love to leave. Sometimes a company creates negative momentum and actually starts losing people just because they are losing people. Turnover is dangerous.

Team members leave, or are let go, most often because they should never have been hired in the first place. The fact that someone got on your team who should never have been allowed in the building is your fault. Once I realized that team problems were my fault I started trying to build a process and a philosophy to stop that problem so we could get back to doing something productive.

The first and often the largest mistake we make in hiring is we don't take enough time. Take more time! Take more time! I know how it is and especially how the first few hires are—you are going along doing business and you look up and realize eighty-hour weeks are becoming a way of life. So you have a revelation: "I need to hire someone to help me." So you begin to hire people quickly because you don't have time to actually do an interview. In your rush to get some help you are extremely naive and actually think after one or two quick interviews that you found someone who will love and rock your baby business with you. Very quickly after they enter your life you find they don't care as much as you or work as hard as you, and hey, they don't even show up on time. If you keep this up you will have a building full of employees. You remember the definition of an employee, don't you? An employee is someone who comes late, leaves early, and steals while they are there. You don't want employees, you want team members, and the process of adding team members requires you to slow down the hiring process. Take more time!

The person hired properly will perform better, will not cause problems, and will be more likely to stay. Once we realized it is much easier and takes less time to go through a lengthy hiring process rather than rehire the position three times, our quality of life got better. When you work with fired-up, talented people who love what they do, you have more fun than trying to gather a bunch of turkeys together and whip some work out of them. The process of building and nurturing a team that has low turnover takes more time per person employed. But it takes much less time than interviewing, on-boarding, training, and then firing three turkeys before you luck into a good person.

I don't care if you are hiring entry-level, low-skill positions or white-collar executives. Each of these human beings has a tremendous ability to bring positive attitudes and infectious hard work to your team. Each of these human beings also has the tremendous potential to keep everyone off balance with so much drama that the place starts to feel like a soap opera. Regardless of the level of team member you are adding, the pay scale, or the job to be done, you must take more time. Make sure you get the rock stars and keep the turkeys out.

I am convinced the mistakes we have made in hiring have cost us hundreds of thousands—maybe millions—of dollars in lost productivity and in lost opportunity. I do know that as we have gotten better and better at attracting, hiring, and keeping rock stars, our life and profits have gotten considerably better.

We use at least twelve components in our hiring process. It takes an average of six to fifteen interviews and an average of ninety days from initial contact to hire. If you had told me to do that when I started I would have laughed and found some reason that all this didn't apply to me and my business. If you are thinking this is overkill I have a challenge for you: try this process, or your version of it, for your next five hires and see if you don't lower turnover and drama as well as increase the quality of your life and the lives of the rest of your team. Just try something new.

Our goal is to find out someone is not a good fit *before* we hire them. My human resources director has a great saying. He says we have a 95 percent turnover, before we hire them. That means if you make it to the second interview you still only have a one-in-twenty chance of getting hired.

Twelve Components to a Good Hire

1. Prayer

As a person of faith I ask God to send me who He wants to work with me to do the work He gave me. I also ask God to keep the crazy people away so I can get my work done. Sometimes He answers that prayer. LOL. If you are not a person of faith at least spend some quiet time in the morning thinking about the type of person you want to work with every day and the type of person you don't want on your team.

Several members of our team have weird stories of how they connected with us at just the right time, and in just the right way, to be hired on our team. Some of the circumstances are such bizarre and unusual methods of getting a job that they are convinced God sent them. Over the years I have become thoroughly convinced they are right.

2. Advertise and Get Referrals

We have found most employment advertising to be a waste of money. We are not trying to collect thousands of résumés. We are instead trying to find someone who fits on our team and wants to join our crusade. We do have an employment section on our website and you will find our ads full of enough information for you to rule yourself out.

You can rule yourself out if you see the position for video editor pays in the $45,000 range and you want to make $90,000. If that is the case you would only want to work for us if you are brain damaged, and in that case we wouldn't want you. You can also rule yourself out if the position clearly states that you must have certain proven skills, like "Two years of accounting experience required" or "Must know ColdFusion." Put too much info in your ads wherever you run them so people can rule themselves out and you don't have to.

We also add sarcastic and smart-aleck things to our ads to represent the kind of culture we have. Our ad might say: "Just because your mother likes your family blog doesn't make you a writer; you really must have professional writing experience," or "Two years of sales experience needed, Girl Scout cookies doesn't count," or "We might be wearing blue jeans and flip-flops, but don't let that fool you, we work our tails off. If you want to join a team that gets it done then you better know how to make things happen."

By far our most successful hiring procedure is referrals from existing team members. We pay our team a bounty of $250 in cash, handed out and applauded in a staff meeting, when we hire someone they sent us and that person makes it through the ninety-day probation period. And every time we hand out that money in a meeting we remind the whole group to be very careful to send us only their friends who are rock stars and not to send us friends who are turkeys or drama queens. We remind our team that we likely will discover their bad friends aren't a fit and we won't hire them, but more importantly, we have a great place to work, so they shouldn't mess it up with their friends who are crazy—and we all have some crazy friends somewhere. Everyone laughs and nods, and I say, "Send only good people, but remember money is on the line, so do send us those good people."

Of course you will have to be doing the things in the rest of this book so *you* create a culture and a company that *your* best people will want their brightest friends to work for. They won't send you their contacts if they don't trust you and don't love everything about working there. More on this later.

3. The Thirty-Minute Drive-By Interview

You should never hire someone in one interview. Ever. Your first interview should be a quick "get to know you" conversation to begin the process or cull someone out quickly.

My team quit letting me do interviews long ago because I am awful at it. The worst thing I do if I am not really careful is spend two hours telling you how great we are, only to discover later that you are not even qualified. I love people and I love what we do so I talk about it too much. It is oxymoronic because I can take a call on my talk radio show and get you to tell me things in two minutes that you never should in front of five million people, but I am a crummy interviewer.

My HR director is a fabulous interviewer, as well he should be. He can learn all kinds of things in thirty minutes that you never intended to tell him. No tricks or fancy interview questions. He just listens and asks questions. He says in a drive-by thirty-minute interview, use the ratio of two ears to one mouth. Listen twenty minutes and talk for ten minutes. Listen much more than you talk. Don't go thirty-one minutes; cut it off, because you two will be talking again, many times, if there is a reason.

4. Résumé and References

This is the most worthless of the twelve components to a good hire, but it's still needed. You need a résumé so you can quickly get to the formal training someone has that pertains to the position you are filling. Other than that a résumé is a great place to begin several conversations where you will discover what the person is really about.

Since most people have the good sense to put down only references who will say good things about them, references are generally useless. We do check references because if the person is stupid enough to list references who don't know we are going to call, or stupid enough to list references who aren't going to say nice things about them, then we consider them too stupid to hire.

5. Testing Tools

Too many companies use testing tools as a key component in hiring. You and your leaders need to have enough relational intelligence to determine who to bring on without giving undue weight to some kind of "magic test" that will tell all.

However, we do use testing tools as one of the indicators of a good fit in hiring. The tool we always order after the second or third interview is the DiSC personality test. This tool gives us a quick look at the personality style of the person. We want to see if their style fits with the job, how their style will fit with the team they will join, and how they will interact with the style of their immediate leader. This is a quick test of twenty-something questions that just takes a few minutes, but it reveals with fairly good accuracy a person's tendencies.

The DiSC Test

I avoid IQ tests and other measures of raw intelligence because they are not good indicators of success. Malcolm Gladwell found in his research for the book *Outliers* that IQ or GPA is seldom an indicator of success. A greater indicator is relational intelligence. The ability to get along with others and work with others to achieve shared goals is huge as an indicator of winning.

The D stands for "dominance." A dominant person is a very task-oriented, hard-driving person who looks to solve problems and is always asking, "When?" Gary Smalley, an author on marriage, assigns animals to these styles and calls this person a lion. They roar, they overlook details, they can hurt people's feelings, but they really get stuff done. They are quick to act and make decisions easily. And if they don't like that decision they will make another. They make great team members because they will always keep the company moving. About 10 percent of the public is the D personality.

The I stands for "influencer." This person is people oriented, fun, outgoing, and generally a party looking for a place to happen. They are very concerned about people and are always asking, "Who?" They are expressive, persuasive, lose focus on tasks, and make decisions quickly, usually because they are impulsive. Smalley calls these people otters, always playing and playful. They are really fun to be around and have on your team. About 25 percent of the public is the I personality.

The S stands for "steady." This person is unbelievably loyal and stable. They detest conflict and are paralyzed by it. They love people and are concerned about how everyone feels. They are a team player, understanding, and amiable. Smalley calls this type a golden retriever, and everyone should have one as a friend. They will be with you to the end and love you in spite of your flaws. They are slow to make decisions because they always want to understand "why," and they want to make sure no people are hurt because they always avoid conflict. They are great team members because they are very loyal and steady. About 40 percent of the public is the S-quadrant personality.

The C stands for "compliant." This person is all about details and is consequently very analytical and factual and loves the rules. You must know the rules and follow the rules if you are a C style. Not following the rules is not only wrong, it represents a failure of integrity. These people can seem rigid and resistant to change, but they will always have high levels of competency. They are slow to make decisions because they must first gather all the facts and details and they are always asking, "How?" People are not so much on their radar and if people show up they should be studied. Gary calls the C personality the beaver; these people are very industrious and all about business. They make excellent team members, and you for sure want some in your accounting department. About 25 percent of the public is the C personality.

We never use this test as a deal breaker on a hire. What we are trying to do with all twelve of these components is to establish a pattern toward or away from hiring. We never hire someone when half of the twelve go poorly. And we almost never rule someone out exclusively on one of the twelve.

Your organization needs some of every personality or you will have serious problems. My three closest leaders and I fall in each of the four quadrants respectively, which ensures that when we make group decisions they are generally wise. If we were all one type or another we would miss all kinds of elements.

There are a few personalities that are wrong for certain positions. You probably don't want an I personality who hates details, loves people, and is impulsive in your accounting department. So the first question we ask ourselves is how the potential hire's personality is going to fit the position interviewed for.

The second thing we are looking for is how they will fit the chemistry of the group they will be working with. If the group is all high energy and artistic, how is a C personality who loves rules going to fit in? They might, but the strengths and weaknesses of the chemistry need to be discussed as part of the hiring procedure.

The last thing we are looking for is how they are going to work with their leader. If you are hiring a sweet young lady who is a high S and doesn't like conflict to work directly for a gruff old D who is blunt and task oriented, she is going to cry every day. That won't work. I am a high D and right on the line of I, so my assistant, who has been with me for years, is perfect as a C with some S. She complements me well but also we share some tendencies.

You also want to keep in mind that lazy is not a personality style, it is a character flaw. Having no initiative is not a style, it is a character flaw. I mention this because we have had people who didn't want to work hard quit and tell us their personality style didn't fit in. Not true; it was that we require a huge work ethic and they didn't have that character quality. Lazy is not a style.

I have trained my leaders to spend time with people in the hiring process to determine if they play well with others. That will be the only way you can build a great culture and actually enjoy your team.

6. Do You Like Them?

In most cases you are going to be working really closely with the people you hire. For goodness sakes, don't force yourself to work with people you don't like or don't have anything in common with. There are some people you don't need to hire—simply because you don't like them. That is good enough.

The last time I hired a personal assistant George W. Bush had just been elected president for the first time. And by the way, I am a huge W fan, which matters in this story. Some of my team had interviewed and narrowed down the candidates to two. One lady came to interview with me and she was very qualified. She had been the personal assistant to the president of a Fortune 100 company and she was very polished and buttoned-down. As I was talking with her I asked which of our books or classes she was familiar with. She said she had listened to me give financial advice on the radio but hadn't read any of the books or been through the classes. That was fine, but it just told me she would have a learning curve about what we do.

Then she jumped in and offered that the advice that we give, helping people with their money, was going to be sorely needed in America now that we had "elected that clown George W." Wow, she was picking on a guy I like. You don't have to agree with me on everything to work on my team. Heck, we've even hired a few Alabama football fans, and I think I saw a Florida Gators shirt the other day, so that is a sign our screening procedures need to be stepped up. (Just kidding, in case you can't tell.) But the moral of the story is my personal assistant works in virtually every detail in my life, so they should be someone I really like. Plus, if you are going to interview with a CEO and every opinion he has ever had is somewhere on the Internet, have enough sense to do some research before you go to the meeting. Had our candidate in question done that, her interview might have lasted longer.

> **I would rather pay my money to, and spend time with, people I actually like.**

Hire people you like; you will be trusting them and spending lots of time with them. There is a ridiculous unwritten rule that if you are professional enough you can overlook vast differences in value systems. You might, but why bother? I would rather pay my money to, and spend time with, people I actually like.

7. Do They Light Up?

We hired a young lady who had been working with troubled teens in a program at the YMCA and before that had been involved with a teen ministry called Young Life. We did not hire her to work with retirees; she is in our youth resources department. And please don't ask her what she does; if you do, an hour later you will leave exhausted, because she is so very fired up about helping teens learn to handle money. She is a rock star partly because she lights up when the subject comes up. For her it is just a bonus that we pay her; she would practically volunteer because she loves, and is passionate about, her role on our team.

When you start talking about the position or when the candidate starts talking about the position, do they light up? Does the mere thought of getting to do the work at hand fire them up? Or are they just looking for a J-O-B? If all they want is a paycheck you will never keep them happy.

We are looking for people to plug into the opportunistic motivation and the philosophical motivation of what we do. We are a successful, moving, and growing company that represents a great business opportunity for team members. Someone joining our team can grow with us, and that is how you should present any position within your team. They need to love the business orientation and speed with which we operate, or they won't fit in.

A potential team member should also fit with the philosophy of what you do. Since I am obviously an unabashed Christian lots of people of faith love that aspect of what I do. Someone should be able to embrace the "loving people" part of our philosophy to fit in with our team.

We have found that people we hire who don't possess some of each of the opportunistic and the philosophical understanding of our company don't last, because they don't fit in. I have had nice Christian people come to work for me because somehow they got the idea "Christian" is code for "don't have to work hard." They were in for a big surprise. They must have thought we sat around all day long singing "Kumbaya." One lady quit because she said we were all about making money. My response to her was that I noticed she kept cashing her paychecks, so she must be all about money too. On the other side of the coin we have had people join us who were only excited about making money, so when we stopped what we were doing and helped some hurting people, it didn't compute in their brain. They didn't fit in either. You have to have both components to fit my company.

8. Personal Budget and Mission Statement

From chapter 2, you know to have a mission statement for your business, and you should build a personal mission statement as well. Very few people are nerdy enough to come to us for an interview with their personal mission statement already done. However, we do show people our mission statement in the interview process and if they go through the whole process and are hired, we require everyone to build a personal mission statement. We want their statement to show how the position they accepted is them living their dream.

Did you know that if you hire people who are broke they don't make good team members? If someone has financial problems they can't concentrate on work because they are constantly worried about their bills. Broke people struggle at work. I found this out the hard way with one of my first hires. I hired this sweet little lady from my church to be one of our first all-purpose secretaries. I had known her for years and she was so sweet—until we hired her. Then she became the meanest woman I have ever seen. She barked, snapped, and snarled at my other team members and even at customers. I was aghast; we were just starting and I was already a failure as a leader.

So I called her into my office and asked her what her problem was. "I'm stressed out!" was her answer, to which I said, "No kidding! What's wrong?" It turned out, as I dug into her situation, that she wasn't making enough to pay her bills. She had a lot of marketable skills and, before she worked for me, had been making really good money but was laid off from that job. When I sat with her and worked up a monthly budget I discovered that I had hired her for $14,000 per year less than she needed to pay her bills. No wonder she was stressed. I couldn't believe someone would take a job that didn't pay enough to meet their obligations, especially when she could have gotten a better-paying job and chose us instead. I asked her why she would do such a thing and she told me she believed so strongly in what we were doing that God would provide a way for her to pay her bills. I told her how much we appreciated her. Then I told her that God says she is fired because he can add. We laughed, and since I could not afford to pay her what she needed, and what she was worth, I helped her find a new job.

I never hired another team member, after that day, without first getting a budget from them to make sure that they could live on what we were paying for that position. As a leader it is my job to serve my team well by making sure they can care for their family and meet their obligations with what I pay.

9. Compensation Calculation, Benefits, and Policy Review

As we go through the different interviews we always go deeper into detail and develop exactly how a team member will be paid.

We unpack the benefits we offer and we go over our core values and operating principles in detail *before* we hire someone.

We will spend a whole chapter on developing creative compensation plans, but for the purposes of an interview, remember that people whose first question is about pay are not people you want. If they are preoccupied by pay and benefits you will never do enough or pay enough to make them happy, because they are just looking for a J-O-B and not an opportunity with work that matters. I have met sharp young people and been disappointed that in the first three minutes of the interview they want to know what I am going to do for them, not what they can do for the team.

10. Key Results Areas

Before you even post a position you need to have a written, detailed job description. We call our job description a listing of Key Results Areas (KRAs). You need to define in detail what winning in that position looks like. What are the key touchstones that will make you, the leader, thrilled you hired them?

Writing out the Key Results Areas really helps you to define who you are looking for as well as clearly communicates what the position entails. I am amazed how many times you can hire the wrong person when you haven't clearly written down what you want them to do. We have hired people who quit when they came on board and discovered what the job really was.

A Key Result Area can be as simple as defining the number of calls and sales volume required in a sales position. It will further define what should happen on that certain number of calls made per week. Our receptionist—our director of first impressions—has as KRA number one: *Answer all incoming calls within two rings with a smile because a smile changes the shape of your vocal cords and your face.* A customer can hear a smile on the phone. Three rings is unacceptable, because the caller thinks no one is home. And her number two KRA is: *No one is on hold longer than seventeen seconds.* Because as George Carlin used to say, "Hold is a lonely place."

11. Spousal Interview

This may be the best advice in this whole book. I mentioned in chapter 4, on making the call, that I get Sharon's input on big decisions, including big business decisions. A hire is a huge decision. The last interview we do is an informal dinner with the department leader and their spouse, and the hire and their spouse. With the first forty people we hired, Sharon and I went to dinner with the hire and their spouse. We started doing this so I could get Sharon's input and see if she got some kind of *feeeeeling* about them. This has given us several other great benefits also.

One, we not only get to meet the hire's spouse and get to know them before they join our team, we can solicit their input on whether they think this position will work for their spouse. You would be amazed by the number of times a spouse, after meeting us and hearing the details of the job, will speak up and say that they don't think this is a good fit. We just saved ourselves a ton of trouble. Also, we get to tell our story with the spouse and share some of how we run our company and let them say if they think it's a good fit.

I have a friend I met in radio who is very talented and I kind of always wanted him on my team. He was a bit of a partier, a little on the wild side, but we really like each other so he and I convinced ourselves that we could work together. At dinner, after covering why we do what we do and who we are, his wife made a brilliant statement. She is definitely a country girl and it went something like this: "Y'all are really religious. I don't think he is going to fit in." We all nervously laughed because we all knew she was right and the interview was over.

One of the biggest benefits I have found in this process, which I didn't recognize on the front end, is by doing the spousal interview you will discover if your hire is married to crazy. Have you ever hired a great person whose crazy spouse completely took away their ability to win because they were doing maintenance on crazy? I was interviewing a very sharp young man for our broadcast department and explained to him that our final interview would be an informal dinner with his spouse. A few hours later I got a screaming and cussing phone call from his wife. She blew a gasket at the very thought that she had to be involved in her husband's hiring. After she yelled and cussed for a minute or two she finally asked me, laced with profanity that I'll leave out, "Why do you do this spouse interview anyway!" To which I responded, "To find people like you." That poor guy gets his backbone ripped out every morning and maybe she gives it back to him at night if she hears a noise outside. Either he is a complete jellyfish, their marriage will end up in counseling, or they will get divorced. None of those options sounds like a productive team member. So the spousal interview might help you discover if the person is married to crazy; if they are, stay away.

12. Ninety-Day Probation

Once a person is hired, they are on a ninety-day probation and we have very little obligation to them during that time. Likewise, we tell them that our company is on probation with them and they have very little obligation to us during that time. They are welcome to walk in and quit. We probably won't release them without lots of discussions because we have invested heavily at this point, but we have low obligation. After ninety days though, we take serving our team and working with them very seriously.

The funniest story about probation is the young man we hired into our call center who had owned a landscape company since he was sixteen. Translation: for ten years he had been cutting grass and doing other miscellaneous landscaping duties. He told our leader that he wanted a "real, inside job." So after going through all the interviewing and other components he was hired and started on a Monday. About eleven A.M., as he was sitting in the call center taking calls, he jumped up, ripped off his headset, and ran out the door. He jumped in his car and drove off. In a few hours our leader got the call from him explaining that he just couldn't stand to be inside that long. I really gave my call center leader a hard time about not asking if working inside was going to be a problem! Oh, brother.

Subtracting

So that is how we add team members, but what happens when we need to subtract? What happens when team members fail? Team members eventually have to perform or they have to leave. There are only three reasons we find team members failing to the point we have to release them. When someone is failing you should start by determining the root cause of the failure.

1. Failure Because of Leadership Failure

At least half of the times we've lost people due to underperformance, it was because of a leadership breakdown. I consider hiring someone who should have never been hired a leadership breakdown, so when someone is failing, ask yourself: did you goof with this hire?

Do you have clear Key Results Areas outlined so that the hire actually knows how winning is defined and measured? I have found that sometimes even a year after a person was hired, somehow a clear description of winning had not been clearly communicated. That is a leadership problem, because the poor team member thought they were doing awesome.

Was leadership in place to train and mentor the new person and continue to mentor them into new tasks? I actually had a VP hire a guy and the guy's first day was the first day of the VP's two-week vacation. Unbelievable! The poor guy sat around having no idea what to do for two weeks and thinking his new leader was a clown, because he made a clownlike move. When a team member is new, or on a new task, our leadership is there to serve them by training and mentoring them through the newness of the process.

Ask yourself if the failing team member was given the tools to win. Were the environment and all the resources in place for them to win? I actually discovered one time that we were taking two weeks after a hire to get a computer and a phone in place for a new team member. IT and HR got the opportunity to do better planning after that. Now when we budget for a hire in a quarter IT gets started building the computer and ordering the phone weeks before we even know the name of the person who will use them.

You have a honeymoon with a new team member when they are very enthused, excited, and energized. Don't let all the air out of their balloon by not having a fast track in place for them to enter your team.

Another leadership failure that will cause a team member to fail is unresolved conflict. The S personality style that does not like conflict can be paralyzed by conflict with team members. Early and often, find out about conflict and demand resolution. You will lose good people when you don't throw water on the drama that is a natural result of humans working together. Part of leading well is creating an atmosphere where justice prevails. That means unresolved conflict is a leadership breakdown.

2. Failure Because of Personal Problems

If a team member has a personal problem that is causing them to fail at their job the first thing you have to do is quantify the problem. Figure out how big the problem is.

A lady on our team walked into my office with tears in her eyes and said, "My baby is sick." What does that mean? What is the illness? Well, that time the tears were because she was a first-time mom whose child had never been sick with the flu and she'd never had to deal with how the day care reacted. In a couple of days everything was back to normal, no big deal.

When Shauna from our accounting department came into my office one day and said, "My baby is sick," it turned out to mean her three-year-old had leukemia. We had a whole different reaction. We let her have time off to deal with the chemo, with pay, and did not count it against her vacation. Some of our guys helped to keep their yard cut and some of our ladies cooked their meals, while members of the accounting team rallied around and covered her work. Why? Because that is how I would want to be treated if my baby were sick. Treat your team like family and they will *act* like family.

Once you know how big the personal problem is you can assess what to do for the team member and what to do about their job while they recover. You may need to pay for some professional help, such as marriage counseling. We have discovered that when a team member goes through a divorce they are useless for at least thirty days before, during, and even after the divorce. Walking emotional zombies are not on their A game. You need to decide whether you can tolerate the lack of performance for a while or whether you need to staff around it.

When dealing with a personal problem, you must see some incremental progress in order to give grace during the downtime. We had a young man go through a horrendous divorce one year after getting married that devastated him. But three months after the divorce he still was not coming back around. We had counseled him and been with him through all the high drama, but he was just wallowing in his sorrow. So I called him into my office and told him that as his friend, not his boss, it was time for him to begin to heal and that he needed to begin to have some good days to go with all the bad ones. He was angry with me, but our little talk started him on the road to healing and now he is in another city, remarried with two cute kids. I am glad for the time he was with us and glad he got better. You have to see that they are going to come back to work after a crisis or you will eventually have to act. Always go too far in extending grace in the case of personal problems because you will never have regrets that way.

3. Failure Caused by Incompetence

If the team member isn't failing because of a leadership breakdown or a personal problem, then it is usually some kind of incompetence. Keep in mind incompetence isn't evil; we are all incompetent at something. Quantify the incompetence.

Many times you can pay for some training and/or mentor someone through a rough spot to get them to where they are able to perform. Sometimes, though, the incompetence is a character or a behavior issue. Is there an integrity problem, or are they stealing? In those cases nothing can be done and you should release them immediately. If they have other behavior issues, that is a *type* of incompetence and you may be able to train them in how to act.

As a hard-charging guy I used to have a tendency to think anyone who wasn't moving at the speed of Dave was lazy. I have discovered, as my leadership ability increased, that a lot of people I thought were lazy really weren't, they just didn't have clear direction. So check first to make sure someone you think is lazy is being led well. But sometimes you will actually encounter someone who is just full-on hound-dog lazy. There is no cure for these folks; just release them as quickly as you can.

The most frustrating type of incompetence I have dealt with is the person who gets their work done but never quite rings the excellence bell, and you come to realize they never will. There are some positions where you can tolerate that, but in a small business there really isn't any margin for that kind of behavior. I had a man who had been with us for about three years and he could just never get there. Any team that had to work with him would come away frustrated and there was always finger-pointing in all directions. His leader recommended several times that we release him but I wouldn't because I couldn't put my finger on an exact behavior that we could demand change for. I like clarity and I always want to give someone clear direction for the change required if they want to stay on the team.

Jim Collins got this guy fired. Jim wrote the book *Good to Great*. In his chapter about getting the right people on the bus he makes a statement that I have used in finance for years. Jim said to ask yourself this about a problem team member: if you hadn't hired them yet, would you hire them again? My answer was a quick no, so the next morning we worked up a generous severance package and my really nice but incompetent guy was released. If I would never hire that guy again in a million years, why was I keeping him? I promise you the air in the building changed the next day. It was as if the whole organization had a splinter removed.

Components of a Release

Isn't it weird that we say phrases like "release" or "let go" when it comes to firing? Even the saying "to fire" someone means "to discharge," which comes from discharging or firing a gun. It is almost as if we were holding something captive and we released it. In truth that is the case, and you will discover when someone doesn't belong on your team you are doing them a huge favor to set them free. The longer I have led, the more clear this truth has become to me.

Always treat people with dignity and be generous as you set them free, but have the courage to do so and you will actually be friends with some of the people you go through that process with. I have actually gotten thank-you notes many times from people we have set free. Sometimes it is a few months later and sometimes years later, but it is not unusual for someone to send me an e-mail or letter thanking me for how I treated them and telling me how they are actually doing much better now that they are somewhere else.

Just like there are components to hiring there are components to releasing someone properly.

Releasing Someone Immediately

If you discover a character flaw like an integrity problem or stealing, the team member has to leave immediately, that day. If there are other character issues like laziness or things you can't let happen in the company, you have to act on that as soon as you come to that conclusion. I have zero tolerance for the mistreatment of ladies. The current culture calls it sexual harassment, but I call it trash and won't tolerate it for one second in our company. I also won't let a team member stay if they decide to have an affair. If their spouse can't trust them, neither can I. Those are the types of things that cause someone who has been with us ten minutes, or ten years, to be let go quickly after we discover it. Of course people with other problems like drug use or addictions can't be part of our team either—gone that day.

The only other time someone is let go quickly is during their ninety-day probation. Once that time is over though, they get the company tattoo and they are part of the family, and they really have to go through many steps to be let go then.

Dignity

James Ryle says, "Truth without love equals harshness and love without truth is compromise." Always treat people how you would want to be treated. I had to release a leader who had an affair, and that was really tough. Not only were we friends, but he left a huge hole in my company. He was so broken and so ashamed but still could not stay. We are friends to this day, partly because of how the whole situation was handled. I was honest with him about how hurt and disappointed I was in him—as his friend and as his leader. But I was never angry or condescending, just hurt. He got tons of severance and we are still friends. But he knew he couldn't work here if he had an affair.

Regardless of the reason for the release, treat people right and with kindness. You are in control and you still have a job; they have neither, so be kind.

Regardless of the reason for the release, treat people right and with kindness. You are in control and you still have a job; they have neither, so be kind.

Reasons to Leave

I have outlined three reasons people fail at their job. The first, a leadership breakdown, should almost never result in someone being let go. If you or your team are screwing up and that is causing the failure, then fix it. The only time your leadership failure should result in someone being released is when you come to the conclusion, hopefully within their ninety-day probation period, that they should not have been hired and can't do the job. Even then we look to see if we can find a "different seat on the bus"*

---

* "Different seat on the bus" reference from Jim Collins, *Good to Great,* p. 41.

for that person. If they have gone through our incredible hiring procedure they are our kind of people, and we may just need to put them in a different seat.

The second reason for failure, a personal problem, should also almost never result in someone being released. We don't shoot our wounded. When we have mercy and give kindness to our team member who is legitimately hurting, we build huge loyalty with the rest of the team. Companies that treat people like a commodity create an "us against them" culture.

A car service driver on one of my media stops told me a wild story. His thirteen-year-old daughter was kidnapped, raped, and missing for thirty days. The police found her wandering delirious at a rest stop two states away. This father called his boss to ask for the day off to go pick up and comfort his daughter. That company said, "If you don't come in today just don't bother coming back." That was the company he *used* to drive for and they will never have me as a customer. That is so extreme it's crazy, but people are treated that way by bad companies every day. You can't shoot your wounded.

The only times we release someone for personal problems is if the problem leaves a customer or a team member at risk, or if there is no incremental improvement. If you are working your way through your junk we will give you a ton of grace, but be climbing the ladder.

Several times since we opened we have discovered a porn addiction with some guys on the team. This filth coming into our offices on my computers makes my blood boil. Plus, I don't want to put ladies at risk working with some guy who is going places in his mind he should never go. When we discover a team member viewing porn we put in place several severe steps to give them one last chance to stay: no computer, pastoral and marriage counseling, and reports from wife, counselor, and team member that he is getting better and staying clean every week. If he trips once, he's gone. I am not going to mess with that filth or try to figure out an addict's lies. We have worked that plan and have managed to keep a few team members, and they have become great guys and great husbands. But most don't stick with the plan, which means they are released.

Almost all of the releases we have done fall under the last reason for team member failure—incompetence. So the process we use if someone has a behavior or competence problem is gentle, progressive, and has lots of blunt clarity.

When I was twenty-two years old, I worked for a company for three months in their real estate department. My boss was a yelling, cussing, angry jerk. One morning he walked into my office, sat down in front of my desk, and said, "You are fired, clean out your desk, see payroll, and get out of the building." Honestly, I probably deserved to be fired, but to this day I still have no idea *why* I was fired, and no amount of asking my boss would get me a reason. Two weeks later my wife of nine months was fired. She worked for a savings and loan as a teller. They asked her to sell a particular kind of loan product and gave her half a day of training on it. A manager from the home office called and posed as a customer to see if she could sell the product. She screwed up completely and was fired the next day. At least we knew why she was fired, but she would really have loved to have been corrected, trained further, and then told, "If you don't get this you can't work here."

So there we sat with both of us unemployed, newlywed, mad, and scared. I have never forgotten those lessons on how to *not* treat people. Maybe we both deserved to be fired, and maybe neither of us would have made it in those positions if we had been trained, given clarity, and given second chances, but we will never know.

My goal today is to never surprise someone with a release and to give someone every opportunity to change so they can stay on the team. So when there is a problem with a team member's behavior or competence, we communicate that very clearly and very often.

Reprimands

We start with verbal course corrections that fall under the heading of a reprimand. These reprimands are not some kind of HR file filler where we "write someone up"; they are paternal instructions on how you must adjust in order to stay. It might be as simple as sitting down and reminding someone that our office opens at eight thirty and if they come in at eight forty-five they are a thief. I am paying them and when they are late they are stealing. Ouch. That makes the point, and it's true. Some people view tardiness as a harmless behavior but when we put it in those terms—that it's stealing—it helps them see how seriously we view it.

A reprimand done properly should do five things:

1. *Be short.* Don't camp out and spend an hour verbally assaulting someone.
2. *Be uncomfortable for everyone.* If you love reprimanding people you are a bully. You should not avoid, but neither should you relish, giving a reprimand.
3. *Attack the problem.* Love the sinner and hate the sin. Ken Blanchard, in his classic *The One Minute Manager,* says to use the "Reprimand Sandwich" when you are doing a reprimand. Praise the person and their good qualities, hit the problem behavior directly and hard, then remind the person of their value to you personally and to the organization.* Praise, problem, then praise again makes a nice sandwich. I have been guilty of serving a reprimand sandwich with no bread, and from personal experience I know it didn't have the long-term desired effect.
4. *Be private.* Never reprimand someone in front of someone else; you will lose their loyalty forever.
5. *Be gentle.* You are teaching and course-correcting in a reprimand, so you owe it to the person to be brutally clear, but you can do that with kindness.

The one I have messed up the most, and seen messed up by others the most, is making sure to do all reprimands in private.

---

* Ken Blanchard and Spencer Johnson, *The One Minute Manager,* HarperCollins (2003), p. 52.

Those of us who are busy, passionate people tend to deal with something when it is right in front of us. When your need for the "now" makes you do a reprimand in front of other people, you have seriously damaged your ability to lead the person you just thumped.

I know it is common sense, but what happens when we are in such a hurry to get a particular project on schedule is we feel the need to deal with problems instantly. This is very efficient for the moment and extremely inefficient over time. If you build a great person who is very loyal to you they can run an entire team for you, which is efficient. You will not keep or build people of quality if you jump on their case in front of others. Worse yet, if the person attacked is not a quality individual they will go so far as to sabotage the job as a favor returned for your leadership screwup. I wish I didn't know this firsthand due to my screwups, but I do.

However, I will tell you that as part of becoming a good leader I haven't reprimanded anyone in public in years. I have been very intentional about taking a breath, counting to ten, and waiting until I can create a private moment to give a reprimand. That is, until just the other day, when for the first time in many, many years I messed this up again. One of our leaders, who is world-class in her field, really made a misjudgment on a project that left me personally hanging in a mess that I had to clean up. I was not happy and went into her office, where three of her team members were standing with her, and told her everything she had done wrong on the deal. Her team members stood and watched, with very wide eyes, this public reprimand. I woke up about five A.M. the next morning with the huge insight that I was a jerk. First thing, I called all four of them into my office and apologized to my leader in front of her team and explained to them how I had violated a basic rule of leadership, and they should learn from the embarrassment of their inept leader (me) to never make the same mistake. That apology made it somewhat better, but I know you can never take back your screwup completely.

More Reprimands

If there is an issue that is causing you, the EntreLeader, concern it should be frequently and clearly discussed and course-corrected. You owe your team member lots of clear, even blunt, communication about what is required to change their behavior.

If you sit down with a salesperson and discuss the fact that you require at least fifty calls a week and their call report is continually showing thirty calls, then they know they have a problem. You can then point out their low closing success as a simple result of low activity. Then if they don't pick up the pace you have to be very clear that in order to stay in your company they will have to get their calls up, otherwise they will be leaving. Simple, pure, and direct communication done with dignity will help everyone in the conversation know what's expected.

Many times, when you are constantly reprimanding and correcting, people will get the idea they are not going to make it and leave as a natural result of your clear and constant parameters. When they leave and you didn't have to release them, you did a really good job leading. My HR director calls this getting them to "participate in the inevitable."

Occasionally we have to go so far as to put a formal reprimand, in writing, in their file. Usually this is the last chance they get and the paperwork says so. The natural consequence of their behavior or activity *not* changing is they will be released.

We hired a really sharp young man named Jordan in our customer care center. Jordan was a rock star and broke all the sales records by almost double in just a few weeks. He was incredible. The only problem with Jordan was he couldn't seem to find his way to work on time. Some companies operate with flex time or the work-whenever-you-want plan, but we don't. We expect everyone to be at work on time or early and to leave *on time*. We don't want to end up with a building full of divorced workaholics. Come to work on time and work your tail off all day long. Novel approach.

My customer care leader sat down with Jordan several times and talked to him about his coming in as much as an hour late.

He had a prima donna attitude that if he was selling like crazy his schedule didn't matter. My leader tried to explain to him that the rest of the team is demoralized when we sanction misbehavior, and we value teamwork above superstars. He would nod his head and agree but two days later come in late. One of the executive VPs finally intervened, but it did no good. I decided I could fix this kid even if my leaders couldn't. So I prepared the final, written, formal warning for him to sign and called him into my office with his leader. I told him how much he was valued and how good he was, but I was at the end of his coming in late. I explained that the paper he was signing said if he came in late again he would no longer work for us. I asked if he understood and he assured me he did and signed the warning. Just to be sure, I told him to think of the warning as "the box warning" and asked if he knew what I meant. He said he didn't. I explained that this warning meant if he was late again he should bring a box with him to clean out his desk—because he was fired. He nodded.

Almost two months went by without Jordan being late. I kidded my leaders that they just didn't have what it took and that I must have the secret to the perfect course correction. But sure enough one morning I looked up at about nine forty-five A.M. and walking through the parking lot was Jordan . . . carrying his box. At least he got that part right!

Sanctioned Incompetence

My friend John Maxwell, a great leadership author, says, "Sanctioned incompetence demoralizes." If you as a leader allow people to halfway do their jobs and don't demand excellence as a prerequisite to keeping their job, you will create a culture of mediocrity. If you allow people to misbehave, underachieve, have a bad attitude, gossip, and generally avoid excellence, please don't expect to attract and keep great talent. Please don't expect to have an incredible culture.

We had several public relations and marketing people from a big corporation meet with our team recently. I got the impression they thought they were there to school us, but the result of the day was they became enamored with our culture. One of the ladies said, "Everyone is smiling on every floor and they are all working really hard too." Another said to me, as they were leaving, that we have the nicest people working for us, and she meant it.

She might have been a little shocked at my response: "Yes, we do have only nice, smiling, and hardworking people here, because if you aren't and we mistakenly hire you, you will change or we will fire you." We don't keep jerks; life is too short to work with them and really way too short to pay them *and* work with them too.

Seems simple, but it requires that you fight to build an incredible team and culture from the moment you post a position until you celebrate their retirement. Every day every behavior, attitude, and execution has to be led well by a courageous, loving leader.

> **Every day every behavior, attitude, and execution has to be led well by a courageous, loving leader.**

When our kids were preteens our family schnauzer Scarlett was on her last legs. We swore we had had enough pets and she would be the last—that is, until I saw a pug with a bow on it in a Sears ad. I suddenly had the great idea to surprise the kids with a Christmas puppy. I began to tease them about the best Christmas ever. I put a padlock on the crawl space, where I hammered and worked on nothing to fool them into thinking I had a big project. Can you tell I love being a dad? I teased them about how thrilled they were going to be with the most fabulous gift ever.

We went to Christmas Eve church service, came home, and put the kids to bed so Santa Claus could come. I drove to my neighbors' to pick up the little six-week-old pug that we had been hiding there for a couple of days. I stored her in her crate all the way in the back of the house, away from the other presents, so her whining wouldn't be heard. Christmas morning arrived and all the presents were opened, but no big-deal surprise. My kids were a little afraid to appear ungrateful, but finally my eight-year-old son spoke up and asked where "the best Christmas present ever" was. Oh, yeah . . . so I went to the other end of the house and put the puppy in a box with shipping peanuts in it. When the kids opened the top of the box her little pug head popped through the peanuts like a little alien. They all screamed and then when they realized what it was they squealed with delight.

They named her Angel because even though she was seriously ugly, she was our Christmas angel. She became my little boy's best friend quickly. Later that summer when Angel was about ten months old we noticed she was having trouble walking.

A quick trip to the vet gave us really bad news. She had an inoperable spinal condition that was going to cause her to lose the use of her back legs and eventually be in pain. We were all heartbroken. Everyone wanted a miracle, but that was not how it turned out. I had to make one of the toughest decisions a parent can make for the good of the sweet little dog. We let her go until we were convinced she was hurting and then the fateful Saturday morning came. The whole family sat on the floor with Angel, playing with her for the last time, with tears running down our faces. Then it was time to go to the vet. The whole family rode there together and they all sat in the waiting room while I cried and stayed with our little Angel.

Some days leadership is unbelievably tough. It requires that you walk through the pain of really rough decisions that are best for everyone in the long term but hurt deeply in the short term. When it comes to releasing someone from your team it is a really tough call if you love people well. Releasing someone should never become too easy, or you are in a danger zone. However, you will learn to pull the trigger gently and with dignity for the good of all involved, your company, its culture, and even the person leaving. Leaders who do this poorly and who don't act are doing damage to all the players on the team. Have the courage to do the right thing, the right way, at the right time, and you will be on your way to becoming an EntreLeader.

Have the courage to do the right thing, the right way, at the right time, and you will be on your way to becoming an EntreLeader.

8

Death of a Salesman

The Art of Selling by Serving

Picture in your mind three upscale custom homes side by side, immaculately furnished. Every detail in these homes was meticulously analyzed to make you want to own one when you walked through. The presentation of the master bedrooms complete with rose petals floating in the oversized Jacuzzi tubs screamed romance. The kitchens were every cook's dream. The studies, with their leather smell and solid wood paneling, made anyone who had ever read a book visualize curling up in a large armchair in front of the fireplace. Nothing was left to chance; every smell, every piece of furniture, and certainly the design of the floor plans made these model homes world-class.

I had the privilege of selling custom homes in my early twenties using these models as a sales tool. Our offices and welcome center were built out very nicely in what would normally have been a garage. The welcome center opened to a parking lot with manicured landscaping. Yes, you could smell the money and the prestige.

It was a hot August day, which was great for business. There were three of us selling that day: Jess, Roy, and me. All three of us worked only on these homes, no outside sales, so we rotated the leads as people visited the models. When a car pulled up the dance began. We learned not only to make judgment calls based on the car they were driving, but to look for other hints of wealth as well. Certainly we looked at the lady's hand to see the size of the rock, looked at everyone's feet to see how nice the shoes were, noticed the condition of the manicure, and of course noticed how expensive the haircut was. We were selling expensive homes so we were looking for money.

That hot August day I noticed my next lead was driving a new Crown Victoria with no hubcaps. Weird. New car, but your grandmother's car, and no hubcaps or wheel covers; it made no sense. I watched through the window as Chris got out. Chris had a full, shaggy beard and wore a white T-shirt with blue jeans that had holes in them (before we started paying extra for that) and flip-flops on his feet. His hair hadn't been combed in a while and I quickly decided that he was just visiting to see how the other half lived, and my new lead was a waste. Oh well, on to the next one. He was a pleasant guy, in a hippie kind of way, and I signed him in and pointed to the models, telling him to make himself at home. I went back to work, but if this had been a real buyer I would have walked him through the models, demonstrating all our unique and cool features.

In a few minutes I looked up and Chris was standing quietly beside my desk asking for a brochure. I have to admit that while I was nice to him, in my mind I was a total twenty-two-year-old snob. I thought to my arrogant self that he should head back to his double-wide trailer so I could get my work done. Our weekend days were by far our busiest and we might have three to four potential clients in the models at once. Those were important days to those of us selling because those were the days we laid claim to a prospect, making them "ours" from then on. In the middle of one of our busiest Sundays Chris showed up again, only this time his wife and five small kids piled out of the Ford with no hubcaps. This time I really was busy so I ignored them completely. After about half an hour there was a lull in the crowd; I noticed the Ford still sitting there and Chris's wife appeared to sweetly ask some questions about the kitchen, which I answered without so much as offering to walk up and show it to her. What a snot I was.

Another hour went by and I was in deep conversation with a lady who had diamonds the size of headlights in her ears when here comes hippie Chris again with another question. I finished with diamond lady and Chris asked how much the third model, a big two-story, would be if we were to put a basement under it. I was starting to worry about this poor guy so I thought I would help him out by explaining how he couldn't afford the home. I explained to him how many thousands of dollars a month that house would be. Chris got a weird look on his face and asked me if it was okay if he paid cash. Cash! Are you kidding me? So Chris and I instantly became best friends. It turns out that he had written some software for the main operations of a start-up company that had just gone public, making him a cash multimillionaire with his stock options. So with Chris and his sweet wife I made the largest sale I ever made while working there. The only consolation I had in my arrogant stupidity was that they really were moving from a trailer; I was at least right about that.

Selling and Selling Properly Matters

Selling and selling properly is not only essential to business but it is also part of life. Henry Ford said, "Nothing happens until someone sells something." Ultimately everyone is in sales. All leaders must learn to sell. Selling is part of human interaction. Teachers sell and persuade their students to learn, parents sell their daughters on who to date, spouses sell each other on where to go eat, and in business money is made by selling. No money is made unless and until a sale is made.

The first thing that will come to mind for most of you is that you don't want to be in sales. Most people view sales from the outside, and sometimes from the inside, as a manipulative, pushy process. When done properly sales should never be manipulative and it should never be pushy. Buying from a great salesperson who is a professional is actually a very pleasurable event, much like having a world-class waiter serve you in a restaurant. By the way, the waiter is making a sale as well.

Counselors sell a better way of living, I sell people on leading better, and when my wife wants to redecorate the house she sells me on it. Everyone is in sales and so it's a great idea to learn how the process of buying works. By doing so you can avoid being pushy or manipulative. My friend the great Zig Ziglar says, "Sales is nothing more than a transference of feeling. If you can make the customer feel the way you do about your product, then your customer will buy your product."

When done right selling is an honorable and noble profession. It is right for your doctor to sell you on taking care of yourself and for your pastor to sell you on the value of a rich spiritual life. Understanding the steps a buyer goes through and assisting them in the process does not cheapen sales as a profession. It is unwise to lump an entire profession under a stereotype just because some don't practice their craft with care. There are a lot of funny lawyer jokes, and in our culture we have a certain view of attorneys. However, a really high-quality attorney is actually a joy to work with. Just because some folks don't practice law with class doesn't mean that the practice of law isn't noble.

Selling is one of the highest-paid professions. In most organizations the top salespeople are some of the best-paid and it is not unusual for them to make even more than their boss. I have several salespeople in our company who make more than vice presidents. Most companies have the good sense to not put a glass ceiling on a huge revenue generator like a great salesperson. Because leading involves persuading the team to follow you in a certain direction, people who know how to sell often end up leading. One of the tracks that most often leads to CEO is through the sales and marketing area of a company. Rainmakers, people who create large amounts of revenue, are always noticed and considered as a leadership team grows.

Every Step in the Experience Is a Sale

Not only do I want to convince you that you as an EntreLeader are always selling, but I want you to convince your whole company that they are in sales. Customer service is sales, shipping is sales, production is sales, and quality control is sales. If the customer has a wonderful total experience they will remain a customer and send you more customers. The chef getting the food out of the kitchen quickly, hot, and tasty might be the biggest marketing arm of your restaurant. The chef needs to understand that or you will be closing.

As I have mentioned, for several years I have taught Entre-Leadership over a weeklong event in a resort setting. We have held the event in Cancún, and one of our activities is to take the attendees on a zip line adventure riding cables through the jungle. We purchased this excursion the first year after a recommendation and after checking them out in advance. We drove down a rocky road deep into the jungle, and from the time we entered their property we were having fun. The young, well-trained team that makes all the trips from tree to tree kept us safe. They were well trained not only in safety, but in making sure this fun and scary experience was truly an adventure. The team joked, played on the lines, comforted us, and instructed us through a day that became a great memory. It probably comes as no surprise that our attendees loved the visit and we remain a customer every time we do an event there.

Wouldn't it be nice if every business you worked with remembered that every step in your experience is a sale? What if your HVAC or plumbing technician understood they are in sales? What if the guy working on your broken car remembered he is in sales? What if you as an EntreLeader, trying to adjust the behavior of a team member, remembered you are in sales? The answer to all these questions is that the efficiency, joy, and profitability of that business would increase exponentially. This is one more reason why it is important for everyone to love their job and be passionate about the whole mission statement of the company. When you read a great book and love it, you can't keep yourself from recommending it to someone and selling them on reading it.

The Steps

Everyone who buys anything, from an idea, to a product, to a service, goes through four steps to make the buy. Everyone who sells walks through four steps with the buyer. There are no exceptions.

Your product or situation is no different. Everyone, every time, does all four steps. The more money is involved in the transaction, the more pronounced the steps. The more important the transaction, the more pronounced the steps. The more time involved in the purchase, the more pronounced the steps.

When deciding to go on a date, you might not realize you walked through the steps. However, when deciding to marry a person you will be able to identify all the steps in detail. When buying a pack of gum you would have to really study the process to even realize the steps are there. But buying a home will usually make the steps very pronounced and very clear. Whether you go through the steps in a nanosecond or whether it takes you months of blood, sweat, and tears, you will go through all four progressive steps.

The four steps are:

1. Qualification
2. Rapport
3. Education/Information
4. Close

If you ignore the steps and/or try to skip one and/or do them out of order you will get a backlash. Your buyer will not like you and you will feel pushy, because you likely are. Any situation that involves successful persuasion is going to flow through these steps intentionally, definitely, and with class. If you prepare your approach to persuading people this way you will see much success.

Qualification

Qualifying buyers is the most overlooked and ignored step in the buying process. Failing to qualify buyers will virtually guarantee a horrible experience for both the seller and the potential buyer. Not properly qualifying a prospect is probably the number one persuasion mistake. Trying to convince an unqualified buyer to buy is irritating, frustrating, and maddening to the buyer and ultimately to you, the seller, as well.

You will waste time, money, and energy trying to sell to an unqualified prospect. You waste time because they aren't going to buy. You waste money because your marketing budget is drained aiming at the wrong target. You also waste money because your wasted time could have been better used to actually make a sale to a qualified buyer. Finally, you waste energy because it is very draining on you and your prospect to be discussing something that is never going to happen. While these statements about waste seem so obvious, there are still some sales trainers teaching people tons of techniques that are supposed to magically make some unqualified prospect suddenly qualified. Don't teach your team techniques to pressure people. Teach your team to serve.

A Qualified Prospect Has the Money

A qualified prospect has the money or can get the money to make the purchase. Not everyone has the money, but on smaller purchases most do; it is just a matter of their prioritizing their money. Even people who appear to be flat broke seem to find $1,000 or so to purchase the services of a bankruptcy attorney. When we want something badly enough on smaller purchases we find the money. So just because someone says they don't have the money does not mean that is correct. That statement can mean some of the following steps haven't been applied to the sale correctly. Some percentage of people who bought one of the millions of books on getting out of debt I've sold were "broke" people. The truth is they weren't really broke, as in destitute and living under a bridge, but they did have more outgo than income. So they were qualified prospects for a twenty-dollar book but had to make it a priority to get some help to change their life.

If you are selling a $110,000 Mercedes, not everyone is a prospect, so you need to do some kind of qualifying in the conversation. You could do what we did selling those luxury homes and make some qualifying assumptions, but be careful, you could have Chris come on your lot like I did. The bigger the ticket for the item, the more you have to financially qualify people, or you will create embarrassment and pressure for both of you. Some of the top real estate agents in the country will have you sit with their mortgage broker to get you prequalified for a home before they show you homes. That way they don't haul you around looking at million-dollar homes when you really can only qualify for a $750,000 home.

A Qualified Prospect Has the Time

In our frenetic culture of go, go, go, we might very well have the money but not the time to engage in a purchase. There are lots of things that fit in my budget, but I simply don't have the time. You can give me a free vacation on a cruise ship, which would be nice of you, but it is likely that I am booked to speak on leadership, be on my radio show, or something else and would have to turn down your nice gift.

If you work for a company, most of the time you can't just leave work in the middle of the day. So a great deal on something that requires you to leave work won't be purchased by you, no matter how cheap or exciting it is; you simply don't have time.

A Qualified Prospect Has the Need/Want

A qualified prospect has the need or the want. Few of us in America have basic needs that aren't met. We often say we "need" something that is simply a want. However, simply wanting something is one of the things that makes you a qualified prospect.

There is a saying among real estate agents that if someone wants to look at a home in a snowstorm they are really motivated to make it happen. To go out in a snowstorm to look at a home says that you really have a pressing need, or you just love the snow. The very act of asking to look at a home in a snowstorm goes a long way toward qualifying you. That is a lot different than driving around on a beautiful Sunday afternoon and noticing an open house, so you walk through, kill some time, and check out your neighbor's decorating. Orval Ray Wilson says, "Customers buy for their reasons, not yours."

You probably aren't going to sell engagement rings to married people or baby clothes to people without kids or grandkids. Given that I have no hair I am not a candidate for a bottle of shampoo. This seems so obvious, but you would be amazed at the amount of sales energy and money that overlooks this simple truth.

A Qualified Prospect Has the Power

A qualified prospect has the power to make the decision. Many salespeople make a huge mistake and assume that the CEO has the power to make all decisions. I don't have the power to purchase computers for my company that I 100 percent own. Why? Because I have given that power to my IT team since I am a computer idiot. The power was delegated.

If you are in the diamond business you are wasting your time talking to me about a diamond purchase. I don't wear diamonds; my wife does. I have been married thirty years, and I am way too smart to make a huge rock purchase without the real decision maker there. I have the money, but I don't have the power to make the decision, so I am not a qualified buyer. If you sell diamonds you can try all the sales gimmicks and pressure closes in the world, but I am not buying. You can say stupid things like how much my wife deserves what you are peddling, but I am not buying. When she approves the sale, there will be a sale, so you need to talk to her.

Very few married people buy a home without both husband and wife seeing the home. Real estate agents who try to pressure someone to make a quick decision without their spouse usually lose credibility by the minute. When you try to sell to someone who does not have the power to purchase you quickly become a high-pressure salesperson and no one will want to do business with you.

Remember that everyone is in sales. Look at problem areas in your business or business model to see if you are trying to make a sale to an unqualified person. One thing our company does is financial counseling. In the counseling office we show people how to change their lives by getting on a plan and getting out of debt. We are selling you on making sacrifices that will cause you to win. If you are married, our counselors will not meet with you without your spouse in the meeting. We have found in twenty years of experience that it is almost impossible for you to be willing to sacrifice without your spouse being on board. If we were willing to meet with you and get you all excited we would cause marriage problems for you. Our counselor would not have a qualified appointment to sell new ideas to your family without both spouses sitting at the table, so we won't do it. We will not allow you to waste your money with us, because the sale made in the counseling room is not to collect fees from you, the sale made is a new set of ideas injected into your family to transform your life.

You might be surprised how much the concept of properly qualifying a prospect can apply to. When a young lady puts on her Facebook page that she is "in a relationship" it says to the guy admiring her picture that she is not a qualified prospect. The concept of properly qualifying a prospect by making sure they have the money, time, need/want, and power to buy from you is far-reaching and not just limited to a straight commission salesman. You should even look at your overall marketing plan through the lens of "qualifying the prospect"; sometimes we call that "knowing your target market." You wouldn't want to target an unqualified market.

Building Rapport

The second step of the buying/selling process is to build rapport. Building rapport gives the buyer a chance to trust you, your company, your idea, and/or your product. When seeking trust, we all know that you only have one chance to make a first impression.

If you want to sell your car and decide to park it in front of your home with a For Sale sign on it, you would likely wash and wax the car first. In a very real way you are allowing your car to build rapport with a potential buyer. It doesn't really matter how great a car it is or how great a deal it is; you will lose most of your buyers by putting a nasty car full of old McDonald's bags in front of your home.

The packaging of your product and your graphics are what builds rapport. We spent a good deal of time on the cover of this book, because we wanted you to see it on the shelf and we wanted it to jump into your hands; we wanted to build a rapport with you.

A great book with a crummy title and cover will increase your chances of failing.

In most cases in a sales situation rapport is built by you personally. You have about one minute to find common ground with a buyer, to establish friendly conversation where they begin to trust you. This is not a manipulative kind of thing but something we all do when meeting a stranger. We size up the stranger to see if we can trust them. Teach your kids to look people in the eye and have a firm handshake. When you go for a job interview wear a belt, unless you are applying with a rap group. Make sure your breath doesn't stink. All these things help build rapport.

You can spend thousands of dollars on TV and Yellow Page ads for your plumbing company and still fail by sending a nasty character with no manners to knock on my front door for my wife to let into our home. To top it off he was thirty minutes late! Even if you give your service away for free, my wife won't use your company after that. Be five minutes early in a neat, pressed uniform complete with little blue boot covers and a pleasant attitude, and you will have a customer for life. You can even charge more if you build rapport like that.

Networking

In addition to building rapport you can and should attempt to find common ground in two other ways. One is networking. You have instant rapport and common ground if a trusted person sent you. If you are sent to me through a close friend you might actually get past my personal assistant for an appointment. If you come to me off the street you will be served by someone else in our company. If you want to build rapport with decision makers you should always be looking for referrals. I am not talking about some artificial referrals gathered by a door-to-door salesperson where you give them your friends' names, wishing the entire time you hadn't. I am talking about real connections of credibility due to you loving your experience with our company. We have all told a friend about a great movie or a great book that they simply must read. That is a genuine referral.

For three years I served on the athletic board for my university, the University of Tennessee. I don't like boards and don't serve on boards, but I took this on because a friend I trust suggested I do so. I was surprised at what a wonderful experience it was, and when a local doctor who is also a friend was asked to serve, I highly recommended he do so. A sale was made to both of us, the doctor and me, by the connectivity of trusted friends, where rapport was instantly established.

We all accept the influence of referrals and make referrals virtually every day. Simply rolling your eyes and curling your lip at the mention of a certain business is a negative referral, without you ever uttering a word. The trick in our business is to create such quality that we go viral with positive referrals in the community and on the Internet, creating instant rapport. And we must be very intentional about pushing referrals into the market as part of our sales plan. That can be as simple as asking for referrals. "Hey, I am just finishing up a custom home-building job for a very happy customer, so I have a slot open; do you know of anyone thinking of building a home you could introduce me to?" Almost no custom home builders ever ask that question. Yet after building a home a couple of years ago I have helped sell many home-building jobs for my builder, who was awesome. And I didn't get a commission; I was just spreading the word as a happy customer. Ask for referrals.

Research

Your best lead is a warm lead where a referral is sent to you. Once you have that connection you should do research on the person to learn additional points of common ground before you meet with them. Again, we are not trying to be manipulative; we're trying to avoid major rapport mistakes by knowing who you are talking to. My personal assistant will have a bio on you on my desk before we talk on the phone or have a meeting. We do that so I do not say something offensive or stupid, not knowing any better. Do a little simple research and find out who you are meeting with before you enter a meeting. To build trust, find places where you have common ground. It might be the car they drive, where their kids are in school, that they like to fish, or a myriad of other things that allow some connectivity and remove awkwardness in the first moments of conversation. Removal of awkwardness is called building rapport.

Sell to Their Personality Style, Not with Yours

Rapport is connectivity and trust. We all tend to trust people and connect to people who understand how we tick. People with relational intelligence attempt to learn how other people process information and make decisions. They will use their observations to meet people where they are and walk with them. That is called playing well with others. If you have a person like me who is hard-charging, makes decisions easily, and hates details, then for goodness sakes don't try to sell me using a three-hundred-page research paper. You better have a one-page summary on the top of that report. I don't care if you like details; I don't, and if your personality style is all about details you can lose the sale by losing rapport instantly with your three-hundred-page research paper. If I am trying to build rapport with you and you are the S—steady—personality who loves people, hates conflict, and is slow to make decisions, I should slow my hard-charging self down. My wife is that style, so I have learned to slow down and allow her to process decisions and make sure all the people involved are okay with the decision. This drives me crazy, but building rapport with my wife is not about me, it is about her.

When I was selling those luxury homes, one of which Chris bought, I had many great opportunities to bend my personality to the customer. I sold one home to an engineer. As you might guess he was a huge detail guy, so I spent a lot of time trying to stay ahead of his next question and make sure all his research was accomplished in order to get that home built. One evening I was the last guy on the property turning out what felt like five thousand lights and a guy drove into the parking lot almost squealing his tires. He jumped out of the car and briskly walked toward one of our largest homes, which we built for the parade of homes. I had to virtually run to catch up with him to unlock the house and turn on the lights so he could walk through. He walked through every room in the large home in just a matter of minutes, hardly saying a word. I hate to admit I was following him and babbling about the features of the home and our great company, answering all these questions he had yet to ask.

As I followed him onto the front porch heading back to his car, he asked over his shoulder how much the house was. I told him the price and he said, "I'll take it." Wow! That was easy; now to get the contract drawn up. We had long contracts and I started trying to fill out the whole thing. He looked at me and said, "Boy, I have a plane to catch, and if I miss it you are going to miss a sale." Finally I grew a brain and asked him how he wanted to handle this deal. We filled in the price, he signed the bottom, and he handed me an earnest-money check for $100,000 as he walked toward the car.

This sale was all too good to be true, so I figured the guy was a con artist and the check wouldn't clear. I was wrong again; the check cleared and the deal closed. He was a corporate executive who had moved many times. He was being transferred and knew he would be transferred again, so this purchase was easy for him. Plus he was a very high D personality. That style makes decisions quickly and is very dominant. If I had been a detail person who demanded he understand every word of the contract I would have missed a large sale.

Our web team and IT team are full of detail guys and they hate seeing a software or hardware salesperson who doesn't know every detail. That person may be selling the best product in the land, but if they don't build a rapport by figuring out the style of the buyer, they miss the sale. Figure out the style of the person you are selling to and make sure you meet them where they are.

People will not buy from you if they don't trust you, your product, and your company.

People will not buy from you if they don't trust you, your product, and your company. They will not trust you if they don't have a rapport with you. Don't try to skip this step in your sales process or you will make a mess in the marketplace.

Education/Information

Serve, don't sell. When someone thinks of themselves as a sales-person they immediately seem pushy. Just like real leaders aren't pushy—they instead pull—a great salesperson pulls someone, serves someone through the process rather than pushes. There is a gentleness, while being proactive, in this approach. As a young salesperson I always thought of myself as the hammer and the client as the nail. I wouldn't want to be treated that way; it is a poor approach.

How do you serve someone properly by assisting them in doing business with you? Think of a great waiter, a server, and how they approach selling you dinner. They can assume you are qualified since you sat down in a restaurant, and they build rapport by smiling and introducing themselves with "My name is John and I will be your server." Wouldn't you feel differently on a car lot or in a clothing store if your first contact had that spirit? Our pretend waiter has now gone through the first two buying steps with you and proceeds to the third, education and information. Our waiter can explain questions we have about the menu, inform us of the daily special, tell us what he has actually eaten from the menu that he loves, or steer us away from items we might not like. He can tell us what is spicy, he can make a wine suggestion within our price range, and he can even compare some of the dishes to those of competing restaurants in the area where he has eaten. What can you learn to do with your sales process from our waiter's example?

Product Knowledge

First, before you sell/serve anyone you must know every detail and the history of your product. You cannot possibly teach someone how great something is unless you actually know it. Study your product line and know it in detail or don't attempt to serve your customer with it—know the menu. It is best if you can have personal experience with the product before you sell it as well.

Remember, if you are a D or an I personality that makes decisions quickly and easily, you will offend a C (detail) person if you don't really know your stuff. If you are a detail person, be careful to know your product intimately, because it will give you the confidence that you are truly serving the customer by assisting them in purchasing it.

Be Proud and Passionate

Second, make very sure you love and believe in your product and your company. Please don't sell Chevys when you drive a Honda. You have to believe, with great integrity, that the best possible thing from the *customer's* perspective is for them to do business with you. This is called integrity. Never sell something to someone that you don't believe they should buy. If you don't believe that vacuum is the best vacuum on the planet in this price range then don't sell it. If you wouldn't want your mother to buy the item or the service then don't sell it.

As an EntreLeader it is your leadership responsibility to make sure your sales team believes to their very core they are serving their customer the best product at the best price. If your team doesn't believe that then you need to change the product. If a member of the team doesn't have a crusade mentality about what you do then get rid of them. A member of your team cannot *serve* the customer if they don't believe in the product, they can only *sell* the customer, because the team member is not on a mission, they are merely working a J-O-B. I tell our team all the time in staff meeting that if they think there is a better financial person, class, or book out there they should go work for them; don't stay and take my money. The only way you can serve is to *believe,* otherwise you just become another pushy salesman.

Your team and your belief in your product needs to be so deep that each person is willing to put their personal endorsement on it. Your team should act just like you do when you see a great movie and are telling your friend about it with great enthusiasm. You really think your friend is crazy if they don't go buy a ticket to that movie. Believe or don't sell. Be very proud of what you do, and if you aren't then change it.

We take this approach for selling my endorsement on our radio show to local and national sponsors. Our ad sellers are told that if you wouldn't buy it or Dave wouldn't buy it, or Dave wouldn't want his sister buying it, then we shouldn't endorse it. So if you hear my voice promoting something, please know that the company and the product/service they provide is something that passed that acid test.

Know the Competition

I had a wonderful experience purchasing a luxury car. I was looking at three different brands. I have owned all three at different times in my life so I knew each fairly well. I had studied the market and knew most of the features of the competing models. However, this particular sales guy knew every detail about every car I was considering and so served me wonderfully in my purchase. He never once used his knowledge to speak poorly of the competition. On the contrary, he told me where each model was better than the car I was considering. Wow. I found myself starting to trust this guy because he was being honest and transparent. He stood firm that his car was the car I should buy because of its particular features and quality, but he brought great information about his competitors to the discussion. It was a really classy way to handle a sales role. A really sad part of my wonderful car purchase was that I was on a competitor's lot the next day and the sales guy there knew less about the car he was selling than my guy knew about the same car.

In order to serve your customer with passion you have to know so much about the competitor that you know why you are better. You can point out the brand differentiation without trashing your competitor. I am sure you have noticed that it is hard for you to trust someone who is selling you by tearing down their competitor. Just point out the differences and why you believe you are a better choice. You cannot do that if you have not studied your competitor in detail, as if you were going to sell *their* product.

Suze Orman and I both give out financial advice over the airwaves. We agree on some things and are polar opposites on others. I think she is a really smart lady and has a heart for helping people. While we are different and believe different things about certain aspects of money, you will not hear me trashing her. That is not classy, and there is no point. There are so many people who need help with money that we are both needed in the market-place.

In this education step the customer is taught about the product and how the product will serve them. In order for you to be a great teacher you have to do more listening than talking and ask more questions as opposed to making statements. A server listens to your questions, follows with clarifying questions, and only then makes a suggestion. When I ask a server what is the best thing on the menu, the best servers always answer with a question about my tastes. If I like beef they will offer a couple of beef options with clarifying points about each. If I am a vegetarian and the server says the best thing on the menu is a three-pound steak, we aren't going to have fun in this transaction. Ask questions, questions, and more questions. Then ask even more questions for clarifying purposes. The customer will tell you what they like, what is most important to them, and will literally tell you how to sell/serve them.

We are trying to give them all the reasons that they will love being our customer. When they have enough education and information to make a purchase, you don't have to hammer them.

When any conversation starts, the customer sees a scale with their time and money on one side, and it is larger than the value of your good or service on the other side.

Our job as a believer in our product, who knows more about it than anyone, is to load the "value" end of the scale so heavily with education and information that the value outweighs the "time and money" end of the scale for the customer and the purchase naturally occurs. Our purpose as we serve/sell our customer is to build the value of our product or service by educating and adding information to the other end of the scale. Once I saw all the features and benefits of the luxury car, I bought one; the rep didn't have to "sell" me.

In the case of a gum purchase, a salesperson did not load the value end of the scale; instead the company's advertising campaign educated me about how sexy and wonderful I would be if I had Dentyne breath rather than coffee breath. In some cases the marketing strategy does the selling and the salespeople become order takers.

People Don't Buy Products or Services

People don't buy products or services, they buy what those products or services *do.* You don't buy a watch, you purchase a mechanism that allows you to manage your time. If you buy an expensive watch you purchase a mechanism that allows you to manage your time that also makes a statement about you to other people.

When I buy my wife a diamond I do not purchase a shiny rock. I purchase a nice way to say "I love you." If it is a large, shiny rock she wears it because it says that her husband loves her and he has made some money, or he did something really bad and bought his way out of the doghouse. (Just kidding.)

Sell and serve by describing the benefits, not the product. What the product does is what matters to the customer. I need a new air conditioner because mine is broken and I want cold air blowing in my house. I like what the AC does, not what it is. I also might like the efficiency that creates lower utility bills, but I have never taken all the guys at a dinner party at my home outside to admire my really neato AC unit. All I want are the benefits: cold air with low utilities.

The great waiter who helps you pick your entrée isn't going to say that the steak is USDA Prime without telling you what that means to your taste buds. Who cares if it is Prime! All I want is a juicy steak that melts in my mouth with all the flavors God intended. I want the benefits, not the product. You must sell benefits, not products.

Sell a massage because of the way the customer will feel after the massage. Sell a financial planning product because of the way the customer will feel with money to relax with at retirement and even with money to leave a legacy. No one *wants* to buy insurance, we buy what insurance does, so sell what it does.

Closing the Sale

If you have a properly qualified customer who you have built a rapport with and you have educated them with the benefits of owning what you sell, they will naturally buy. The closing of the sale should be natural and very smooth. There are sales trainers who make ridiculous statements telling people to close early and close often. Don't do that; you will just be pushy.

If you have a customer who is able to make the purchase, they trust you, and you have shown them the benefits of the purchase, they will close themselves; you do not need some arm-twisting technique. If you have walked through the first three steps properly the next step will be a purchase—without the customer feeling pushed or you being pushy. Pushy is embarrassing for everyone involved.

A great metaphor for this is the single guy who walks up to an attractive girl he has never met and spouts some pickup line that gets his face slapped or, at a minimum, a big turn-down. Instead he could walk up and simply say hi, and ask if she is at the party with her boyfriend. If there is no boyfriend, then maybe he has a *qualified prospect*. First step. Then he needs to build *rapport,* which consists of finding common ground and finding out all about her. The *education/information* step is when he talks a little about himself, but not too much. The *close* is that she now actually cares whether he asks to have lunch with her sometime, and she is probably reasonably open to that idea. Life really does work this way, and you really do buy things this way every day of your life.

Just before the buy occurs there is a moment of increasing agitation and even frustration. The process has been a steady climb up a gradual incline to this point, but there is an apex, a point where we roll downhill quickly into the actual close. At this apex the customer will physically feel changes. The more important the purchase the more pronounced and identifiable this apex moment is. At this apex the customer will turn away from the buy if the other three steps were not prepared and executed properly.

It is not unusual at all for your salesperson to get here faster than their client. If you are feeling resistance and are feeling pushy, don't push, just start retracing your steps from the beginning. Start asking questions to be sure you have a qualified prospect. Again, you will never get an unqualified prospect to close because they are, after all, unqualified. Make some small talk and reassure yourself and the customer that there is rapport and trust. Reload the value end of the scale and ask new questions, lots more questions. Very often you will find you didn't have a good solid completion of one of the steps and you will get the opportunity to fill in the gap. When the gap is full your customer will tell you to write the order up. The close will naturally occur when you have done the other three steps well.

Different personality styles will approach the apex of the buy based on their styles. The D (dominant) personality will likely go over the apex so quickly that even if you are a D you will have trouble keeping up. You should remember the story of the corporate executive buying a home very quickly to make his plane. He was a high D personality.

The I (influencer) personality will be very celebratory as they make the purchase. They see buying as a party and will also launch over the apex.

The S (steady) personality will slow down when they get to the apex. They often feel conflict in the air. You will need to reassure them that all the people involved in the decision are going to be very happy with the purchase. They may need some more rapport-building from you just as they reach the sales peak. They will likely give a great sigh as they roll down the other side.

The C (compliant) personality will likely become a little insecure at the apex and slow down as well. They are analytical and always want more details, so you can never put out too much information for the C personality. They are not concerned about rapport and you will offend them if you get warm and fuzzy at the apex. They are all about doing the right thing and more information is all that reassures them. As they break over the top of the apex and make the buy you will see their body relax and maybe even their clenched teeth form a slight smile. This type is very tense at the top of the apex.

The Closer

There is so much written and taught on closing the sale— improperly and with manipulation—that it is important to make sure you understand the EntreLeader closes the sale, but not with the wrong spirit or process. The garbage of a poorly closed sale I am talking about is like something I witnessed in a sales training once. The guy at the front of the room actually suggested that we fill out the contract, hold the pen above the paper, and release it in front of the client so that the client would catch the dropping pen. He suggested that since the client now had the pen in his hand he would sign the agreement. You might get some spineless custom-ers to respond that way but you won't win customers for life with that kind of trash.

It can't be said often enough that a properly executed sale will naturally close if you have prepared the first three steps thor-oughly. You don't want to use techniques as arm twisters to push people into a pressurized sale. The customer an EntreLeader serves becomes a customer for life, and that doesn't happen by pushing, only by pulling, only by serving.

However, with the serving spirit the sale still must be closed. The order must be finalized. You don't stay in business if you don't collect the check. Learning to finalize the order in keeping with a serving spirit means that you need to look at some of the standard closing techniques to allow you or your team to close smoothly and with class.

Feel-Felt-Found

Some simple little rules will help you and your team to put a bow on the package and finish the order. The most basic techniques are the best because they are real, they are not manipulative. The "feel-felt-found" verbiage can help you pull someone over the apex of frustration. This verbal process is simply a method of reassuring a hesitant customer that they are doing the right thing. It might sound like this: "John, I understand how you **feel** about this purchase and I have had many clients who **felt** the same way. What they **found** was that after they became clients, they were glad they did." Let's try it again: "John, I understand how you **feel** about taking your wife to a chick flick. I know several guys who **felt** the same way—they would rather see a movie that has things being blown up—but what they **found** was that their wife didn't like those movies and so it defeated the purpose of a date night." Remember everyone is in sales.

The Assumptive Close

The assumptive close technique is what the EntreLeader and his team use most of the time. You are simply filling out the paperwork, gathering the information needed for shipping etc., and assuming the prospect is going to become a customer. You simply take the order. A waitress uses the assumptive close and doesn't even know she does. Just take the order. If the prospect isn't ready to buy, they will tell you and you'll retrace the other three steps. It is interesting to remember that when you are ready to order your food in a restaurant, if the marketing representative (the waitress) isn't there to take your order you feel underserved. So closing the sale truly is serving. Most of your sales should be closed with the assumptive close: just take the order, serve the customer.

Shut Up

When you give someone a title that involves marketing or sales they immediately get a disease that causes them to talk too much. Teach your team to ask questions and *shut up*. More sales are lost by yakking salespeople than will ever be gained by them yakking some brilliant statement. Ask a question that implies the purchase is going forward and *shut up*.

You should *shut up* after you ask the question for two reasons. One, it is good manners in conversation to ask a question then wait on the response, even if there is a pregnant pause. But some rookie, poorly trained salespeople feel the need to jump into every pregnant pause and add more not-so-brilliant insights. To ask a question and add more unsolicited information before the question is answered is rude. If your waiter comes to your table and asks, "What would you like, sir?" and while you sit there quietly pondering your selection the waiter jumps in with six more unsolicited suggestions, that is rude. Be comfortable with pregnant pauses after questions.

If you will be quiet and listen, the prospect will tell you how to sell/serve them. Proverbs says, "In the multitude of words sin is not lacking." Even a fish can't be caught if he keeps his mouth shut. The second reason to be quiet after asking a question is there is a natural pressure that builds with the pregnant pause. This is the exact moment in the transaction that the sale is made, the moment we roll down the other side of the apex of frustration. The reason the pause is called "pregnant" is because it gives birth. The pause, the moment of silence, literally gives birth to the sale. Be quiet, a baby sale is coming into the world.

The Alternative Close

The alternative close is a brother of the assumptive close. During the first three steps of the buying process you discover what the customer's needs are and are able to narrow the selection down to two possible options. The alternative close presents the two options to the customer, and both options involve buying. This close might sound like "Did you want to purchase one item or all five to get the quantity discount?" Or "Did you want that in green or do you prefer the blue?" Or "Did you decide on the fish special, or do you have a taste for the lamb tonight?" Either alternative involves the prospect becoming a client. The obvious point is that a yes-or-no question was not presented. "Do you want to buy this home?" is by definition, in this discussion, a stupid question.

The Calendar Close

The calendar close is a combination of the assumptive close and alternative close done by using the calendar. You simply present two days or dates that you might do business. It might sound like this: "We have two days open for marriage counseling the week of October sixteenth, a Thursday and a Tuesday; which will be better for you? Tuesday? Great, we have a ten A.M. slot and a two P.M. slot open; which is better? Great, we have you down at two P.M. on Tuesday; we will see you then." Use the calendar to create options for delivery of the product or service—and all the options involve doing business with you.

The Integrity Close

The integrity close is sometimes known as the puppy-dog close or the test drive. You let the prospect experience the product or service in hopes, or with the promise, that if pleased they will do business with you. It is really hard to take a new car home overnight, let your kids and neighbors ride in it, then take it back the next day. In the old days the pet shop owner would let you take the puppy home to test-drive it. Almost no one can bring a puppy back.

I allowed a high-end pawnshop to advertise on my radio show locally for free for a week with the understanding that they would buy ads if we sold stuff for them. The first day they sold a $12,000 diamond ring four minutes after the ad ran, which resulted in an annual contract. They still advertise with me over fifteen years later.

This close is called the integrity close because it depends on the integrity of your prospect. They have to follow through on the purchase if the product or service proves to be what is represented. Sometimes you may have them sign an agreement stating they are test-driving with the promise to buy if certain criteria are met during the test drive.

http://www.entreleadership.com/benfranklin

Money in the House

Regardless of the close, no sale has occurred until there is money in the house. Invoices are promises, not money. We don't pay commission or count the sale until the money is collected. We are so hard-core about the collection of the check to confirm a sale has been completed that it set up a practical joke by one of our leaders. A new rock-star young sales guy collected his first check and his leader convinced him that we have a tradition in our company with the first check. The tradition is to make a copy of the check and tape it to your forehead, wearing it until lunch to tell the world you made your first sale. I came walking through the sales area and there this young guy sat with a check taped to his forehead. "What is that?" I asked. He then realized he had been tricked and has since spent a lot of time paying back. Have some fun with it, but make sure you count the sale when you have the money.

Conclusion

An EntreLeader makes sure he loves his product and loves his customer and wants to see them married. Doing so removes the frenetic attention to the transaction just for the sake of money, and the EntreLeader sees business as more relational than transactional. We serve, we don't sell, but in order to serve well we have to be intelligent and intentional about the process that humans go through in order to buy. So whether you are trying to get a date, persuade your children to get good grades, or do a business deal for money, approach the process with the good of the other person in mind. When you use that approach you will become a servant-seller and will get customers for life.

9

Financial Peace for Business

Bulletproof Principles for Money, Debt,
and Funding Your Future

In the fall of 2008 the stock market was in a free fall and there was panic in the land. There has been and will be a lot of discussions about why our economy appeared to walk to the edge of a cliff and contemplate suicide, but most believe the crack in the foundation was the subprime real estate debacle.

Broke people were sold crummy high-interest mortgages with bad terms by greedy bankers. Stupid politicians in both parties had encouraged government-backed mortgage lenders to accept the bad deal as if it were a good deal. So a formerly reasonably run mortgage industry cracked open and fell in on itself when broke people couldn't pay their bills—which should not have surprised anyone.

The crash in the fall of 2008 was more complicated than that, but when fear left Wall Street, by the time it reached Washington, DC, it was panic. When the so-called leaders of our nation, in both parties, panicked, the panic left DC and by the time it arrived in the national media it was full-on hysteria. Fear, panic, and even hysteria about the future of our great economy was on the news every night. As one of the loudest voices regarding money in America I found myself on every major news outlet hour after hour giving advice and trying to spread some calm.

I finished doing three shows on Fox News in one day and went out to eat that evening at a great New York steakhouse. As I sat with my wife and my friends discussing the news of the day I had a strange moment of clarity. People supposedly smarter and more sophisticated than me were literally panicking. The thought, among formerly sane people, was that if Congress didn't pass a huge, trillion-dollar bailout our economy would crash and life as we know it would cease on the planet. Emotions were way out of control. I have a very learned friend with a PhD in economics from Stanford and an undergrad degree from Yale who says you should never make big decisions when afraid or drunk. It seemed in the fall of 2008 the vast majority of people were drunk on fear.

My moment of clarity came when I struggled to figure out why I wasn't panicking. Why was I not afraid? Was I just not smart enough to really grasp the implications? I began to doubt my own intellect and beliefs for a few moments, and then it struck me. I was not afraid because I run my life and my business by commonsense biblical and financial principles and I was not vulnerable to the mess that seemed to be looming. I had peace in the midst of the storm because I was like the little pig who built his house of brick, not hay or sticks.

The big bailout passed by Congress was followed by a super stimulus that didn't work. There are those who believe that we would *not* have crashed without government interference, and I am one of them. We will never know. What we do know is in spite of government "help" the economy still hit a wall. Unemployment shot up as the economy slowed and home prices dropped by record amounts. Entire industries came to a screeching halt due to fear. This downturn created record foreclosures, and financial pain hit the unprepared like a flood from a broken dam.

Just like in other recessions or even in the Great Depression, the prepared prospered and bought during the downturn, adding to their wealth. Warren Buffett says it well: "When the tide goes out, you can tell who was skinny-dipping." Those who do not follow commonsense, conservative money principles leave themselves and their businesses vulnerable to the whims of their competitors, every little ripple in the market, and certainly to big shifts in the economy.

I had peace in the fall of 2008 while standing in the midst of people who were freaking out because, from the first day of operation, we have followed the money principles in this chapter.

We were sitting with lots of cash, no debt personally or in the business, with great margins on products and a spirit of generosity. This ultra-strong financial condition allowed us to grow and make investments as others were shrinking. We invested in people by hiring talent that was now on the street. We bought things that were on sale for the first time in years, like real estate, and we invested heavily in the stock market. Warren Buffett also says, "Be cautious when others are greedy and greedy (in a good way) when others are cautious." Buy stuff when it is on sale. But remember you can't buy things on sale if you are one of the broke ones selling stuff.

I can show you how to make your business prosper in great times and in the midst of storms. I can show you how to follow some time-proven financial principles that will help you remove the primary area of stress from your business. The problem is, these principles are the opposite of what most people believe and do. Most people are stressed-out, freaked-out people who are out of business, or wish they were. So be prepared to enter the "never be normal again" zone.

Basic Principles Work

Academics in the world of finance have a certain arrogance about themselves. Those of us who have been formally trained in finance have a spirit of disdain for the simple. We have been taught that *simple* is primitive and unsophisticated. In practice I have to be willing to look at complicated financial options and also learn deep respect for the simple. Some of the most profound truths in any field of study are very simple yet deeply profound. The principle, and the practical application of said principle, does not have to be complicated to be correct. The more education you have, the more careful you should be as you read this chapter. You could be so smart that you miss the opportunity to

You could be so smart that you miss the opportunity to be wise.

be wise. I have fallen prey to that disease and it has cost me dearly, so I recommend giving these ideas a fair hearing.

Do the Accounting

Most small businesses fail because of poor accounting. They start without enough money (undercapitalized), they miss projections, they don't pay their quarterly taxes or their payroll taxes, and they run into "cash flow problems." All of these so-called problems are really symptoms of not doing the accounting required to run a business. Proverbs 27:23 says, "Be diligent to know the state of your flocks and herds." At night as the flock beds down the shepherd counts the flock to make sure he hasn't left someone behind. He counts, does an accounting. That is all you have to do in business, but you *have* to *do it*. If you want to know more, there is a full rundown on basic accounting in the bonus online resources for this book. But we do need to look at some basics.

Microbusinesses

Start-up home-based businesses often forget to do even the most basic and primitive proper accounting. These businesses are often the hobby that ate the garage or the part-time income source that took over the living room. When you are at that stage you can unknowingly commingle (mix) your money, effectively embezzling from yourself.

Your first accounting step should be to open a separate checking account for the business. You don't have to incorporate or get a tax ID number to do this. You can open a simple sole proprietorship account in the DBA (doing business as) form using your Social Security number. Your little checking account can read "Sally Jones DBA [doing business as] Sally's Crafts." You don't even need to purchase those big expensive business checks; you can use a simple little checkbook, like what's used for a personal checking account.

Then you should deposit every single dime of business income into that account. Never pay any business expenses except from this account, and only pay business expenses from this account. In other words, don't use your personal finances to pay business expenses, and don't use your business account to pay personal expenses. Income in, and expenses out, makes your checkbook register a simple profit and loss statement for cash-basis accounting. This simply means the checkbook balance is your profit. No cheating allowed. Run this accounting like it was someone else's business—you would never steal from them or pay *their* bills from *your* personal account. This simple step will show you if you are profitable, if you are winning.

Taxes Will Kill Your Business

I hate taxes, but I hate unpaid, unfunded taxes even more. If you don't keep up with your taxes, that alone will close you down. If you are in a product business where you collect, and deposit, sales taxes and you "borrow" that (sales tax) money to operate, you will fail. If you have employees and don't deposit the proper amount withheld from them for taxes, you will fail. These simple ideas about staying ahead of the tax man are backbreaking for those who don't follow them.

When you take some of your profit from your separate business checking account and bring it home, you should set aside 25 percent in a savings account so you can pay your quarterly estimates as required by the IRS. So open a "tax" savings account that you deposit money in every time you write yourself a check (from your business account). I started my business all those years ago doing this very basic step and I have never had the tax man after me. For example, if you are going to pull $2,000 from your business checking account, you would write yourself a personal check for $1500 and another check for $500 to deposit into your tax savings account. You are withholding taxes on yourself at a very basic level, but you must start here.

Budget

Almost all small businesses will have their tax preparer or CPA prepare a profit and loss (P & L) statement at the end of the year for tax purposes. If you do a slightly better job you get a monthly P & L, or even do your own. For many small businesses the P & L is the full extent of their accounting system. If you want to win you will have to do more accounting than just the P & L. Most pure entrepreneurs are not detail people and hate accounting, so they don't tend to do a good job with it, especially in the early stages of business.

The profit and loss statement tells you what happened last month, last quarter, or last year; it does not tell you what is going to happen. You should do the P & L, but you must also do more. The P & L is like driving your car using only the rearview mirror. However, the very first accounting you should do is a budget, which is like driving while looking out the windshield, looking forward.

All a business budget does is project or forecast income and expenses and thereby profits. The first time you do a budget in a brand-new endeavor it won't be accurate because it is an educated guess. The longer you run your business the more precise your projections will become. You can't drive from New York to Florida without projecting the road you will travel. You will look stupid, and fail, if you leave home on a trip with no destination. Zig Ziglar says, "If you aim at nothing you will hit it every time." John Maxwell says, "A budget is people telling their money where to go instead of wondering where it went." Jesus said, "Don't build a tower without first counting the cost." (Build with a blueprint.)

Doing a budget will make the obvious become a reality and force you to prepare and think of options. If you have a landscape business, budgeting, and thereby projecting income, will force you to recognize that winter is going to be slow and like the squirrel you should put some nuts in the nest. All I am asking is that you be as smart as a squirrel. That is a fairly low bar, the squirrel bar.

Act Your Wage

Once a businessperson starts to make some money they tend to get really sloppy. Just like we do at home, businesses overspend on lifestyle items, but their rationalization is much more sophisticated. They can rationalize all kinds of toys and equipment that they don't really need all in the name of "adding credibility" or supposed "increased productivity."

I know a lot of real estate people who buy nice new cars, and stay in debt to do so, because they have falsely convinced themselves that people buy homes from real estate agents based on the car they drive. A clean, reliable, older luxury car is the most any real estate person should ever drive on the job, no matter how much money they make.

The number of thirty-to-forty-thousand-dollar brand-new four-wheel and dually trucks on a construction site—just like the TV commercials—is absolutely stupid. No one has ever hired a plumber, electrician, bricklayer, or carpenter because of his truck! These nice trucks get torn up on the job site and the driver is usually deeply in debt with a destroyed truck that was in no way needed to operate his business.

The purchase of electronic gadgets and hardware upgrades in the name of "needing it" to win in business makes me want to scream. You can buy toys when you make lots of money, but you don't destabilize your business or go into debt buying crap and then look stupid by trying to convince all of us that you had to have that new item to make a profit.

The most profitable businesses and the most stable businesses are those that have avoided the need for toys or the emotional need to impress visitors. Get some nice things and toys, but only with surplus money, and never with the rationalization that they are actually needed to conduct business.

I visited a billionaire's business to do a multimillion-dollar transaction. In his lobby was a couch that the Naugahyde had been stripped from so long ago, the couch was shedding. When we sat down to have our big meeting we sat around a folding table on stacking chairs. He had no need to impress me with his furniture, since he knew it was access to his business I wanted. If you and your business are attractive you don't have to impress anyone with your furniture or toys. No deal was ever made or lost based on the couch in the reception area. That is ego.

Tax Savings Rationalization

The wise EntreLeader never rationalizes a "tax savings" on unnecessary purchases in order to make a profit. If you need something to make a profit and want to buy it and pay for it a few months early to throw the expense in one tax year versus another, that is wise. But making not-needed purchases and then strutting around like a peacock in your new Hummer saying stupid phrases like "My CPA told me I needed to spend some money to save on taxes" is stupid and will set you up to fail. Yes, you should always take appropriate deductions for expenses associated with the proper operation of your business. However, if your CPA says you should spend money you don't need to spend buying items not needed for the business to "save on taxes" you should fire your CPA because they can't add.

Do the math. If you are making $75,000 per year you are in a 25 percent tax bracket. If you spend $10,000 that you didn't need to spend solely to save on taxes you create a $10,000 tax deduction. A $10,000 tax deduction saves you 25 percent, or $2,500. So the "tax savings rationalization" has you spending $10,000 you didn't need to spend in order to save $2,500 in taxes. If you think that is good math you will definitely fail at business.

Debt

If you have been in business very long you will soon realize that we make mistakes. We all make mistakes and have some really dumb ideas. Most of us have an idea a day, and most of those ideas stink. After being in business several decades and achieving national prominence with the Dave Ramsey brand, I am convinced that our company makes almost all of our revenue and enjoys all of our success on about 10 percent of our ideas. We survive the other 90 percent of our ideas. Maybe the percentages are wrong, but those of us who have been around awhile can testify that most of our ideas, brainstorms, and revelations prove to be stupid, or at least wrong.

Debt Magnifies Mistakes

Since I don't know which one of my "brilliant" ideas is going to be a mistake, it becomes a huge error to borrow into and increase the size of my mistake. We have made so many errors and miscalculations there aren't enough pages to recount them. I am sure our gleaming mountain of success is actually a pile of garbage, a pile of mistakes and missteps, only we are standing on it rather than lying buried under it. If you are standing on mistakes you are a success. However, if you have borrowed to increase the size of your mistakes you will be out of business. Nonfatal failure is encouraged and is how you learn to ride a bike. But when you borrow to implement your latest "brilliant" plan, you exponentially increase your chances of fatal failure.

Space Camp

We have a wonderful series of children's storybooks that teach financial principles to children ages three to twelve. They are world-class stories illustrated by my cousin Marshall Ramsey, who is an editorial cartoonist and has twice been nominated for a Pulitzer Prize. When we started we originally had four books in which our character "Junior" (Financial Peace Jr.) went on four adventures where he learned to work, save, spend, and give.

Our friends at Chick-fil-A asked us if they could license five children's books to put in their kids' meals. Their plan was to put one book per week in the meals for five weeks, about 2.5 million books total. License fees for opportunities like this are not much so we wanted to come up with an idea to make some money off this fabulous exposure and brand lift. Since we had four books, and they needed five, our plan was to create three more books.

With three more we could provide five books to Chick-fil-A and have two more to advertise on the back of all 2.5 million. Our plan of course was that we would sell several gift boxes of all seven books in hardback, or at least sell the two extra books they didn't get in the meals. So Junior went on three more adventures where he learned about debt, integrity, and contentment.

The new book on contentment was called *Adventures in Space*. In this book Junior wants to attend Space Camp and isn't able to attend because it is so expensive and his parents are on a budget. Junior is very sad, but his dad goes to the big-box store and gets some leftover boxes to build a spaceship. Junior and some of his other friends who couldn't afford the expensive Space Camp have a blast playing in the boxes. Junior's friends who attended the big, nice, expensive Space Camp got rained on all week and didn't have fun at all. So Junior learned the wonderful lesson of contentment. What a wonderful, inspiring story until . . .

The director of the real Space Camp from the Huntsville Space and Rocket Center called to ask why we were stealing their federally trademarked term "Space Camp." He was nice, but then their attorney started sending us threatening letters. We were stupid, we were wrong, and we had completely violated their trademark *accidentally*. I own many trademarks and copyrights and would never steal from someone. We had no idea "Space Camp" was trademarked. The story gets worse. Apparently the director of the real Space Camp's wife listens to me on the radio and respects our mission. So when she discovered that Dave Ramsey had said that Space Camp was bad and too expensive she confronted her husband about why he would do such a thing. Ouch.

We were completely in the wrong, even if it was by accident. They could have taken huge chunks out of us and it appeared their attorney was suggesting they do so. I personally called the director and profusely apologized and offered to personally tell his wife this was a huge mistake. He was understandably upset, but the more we talked the more he realized I was not a crook, though possibly me and my company could be accused of stupidity. He graciously allowed us to certify that our remaining stock of Space

Camp books had been shredded, and now any of his team is allowed to attend our events free, forever. Oh, brother.

We were so excited about this project that had we been willing to borrow we would have shredded 250,000 books, but since we don't borrow we don't magnify our mistakes. We only had to shred about 22,000 books, which we were happy to do to avoid any further theft on our part. Actually we weren't happy about losing the money, but it was the right thing to do and a gracious settlement on the part of the real Space Camp. For the record, the real Space Camp, which I didn't previously know existed, is a fine camp and is *not* expensive for what you receive. And they didn't have to threaten me to get me to say that.

Debt Kills Cash

When small businesses fail it is usually blamed on "cash flow." As I have said this "cash flow" problem can actually be translated as "tax problems" and "debt problems." If a business has no debt, by definition they have more cash than a competitor running the same business model down the street in debt. The dry cleaner who has $300,000 borrowed on an SBA loan and a second mortgage on his home is much more likely to fail than the dry cleaner who is debt free. So debt is a destabilizing force that exponentially increases risk and the probability of fatal failure.

Companies that carry debt and are publically traded are devalued in the marketplace due to their increased risk. Even an undergraduate investment finance class teaches this basic principle of finance. Yet, supposedly sophisticated and educated people spend an inordinate amount of energy trying to say debt is good when used properly. Debt is needed to open and operate a business, they say. The reality is there are many, many debt-free companies that are small businesses that last generations. Even among the large companies there are many that are debt free because they don't want the risk or the drain on cash. All

> **What kills companies is debt; without debt, companies have the wherewithal to survive.**

these debt-free companies seem to fly under the radar of what the culture has come to believe: that debt is most often used in business to win—which turns out to be a false belief. Large, debt-free companies you may have heard of include Cisco, Microsoft, Chick-fil-A, Hobby Lobby, Bed Bath and Beyond, the Gap, Electronic Arts (EA Games), eBay, Apple, Google, and Wrigley (gum). Peter Andrew, a former analyst with A. G. Edwards, says, "What kills companies is debt; without debt, companies have the wherewithal to survive."

Mythology

There are several myths about debt that float around in the air and in conversation about business that need to be addressed. The first one says you can't start or expand a business without debt. The truth is, according to the Bureau of Census's data, 60 percent of all small businesses opened in a given year needed less than $5,000 to get started. The reality is most people do not start their business (nor do they need to) with a huge loan, a huge amount of brand-new equipment, and a building with a mortgage. The truth is that starting small and gradually expanding is what most businesses actually do, and they survive. The truth is that by starting small and gradually expanding you lower risk and minimize the size of the mistakes you will make.

The Line of Credit Myth

I often hear that a line of credit is needed to cover cash flow fluctuations: "My business is seasonal or unpredictable, so I have to have a line of credit to make it." Once again the truth is very different from the mythology that the culture believes. The longer you are open the more you should be able to predict normal cash flow fluctuations with decent accounting and budgeting. If you are smart and run your business well you will catch on quickly to what cash drains are due to seasonal or cycle-caused problems. Also when you have some retained earnings and/or just some liquid cash you become your own line of credit.

Credit Card Debt in Business

It is really hard to imagine but people actually think using a credit card to finance a business is smart. The person who thinks that is a very naive businessperson—basically, a gambler. Yet according to *Businessweek* 50 percent of small companies use credit cards, with 71 percent of them carrying balances. This extremely expensive form of debt is an indicator that the person running or opening the business isn't putting much thought into the finances. They are under the illusion that they can outearn their stupidity. As I have counseled small-business people I've found, in most instances, the credit card user is reactive. They are reacting to a slow time or an opportunity, or worse yet, they did not think through their launch very well and are reacting in the fashion of a dreamer thinking automatically that it will all work out. I am convinced the failure rate of small businesses is largely influenced by the number of them who break the back of their dream by using credit cards to finance their business.

They are under the illusion that they can outearn their stupidity.

I also counseled people who rationalize the use of credit cards in the operation of their business by saying, "We don't carry debt" or "We use them to do our accounting." First, if you don't carry debt, then use business debit cards. We use debit cards exclusively and we find we watch them a thousand times more closely because they represent real money. The irony is that credit cards also represent real money, but using them just doesn't hit your emotions the same as using debit cards. Owners look at me, horrified, when I suggest debit card usage and say, "I would never trust my employees with a debit card!" This stupid statement lets me know two things: One, they don't think they are liable for the company credit card if an employee misuses it; that is stupid, of course. Two, they have employees they don't trust who are helping them grow their company. I don't want an employee, a team member, who I don't trust trying to make a $100,000 sale. So this isn't a credit card issue, it's a leadership issue; you have employees you don't trust but you're keeping them anyway.

Lastly, if your only accounting system is your corporate credit card you are an inept businessperson and you must do some work to put a real accounting system in place. I know credit card companies sell the accounting function as one of the supposed benefits of using their plastic, but if you stop and think for one moment you will realize how lame that is.

Myth: Large Purchases Require Debt

Bill is a good man, a hardworking man, an honest man, the kind of guy you really want to see win. He is good to his wife, loves his kids, and runs his business with integrity. He was sitting across the table from me with his wife, Sonja. His Caterpillar ball cap was tilted back but his eyes were looking at the floor in shame. Bill runs a successful small company as a plumber and found himself on the verge of bankruptcy. He was asked by a general contractor to dig a ditch from a street to a building and he rented a backhoe to do it. The rental fee was about $450. The customer was a good customer, so he paid for the rental and took care of the job. The next month he ended up renting a backhoe three more times, and the next month four more times. When all the rental bills came in, he saw how much he was spending and decided it was time to invest in a backhoe, because, he said, "the rental fees were killing" him.

So Bill went off to the heavy-equipment store, where he financed a new $52,000 backhoe and a $16,000 trailer to deliver it, and later that day bought a $64,000 dump truck to pull the trailer containing the backhoe. Bill is a good man who made some really stupid decisions. It is ridiculous to think that a few $450 rental fees mathematically justify these purchases, but businesspeople do it all the time. Medium-size businesses borrow $500,000 to buy equipment to "stay ahead of the competition" or to "land that big job" they think they couldn't do without the large purchase.

The reason Bill and Sonja were sitting in my office for counseling was the equipment payments were quickly sinking their otherwise profitable small plumbing business. After selling off the equipment Bill took a loss of around $20,000, which he financed and is still paying on. However, that move was the only move that prevented him from losing everything. Most business leaders are optimists and so they often only see, and digest emotionally, that everything is going to work exactly as projected. I have had the displeasure of sitting with thousands of businesspeople who hit the wall and the big purchase that was financed was the reason for their failure rather than the reason for their success.

I suggest you don't borrow for these large purchases for many of the reasons we have already discussed. Risk is increased exponentially, mistakes are magnified, and cash flow is destroyed by debt payments. You might ask, "How in the world am I supposed to grow my business if I don't buy this equipment or this building?" First let me remind you that slow and steady wins the race, so it is preferable to grow slowly and gradually rather than go deeply into debt.

It is preferable to grow slowly and gradually rather than go deeply into debt.

There are four principles we follow when making large purchases.

1. *We pay cash.* We systematically save toward a purchase goal and put that very specific amount as a line item in our monthly accounting—almost as if it were an expense. Saving is not tax deductible but I still treat it emotionally and mathematically like it is an expense. So save $28,000 a month for eighteen months and you can pay cash for that $500,000 piece of equipment. Note: if you can't save the money you won't be able to make the payments anyway, and don't think you will make the payment with the increased income, because that doesn't always happen like you plan.

2. *We rent until we can pay cash.* If Bill were still renting the backhoe instead of having purchased it he wouldn't have nearly lost his business. When I started my business in my living room I didn't have a copier, so I rented one from Kinko's by paying per copy. Rent until you are so profitable that you can afford to pur-

chase with cash, and by then you may not even want to own the stuff.

I have a wonderful TV and radio studio with about $500,000 worth of equipment in it. We did not start there, however; we started in radio using the studio of the local station I was broadcasting on. That means that for four years I drove across town every day to do a radio show. It was a pain, but during that time I learned a lot about equipment, which meant when I did purchase I didn't make mistakes. And of course I didn't have debt payments on equipment driving me to make bad decisions out of desperation. I will never forget when we finally saved up the money to build our first little studio. We put the proud new addition in two closets, installing a piece of glass between them. We had several pieces of used equipment and furniture. The rooms were not even soundproof so we had to rope off that end of the office when we were on the air because people talking down the hallway could be heard over the air. We bought a good microphone, but my first broadcast table was a small, round pressboard Formica table covered with scratches and dents from the back corner of the local office supply store. We drilled holes in the "wood" for the microphone stands and we were off to the races.

Slowly, gradually, we saved the money to build a slightly better studio, then another, then we added TV studio equipment, and now we are making enough money to do continuous upgrades as we go along. But we never borrowed and we never had to; we started by using someone else's equipment.

3. *We outsource to avoid going into debt.* Every company outsources something, and when you can't dig the hole there is a guy somewhere who has a backhoe and would love the work. We purchase well over ten million dollars a year in printing and don't own a single printing press. We purchase meals for our team

every week and provide catering for monthly events in our conference center, and we don't have a chef. It makes more sense to outsource—economically, from a management perspective, and to avoid debt.

When your business is just starting or is still growing fast you must outsource the ownership of real estate. I love real estate as an investment but I find most of the time owning it is a really bad idea, until you have stabilized the business. So many businesses are affected by location, and when you are just starting you can mess up selecting the location. Owning the wrong location will cause you to stay longer than you should. I've seen businesses try to make their business fit their building instead of making their building fit their business. I have actually heard people say they didn't want to grow any larger because they would outgrow the building they own!

After you have been in business at least five years and your growth is predictable you might be ready to save and purchase something with cash. As I mentioned earlier I got a great deal on the building we are in but the repairs and operational functions some days cause me to be a landlord (to myself) instead of concentrating on what makes me money, my business. If I have to review bids to put a new roof on the building I own, that is not a revenue-producing activity. There is something to be said for letting a landlord be in the real estate business and letting you focus on your business. Once you have the money and are not going to quickly outgrow your purchase, then you may want to consider buying a building if you get a great deal. Otherwise it is okay to rent the entire time you are in business.

4. *We buy used.* When we started out and when we purchased our first big items, we purchased high-quality used stuff that was pennies on the dollar, great deals. The very first counseling table had very nice Steelcase-

brand chairs with it that were probably $400 new but I bought, used, for $10 each, though they were an ugly green. We just needed something presentable and functional to start with. I think we still have that table, but the chairs are long gone. We don't buy used things like that today, but those purchases now represent a small portion of our revenues. Don't be so proud you can't or won't start with used equipment.

Saving Makes the World Go Round

On Mondays, midmorning, we have a leadership meeting of my top four leaders. In the first few years of the business we called it the "managers' meeting" and we discussed every detail going on in the business. We'd talk about personnel issues, cash position, purchases, technology, and anything else we needed to look at to keep the business running.

There are three very important things I have applied the "wisdom of the wife" to. One is hiring, as I described earlier; two is large decisions, like the time my wife, Sharon, got me to move into the building we are in; and three is the managers' meetings, which in the early days Sharon attended. She didn't want to come and honestly was quiet most of the time. We would sit and try to figure out what phone system to purchase and she would yawn. She does not attend those meetings today because they got to be just too much, but her wisdom in those early days is legendary in our company culture.

One Monday we were whining. I know you never whine, but we were sitting in our managers' meeting, whining. We were whining about how tight the money was and how it seemed we would never get over the top. We were whining about the fact that if we didn't collect from some of our customers we were going to have a hard time meeting payroll on Friday. We were having a full-on pity party about how tough business was. My wife spoke up and said, "I know why you don't have any money." I kind of rolled my eyes and asked my wife, the homemaker, to enlighten

us. She said, "The reason you don't have any money is you guys
are hypocrites." Then I was getting mad, but I said, "Okay, what
are you talking about?" "You go on the radio, in books, and all
over the country in seminars telling people to have an emergency
fund and yet you don't have one in the business," she said. Oh
crud, she was right. I hate that.

I immediately knew that she was applying common sense and
was saying we didn't have any retained earnings. When you can't
see the forest for the trees it is always handy to have a lumberjack
around. That month, and every month since, we put a percentage
of our net profits aside as retained earnings. Proverbs says, "In
the house of the wise are stores of choice food and oil." In other
words, wise people save money. To this day the retained earnings
account is nicknamed "the Sharon Fund" because that is actually
how it got started.

More Than Just an Emergency Fund

Retained earnings are used for three things: emergencies, invest-
ing into the business, and capitalizing on opportunities. The goal
should be to have about six months of operating capital saved in
cash. You likely aren't there now and it will take you a while to
achieve this much in retained earnings, but it is a great best-case
scenario goal.

It is not simply an emergency fund, but that might be the retained earnings' most important function. When you have built
some liquidity (saved cash) your business can weather the storm.
The storms in business are different than in
our personal lives, but in some ways they
are the same. The storms are the same in
that they are unexpected, but they do come
from different directions. In your personal
life you might lose your job, where in business you might have a horrible month or two
collecting from your customers. Both mean
unexpected lost income, but both are still a little different. In business you might have unexpected expenses like cost overruns on a

**It is wise to
expect the
unexpected
loss in revenue
or increased
expense.**

job or a piece of equipment that goes bad, where at home it could be the car transmission going out. So emergencies, unexpected events, really aren't unexpected, we just don't know what flavor they are going to come in. It is wise to expect the unexpected loss in revenue or increased expense; that way you will stay open and operate with a ton less stress.

Investing in Your Favorite Company

Retained earnings are used for more than just the emergency fund. You can also grow your company without debt by simply designating some of your cash for future growth. You can launch a new product, or hire some very talented people, or try a new marketing approach when you have the money. When you do so with your hard-earned cash you will be much more careful and wise with any growth-oriented investment than you will be with borrowed money. Borrowed money just doesn't feel real.

I have a leader who has been with me for over a decade who is very cash conservative, too much so. We were meeting with one of his department leaders who was not taking any marketing risks and I was trying to get them to make some nonfatal errors to get the marketing machine moving. I suggested that within the next sixty days I wanted them to find $10,000 worth of marketing ideas that did not work. I told them to get out there and try something, because nothing moves while you sit in your office counting coins. I was being a little bit sarcastic but I think they took me literally, because they promptly bought $10,000 worth of marketing that did absolutely nothing. Well, I guess I asked for it, but at least we had the money to invest into the business and try some things. I am not seriously suggesting that you be rash or impulsive, but saved cash allows you to take the calculated risk safely.

Opportunity Is Knocking

The other thing cash is good for is to take advantage of huge opportunities that come along. You can buy inventory for pennies on the dollar off a failing vendor. You can buy out a competitor completely, with cash, for pennies on the dollar. For me opportunity is spelled D-E-A-L. Sometimes bargains of all kinds float before your nose and you can't jump on them unless you have the cash.

In the late nineties we were providing content for a financial website start-up during the dot-com boom. The start-up was a classic dot-com deal: they were using venture capital to build an idea to take public. The idea was burning cash at an unbelievable rate and had yet to take in a dime of revenue. You know the story . . . they didn't make it.

The guy running it called to tell us he was closing and we should buy out their brand-new office furniture. We didn't really need any office furniture, but he insisted it was a great deal. I went to look at the furniture and it was all top-grade Steelcase workstations, some fabulous executive conference tables, and executive desks. They had not even moved into the building yet so the furniture had never been sat in. He showed me the invoice of just under $300,000. I assured him I didn't want the stuff and I sure didn't need him wandering around town telling people how I had kicked him when he was down. He told me repeatedly it was venture capital money and no one cared; he was tasked with the cleanup and wanted to get it over with.

My leaders and I discussed it and tried to figure out at what price we'd be stupid not to take the furniture. We decided $21,000 was a comfortable figure considering our cash position, especially since we were just going to store the stuff until we needed it. He took our low offer so we bought that furniture at about seven cents on the dollar. You can't, or at least shouldn't, do that unless you have the cash. When opportunity knocks, if you keep some cash you can answer the door.

Be Generous

Be generous with your products, services, and profits. In his book *The Little Red Book of Wisdom*, author Mark DeMoss tells a story about John D. Rockefeller. The Standard Oil founder, who died in 1937, was one of the world's richest business barons. In his lifetime he gave away today's equivalent of $5 billion. He told his story this way: "I had to begin work as a small boy to support my mother. My first wages amounted to $1.50 per week. The first week after I went to work I took the $1.50 home to my mother. She held it in her lap and explained to me that she would be happy if I would give a tenth of it to the Lord. I did, and from that week until this day, I have tithed every dollar God has entrusted to me. And I want to say that if I had not tithed the first dollar I made, I would not have tithed the first million dollars I made."*

Being generous is the hallmark of people who live successful lives and who operate business with soul. If your exclusive reason for operating your business is personal gain, you will find yourself empty because you are shallow. Some of the greatest joys of becoming successful are associated with acts of generosity to your team, your customers, and your community.

As an evangelical Christian I believe in tithing on my income. Which means Sharon and I give a tenth of our personal income to our local church. We do not find it in the Bible to tithe on business profits until we take them home. So we do almost no giving directly from our business. We take the profits and income from the business home, where we tithe and do other giving.

Giving from home keeps us from giving from the business as a form of advertising how wonderful we are. The math is the same when you tithe and give from home but it keeps our motives more pure and allows us much more anonymity as well. In our case we use a family foundation to keep all this separate.

However, while we do most all of our cash giving from home, we maintain a generous spirit in our business. We want to be generous to our team, donate books to silent auctions, those types of things. If you are a dentist your team should have free dental care for their immediate family. If you own a tire store your team should not be riding on bald tires. Allocate money in your accounting process to constantly push a spirit of generosity. You will find the dividends in terms of smiles and personal satisfaction far outweigh the few dollars committed.

---

* Rockefeller quoted in Mark DeMoss, *The Little Red Book of Wisdom*, pp. 96–97.

My friend Rabbi Daniel Lapin describes the Jewish tradition of the Havdalah service in his book *Thou Shall Prosper.* It is possibly one of the more beautiful metaphors I have ever seen for having a business and properly viewing prosperity. He says it this way:

> As the Sabbath ebbs away each Saturday night, Jewish families prepare for the productive work week ahead by singing the joyful *Havdalah* service . . . The *Havdalah* service is recited over a cup of wine that runs over into the saucer beneath.
>
> This overflowing cup symbolizes the intention to produce during the week ahead not only sufficient to fill one's own cup, but also an excess that will allow overflow for the benefit of others. In other words, I am obliged to first fill my cup and then continue pouring as it were, so that I will have sufficient to give away to others, thus helping to jump-start their own efforts.

I think he is saying that we first earn to take care of our needs and reasonable wants but keep earning simply to give. This formula will make your business vastly more satisfying if you follow it.

Applying the Principles

You might now be wondering what to do first and how to apply some of these principles. Most are obvious, like you have to do a better job than you have been doing with accounting, including developing an accurate budget. Simply stop buying things you don't need to make a profit or that are purchased exclusively to save on taxes.

If you find your business in debt or without enough retained earnings, follow my suggested formula: First, drop your personal income from the business down to a simple living wage, the minimum your family can live on. Then, apply most of the profits that are left after you pay yourself that minimum wage to debt reduction and use some smaller percentage to grow cash.

I recently had an attendee at one of our EntreLeadership events who was running a nice printing business. He was making a profit of about $200,000 per year and took it all home, so he had no cash in the business and had equipment debt of $150,000. We counseled him to cut his take-home money to $60,000 a year (ouch) and he decided to apply 80 percent of profits to debt and 20 percent to cash reserves. If his business continues like it has he will apply $112,000 to debt per year, making him debt free in seventeen months, and will also have saved $40,000 in cash by then. At that point he can bring more home, and he decided to continue to grow cash at 20 percent of net profits until he has six months of operating capital.

Wrap Up

It sounds so primitive and unsophisticated when I state it again, but business is really not that hard. You are, however, required to do the basics or you will not win. Budget and do the accounting, stay out of debt, don't buy what is not needed to make a profit, save cash, and always be generous. When you do these basics with a steady hand and increasing sophistication you will find yourself running a stable and satisfying operation.

Business is really not that hard. You are, however, required to do the basics or you will not win.

10

The Map to the Party

Grasping the Undeniable Relationship Between
Great Communication and Great Companies

When I was in college my grandparents allowed me to live in their summer lake house for free. Get this . . . college student on the lake and it's free! The only drawback was that it was twenty-seven miles from campus, and not an easy twenty-seven miles. This particular stretch included cattle crossings, curves, twelve turns, country lanes, and all kinds of wildlife. Every commute was an adventure. Being in college and being on the lake meant that we were required by federal law to have frequent parties at the Ramsey lake house. Before the days of the Internet, cell phones, and GPS, we were required to learn the art of "giving directions." The directions to these parties were a sheet of paper with a crudely drawn map that resembled a treasure map and a list of directions, statements like "When you cross the railroad tracks you will see a road to your right, don't turn there." We were famous for our maps.

The parties were awesome, but the trips to and from the lake house by first-timers created real legends. Getting lost is one thing, but getting lost in backwoods Tennessee and being really late for the party is another. Over the years the number of times I have gotten to a party late and been really mad because of bad directions or no directions is ridiculous. Just this week we had a dinner party at our home and the guests' GPS sent them ten miles out of the way, so we ended up talking them into our home by cell phone, and they were thirty minutes late. All was well, but it reminded me again how frustrating, even maddening, bad or no directions to the party are.

Your business is a party. You have invited your team to the party. If you give really good directions everyone will have a great time at the party. If your business is like most businesses you are awful at the art of giving directions and the only communication is poor communication. Communication in a business is the map to the party. If you have a great map, expect to have a great party. But most don't.

One of the hallmarks of winning companies is they are very intentional and effective at communication. As a matter of fact the EntreLeader's goal should be to create a company culture of communication. Communication is the grease in the gears. You can have great gears in your company and it will still freeze up, grind to a halt, if you don't put the grease of communication into the engine. When the right hand doesn't know what the left hand is doing, great frustration and distrust sets in.

If you want to create a company that is fun to work for, where productivity and creativity are high, and that you are actually glad to lead, you must create a culture of communication.

Lack of communication is caused by many things, but there are two main reasons for it: one, companies don't make communication a priority, and two, leadership is so arrogant or fearful that they intentionally *under-*communicate. In either case the lack of communication starts to sow the seeds of discontent and distrust within the team. If you want to create a company that is fun to work for, where productivity and creativity are high, and that you are actually glad to lead, you must create a culture of communication.

Lack of communication first breeds frustration. The frustration will convert to outright anger and then morph into team members' distrust of each other as well as the leadership. The distrust will finally end in fear. Deloitte's 2010 "Ethics and Workplace Survey" revealed that 48 percent of employees who plan to leave their current jobs want to leave the company due to a lack of trust in their employers, and 46 percent say a lack of transparent communication from their organization's leadership is their main point of dissatisfaction at work.*

Many companies use "mushroom communication" with their team: keep them in the dark and feed them manure. This is really shortsighted and has catastrophic results when it comes to trying to create an environment that attracts and retains talent, is creative and productive, and allows you to confidently delegate.

When the team doesn't know what is going on in the company they are by definition not a team, so you end up with employees, not team members. When the team doesn't know what is going on fear and anger set in. When people don't know the truth they generally will grow a huge pile of negative garbage in their minds that is ten times worse than reality. If management doesn't have a reputation for transparency and quality, complete communication, a simple statement gets blown up into a catastrophe in the employees' minds. If the team can't trust leadership for complete information a simple statement like "We are over budget and need to get sales up" will create rumors by the end of the day that half the workforce is being laid off due to sales being down. Most people assume the worst times ten when leadership hasn't built trust with them by telling them the whole truth. Fear, frustration, anger, and distrust become the company culture when there is poor communication. That all leads to a culture of secrets, gossip, and tons of missed opportunities. Sadly this describes most companies.

> **Most people assume the worst times ten when leadership hasn't built trust with them by telling them the whole truth.**

If you are the kind of leader who has poor communication because you are not proactive about it, I can help you quickly change your company culture with some basic processes to create quality communication. The main thing that will change your company

---

* *New York Post,* July 26, 2010, www.nypost.com/f/print/news/national/gets_third_economy_americans_will_fdKUJmux9W0r04dJc43cnN.

is *your* commitment to create a culture of communication. You must *really* want the left hand to know what the right hand is doing.

If you are the kind of leader who has poor communication due to your lack of trust in your team or your arrogance that "the little people" don't need all that information, I probably can't help you. Hiring the right team and then trusting them with information and trusting they have the emotional maturity to hear the whole story is one of the hallmarks of an EntreLeader. So if you are guilty of being the other kind of leader you will need a change of heart on how you view your team before you will become an EntreLeader, a real leader; for now you are just a boss.

Methods of Communication

Share the Dream—Tell the Story

Your team can't manage their time toward building your dream if you don't tell them what the dream is. Communication moves the ball, for the whole team, from dreams all the way into time management, which means productivity. Leadership has to repeatedly share the dreams, visions, mission statements, and goals with their team. Remember Andy Stanley's warning that when sharing your vision you must do so twenty-one times before your team actually ingests it and starts to believe. The EntreLeader is constantly stating and restating the organization's dreams and how their team is going to get there. As a leader, if you are not sick and tired of saying the same thing over and over, you have likely not communicated with your team.

As a leader you must learn to tell the story of your company and its history. As you tell the story of struggle and victories to your team over and over you are accomplishing many things, such as teaching the team the value system of your company as they see how you reacted rightly or wrongly in a given situation in the old days. You also let them know they are part of something that is bigger than them. If your team members know they are participating in a big deal it gives them energy and creativity as well as lets the occasional prima donna know you can probably pull this off without him if he doesn't plug into the culture.

I often tell stories to our staff meeting of victories won in battles past. I always remind the existing team they are valuable, but the future is ours. The future is ours based on how we have won in the past. I recently held up a British pound and read the inscription around the edge of the coin, which says, "Standing on the shoulders of giants." I then went on to tell of the sacrifices and effort put out by some of our team members who have been with me for decades. I wanted all the great young talent to get the message that we will win, they are important, but standing in their midst are great warriors of old, so they should be respectful.

http://www.entreleadership.com/history

Communication in Times of Trouble

Trouble is going to come to you. Trouble is going to come to your company. No one is exempt, and so deciding how to communicate about it before it comes is absolutely vital. People who have emotional and spiritual maturity as well as good mental health can handle problems and can communicate during a crisis.

When there is garbage to deal with, it might be the most important time you communicate with your team. We use a couple of rules when we are dealing with garbage.

First, when in doubt, *over*-share. Tell more details and more of the story than you are really comfortable doing. This is risky and must be done with class—and a warning. I have had to do this several times over the years and I always start with a disclaimer. I let our team know that I am over-sharing and I have an expectation that they will be mature enough to hold this sensitive information. I remind them that we have a no-gossip policy, so if they have any comments or questions they should bring them to leadership or keep them to themselves. I remind the team that we want to be a special company with high levels of communication and I am honoring that by over-sharing, and their part is to be emotionally mature enough to honor the process by acting like classy adults. Over-sharing scares me, but having a normal company scares me even more.

The need to communicate about problems can be brought on by many different kinds of situations. For the first time in the history of our company we had a couple of quarters where sales turned down. I dealt with the core problems directly with the leaders and with some particular departments within our company. I also shared in general terms, not actual dollars, with the whole team that we had to pick it up. We don't borrow money, so we had to catch this downturn early and fix it, because we would not be able to keep everyone if the trend continued. I explained again that we were all ultimately self-employed, so we better all act like it and turn sales around. Every team member was called on to improve everything they do by at least 5 percent and I promised we would see a turn. I worried out loud in front of the whole team that sharing this information openly would create illogical fear, but I was willing to take that risk because I believed I was working with adults who could carry reality, not children who must be made to believe everything is okay, even when everything isn't okay. As a leader those conversations are scary, but I will always risk having them.

Second, never publically harm or embarrass people while over-sharing about problems. Several times over the years I have had to deal with guys getting addicted to porn on the Internet. In the instances where we couldn't walk them into a place of healing, we had to let them leave our company. I have never named a person when discussing this subject with the team. However, I occasionally remind our team that people have left our company over the misuse of the Internet. I remind them that the computers and e-mail they use are owned by me and they have no right to privacy when using my equipment. That sounds so controlling and offensive as I write it, but privacy isn't a big deal to people who are living a clean life and doing the right thing.

Mechanical Communication Systems

Once you have decided that huge amounts of communication are going to be a priority for you and your team, then you have to use some basic methods to communicate. Remember that creating a spirit in your culture that yearns for, and seeks, communication is the only way you can really create a winning environment. Don't put these processes or systems in place in a company where leadership doesn't continually talk about how important communication is. The methods of communication have no energy if they exist in a culture that doesn't highly value communication. On the contrary, when you put systems in place without the driving spirit for communication, the systems will bring your team down instead of up. Budgets and reports become paperwork I hate if I don't understand how valuable they are.

Staff Meetings

When we were first starting and reached the level of about ten team members, we all got in a huge argument one day. The stress and the frustration boiled over and it was not pretty. Once we cooled off we sat down and dissected what had occurred. We figured out that we really did trust each other's competency and integrity. We figured out that we had some very passionate champions pushing to make sure their area won. We also figured out that the right hand not knowing what the left hand was doing caused us to distrust each other's competency, integrity, and even intent. That moment is when our staff meeting was born.

We drove a stake in the ground and made eight thirty to nine thirty A.M. Monday morning a mandatory meeting for every member of our little band. Our first meetings were very primitive and simply consisted of each person saying what they worked on the week before and what they were working on the coming week. At least each of us knew what the other was doing. Immediately, even at this very primitive stage, we began to see the frustration and distrust leave. We also started seeing something we didn't see coming: synergy. When you know what battle your fellow warrior is fighting you can often offer great insight and connections to your network, and even join in the battle. None of that was happening. The loss of one hour a week of "work time" increased our productivity tremendously. The productivity went up due to the synergies created, but also because we all liked and respected each other more.

So today, with over three hundred team members, we still gather on Monday mornings. Each department leader is called on to share something good or bad going on with their area. We celebrate the victories together and we mourn the losses together. Today a departmental report to the group may include photos or video shown on the screens. We introduce new hires to the whole company and clap welcoming them. We talk about profits and sales. We read hate mail and brag letters recognizing awesome customer service internally or externally. I teach from our core values or operating principles to remind everyone who we are as a tribe. We announce birthdays once a month and sing happy birthday (that's corny, isn't it?), serving cake after the meeting. We give away NHL or NFL tickets by random drawing. In general we leave that room first thing every single Monday morning on the same page and pumped for the week to come.

On Wednesday morning we meet again as a group for an hour. This is our devotional time, when we have a local pastor, a motivational speaker, or even a big-time recording artist come and inspire our team. In addition to lifting us all up it gives us another time to make company-wide announcements in person. These two hours of shutting down our company to make sure we are all singing from the same sheet music has yielded tremendous results.

There are a lot of reasons we have a fabulous culture, but if you were to interview and ask my team what they attribute it to, many of them will tell you they value these times together. If you are running a business you must do physical group meetings as often as is possible and reasonable. If you are a huge business, meet departmentally. If your team is spread out geographically, meet by Internet and force a physical gathering at least a few times a year.

Static Meetings

You never want to have so many meetings that you can't get any work done. Many companies that have lost their soul are often guilty of that. On the other hand most start-up entrepreneurs never have a regular meeting and consequently end up running from fire to fire to fire in some kind of ADD fashion that exhausts them and isn't productive. I know; I did that. When I first started leading I would show up at one of my people's doors every time I had a question or something to work on. None of us could get anything done because we spent all day interrupting each other.

When we started having set meetings at the same time on the calendar every single week, we quit bothering each other. Every Monday morning from eleven A.M. to noon, I meet with my two EVPs, my COO, and my CFO. The five of us are the core team of leaders. We discuss all kinds of things in that meeting. These are some of the most highly paid people in our company, so to pull all of them together every time there is a question would really be costly. So each one of us comes into that meeting with a list of things to discuss with the group and we have a very productive hour. With the exception of illness, vacation, or some really big deal, we never miss this meeting.

I also have a set meeting with each EVP for an hour a week and my COO for an hour a week. This keeps me (and them) from wearing me out with e-mails, voice mails, and drop-ins all through the week. These fixed meetings are not only very valuable for productivity; they have another benefit that at first I didn't realize. Having the same meeting at the same time for almost two decades has created a rhythm to my/our week. If something causes one of those meetings to be canceled a couple of weeks in a row we start to sense something wrong down inside. No, the meetings are not a security blanket; they serve a very valuable role, so when we miss them we start to emotionally register that something is wrong. Because something is wrong, we lose touch with our operation and with each other.

Mail

Voice mail, e-mail, and texting are efficient but dangerous ways to communicate to your team. They are efficient because you can fire off a quick message to one or more players. However, they are dangerous because body language and tone are missing. Nonverbal communication accounts for 80–90 percent of the message. When you forget this you will engage in e-mail fights with people. I am guilty of doing this and it is stupid. Worse than fighting by e-mail is fighting by e-mail while hitting "Reply to All." E-mail seems very efficient but the loss in meaning requires more meetings to correct the imperfect communication, so be careful.

Weekly Reports

We resist anything that feels like the bureaucracy in many large organizations. When something is petty, useless, political, or doesn't love people well, we call it "corporate." If you hear one of our team say something is "corporate," that is an insult. We certainly understand that not all large organizations fall into that insult, but enough of us have worked for jerks requiring stupid do-nothing work that we resist that feel in our culture with a vengeance.

When our company got large enough that I couldn't look over people's shoulders, I found myself wanting to know what they were all doing. I also wanted to make sure they were doing something. I started thinking that I would like to have each team member do a weekly report stating what they had done that week, but the instant I had that thought I recoiled against myself as becoming "corporate." "Weekly report" sounds like useless paperwork done by a drone in a cube that hates his job. Yuck. But I was teaching my team time management and goal setting, so I wanted to be able to verify that these things were happening.

The more I thought about the weekly report idea, the more I realized that it wasn't the report that I hated, it was the fear that it would be "corporate." So our weekly reports are not written to me; the team member does a one-page summary of their week, written to themselves. If you are on my team you need to be the kind of person who wants to win and measure yourself to make sure you win. What is the point of losing weight if you don't get on a scale to prove it?

So each week our team writes a report to themselves answering the question "Why should Dave be glad I work here?" We allow team members to design their own report with the few guidelines listed below. The report must be no longer than one page. At the top of the report is what I pay them and they spend the rest of the page describing why I should be glad of that.

High Point, Low Point

Each report must contain the high point of the week and the low point of the week. When I first asked our team to do this I was so naive I assumed that the high and low points would have something to do with our business, their job. Nope; our team members put some of the most bizarre personal information there you can imagine. I was tempted to go back to them in staff meetings and tell them to confine their highs and lows to business, but then I began to realize all this insight into where their head was is valuable for building relationships and leading them well.

If the high point of the week is "Going to my first NFL football game of my life this weekend, thanks for the tickets," what did I find out? First, I need to see that person for thirty seconds as we leave staff meeting and talk football and find out how the game went. Second, my human resources guys who arrange for us to purchase tickets to give away need some positive feedback because their program is touching our team in a good way. Third, as a season-ticket holder, I need to remember how many people consider something like that a huge deal. Perspective. All those conclusions from one little bit of communication.

If the low point is "I am bummed that my dad didn't call me on my birthday," what did I find out? How that person's father issues have to be considered. Make double sure we do something cool for his birthday next year. Depending on my relationship or his leader's relationship with them it might be appropriate to stop by his office and just give him a hug.

"My dog is sick," "My mom is sick," "I just got the biggest

check of my whole life," "I just got out of debt," "I'm struggling with my marriage," "I broke up with my boyfriend," "I lost thirty-two pounds," "I ran my first marathon," and "I love my job" are just a few of the real-life highs and lows I have read in reports. This stuff is extremely valuable because your team consists of people who have real-people stuff going on all the time. I never asked them to get personal, they just did.

http://www.entreleadership.com/weeklyreports

Report Must

If you and your leaders do not read and react to the information in the reports you are sending a message that communication and reports are not important. If you read a person has broken a sales record, give them a personal attaboy within minutes of reading the report. If there is a problem mentioned in the report, address the problem, but most importantly let the writer of the report know you did. If you value the information you are getting—and you should—let the writer know by acting on it. Read the reports and react to them every single week, or don't do them.

Annual Reviews

Here we go again . . . a process some "corporate" companies do that we didn't even want to get close to. Annual reviews are often the one time a person gets real feedback on their job and personal performance, and the time that a raise is given.

At our place job and personal performance get continuous, almost weekly feedback, positive or negative. I do not wait a year to course-correct mistakes. Team members don't need to wait a year to bring problems to leadership either; that is silly. Team members don't even need to get a raise only once a year on their anniversary date; they might not deserve a raise or they might need to get two or three in one year.

For these reasons we don't do annual reviews, but we have found the annual checkup to be valuable. Throughout the year, we will address performance, a team member has plenty of opportunities to present problems, and we will give raises. However, we have found that scheduling a set meeting at least once a year further ensures that we review every team member's income and that we give them yet another time to present problems or ideas about the future. We find that sometimes people who won't schedule a conflict-oriented meeting will open up in this meeting. We do *not* use the annual checkup as a job-performance discussion; I require my leaders to make that a fluid ongoing discussion.

Key Results Areas

A job description is communication. When you state in writing clearly what the Key Results Areas are for the position, you have communicated. KRAs are a vital type of communication because we have to continually define what winning looks like with our team. We are communicating that doing these three or four things with proper passion, creativity, and attitude is winning. If team members aren't doing them, they are losing, and they'd better change. That kind of communication is most often missing in companies.

Management by Walking Around

There is no better quality of communication than in person. You have the benefit of body language, touch, tone, eye contact, plus a ton of other nonverbal cues that make communication complete. Tom Peters, in his wonderful book *In Search of Excellence,* studied excellent companies to discover their attributes. I read the book decades ago and still remember several of the points. One thing that he mentions is MBWA, Management by Walking Around. I like to think of it as simply hands-on leadership.

The way I implement this type of communication is at least a couple of times a week I grab my cell phone and tell my assistant jokingly that I am going to walk through the building to spread hate and dissension. With my small yellow pad I slowly walk through the building and feel what the vibe is. I use some of the highs and lows from reports to congratulate or console someone as I run into them. I look for dirt and disorganization. I eavesdrop on phone calls. Sometimes I just plop in front of someone's desk and find out about life and business from them. In thirty minutes I can wander through our company and take its temperature. This is the culture of my company communicating with me. The feel in the air is communication. I have also deposited with my team, by wandering through, that I care and I don't live in an ivory tower.

Sam Walton was known for riding with his delivery drivers and wandering through a Wal-Mart spontaneously. Legend has it that he used to say he learned more about his company from truck drivers on a ride, checking out people on a visit, than his reports could tell him. He was communicating and being communicated with using MBWA.

> **The greatest problem in communication is the illusion that it has been accomplished.**
> **—George Bernard Shaw**

Conclusion

Chaos that is unhealthy and breeds failure happens in companies that don't make communication a big deal. Your team, by definition, can't be called a team unless they have a shared dream, vision, mission, and goals. The only way these things become shared is with intentional, quality, constant communication. Seth Godin says, "A crowd is a tribe without a leader, without communication."

My mandate to the EntreLeader is to lead the way mechanically and culturally, creating quality communication.

11

People Matter Most

Building Unity and Loyalty with Your Best Resource

My personal assistant is tough as nails, so when I looked up from my desk and she was standing in my door with tears running down her face and a highway patrolman standing next to her, my stomach went into my throat. In an instant I was worried about my wife and my kids. What in the world was happening?

It is amazing how fast your mind can process situations and visual stimuli like that. The patrolman said he was there to deliver some really bad news. There had been an accident, a head-on collision, which took the life of a young mother and her little girl; only the younger child, a baby, had survived. This was the family of a young man who worked for me. We asked the officer if we could tell him, which he said was fine, but he needed to be there to make sure the sad news had been delivered. My heart was beating wildly, and my head was spinning. How in the world can you tell a young man that his wife and child are gone? I could hardly breathe. We sent word up to his department for him to come to my office and that was when we discovered he wasn't in the building. Where was he? Man, this was getting messy.

Finding his leader, we figured out he was working with our live events crew that week and so he was over a hundred miles away setting up in an arena. Because the wreck was so big it was going to play on the evening news, so the officer was insistent the young husband get the news very soon. We chartered a jet to go pick him up and got it in the air in a matter of minutes, so that by the time we could get ahold of our young man the jet was almost there.

We called a leader on-site and had him plus a few others gather in a hotel room with our young husband. Sadly we had to deliver this horrible news over the phone but then sent him straight to the airport with a leader riding the jet home with him for comfort. We got his family and pastor to meet the jet as it landed so he had as many people as possible who loved him around him in that horrible time of need. That was one of the toughest days of leadership that I can ever recall.

How did we make decisions quickly and wisely in such a stressful situation? How did we know what to do in that wild crisis without hesitation? Simple. We handle all of our interactions with our team, in any situation, based on one simple rule: The Golden Rule. I know I have mentioned this before, but you have to learn to treat other people like you would want to be treated if you want loyalty and unity in your company. I knew exactly what to do: everything within my power to minimize the extreme pain that life had brought to our young husband.

Leading for Loyalty

Do you know why most employees aren't loyal to their company and leadership? Because their company and leadership aren't loyal to them. My wife always told my children growing up that if you want to have friends you have to be a friend. If you want loyalty you have to be loyal. Too many people in business have abandoned sight of the fact that their team members are humans, they are people. Too many people in business have become so shallow that they are merely transactional, not relational. The people on your payroll are not units of production, they are people. They have dreams, goals, hurts, and crises. If you trample them or don't bother to engage them relationally you will forever struggle in your operations.

"Treat others as you want to be treated" is a core Entre-Leadership principle. When you would expect to be praised, praise. When you would expect a raise, give a raise. When you would need training, train. When you would need some grace, give some grace. When you would expect a reprimand, give one. When you would feel competent and want the dignity of being left to do the job, back off and let the competent execute.

Quality people—really all people—have a need to be treated with dignity. If you want your team to buy into your dream and execute with every ounce of passion they have, you must be caught caring about them personally and treating them with dignity.

We hired a superstar marketing guy to reel in some large relationships. We clearly defined his Key Results Areas and set up his compensation so that when he landed a whale or two he would make some great money. About six months into his employment he brought in a one-million-dollar deal. He got creative with a client who was nibbling and sold them on something completely outside of what we hired him for. We realized, and so did he, after the deal was signed that his compensation structure specifically said he would not be paid on deals outside his area. The decision was made instantly to pay him anyway. This poor guy had been in bad companies for so long he had become cynical and could not believe that some company would actually pay him money that was not technically due. He cried when he opened his check; it was awesome.

If you want your team to buy into your dream and execute with every ounce of passion they have, you must be caught caring about them personally and treating them with dignity.

We made that decision instantly. How? That is what I would want someone to do for me if I brought them a million-dollar deal. Do you think this guy is pumped? Sure. Do you think this guy will be loyal? Of course. Do you think anyone anywhere anytime can say something bad about me within earshot of him and not have a fight on their hands? Loyalty. Possibly best of all he will be motivated, highly motivated, to bring in some more million-dollar deals, because he knows I have his back, he will be paid. Sadly some shortsighted companies do the exact opposite. They save the money they would have paid him but lose his trust, loyalty, motivation, and creativity. All that loss for a saved commission check is really bad business.

http://www.entreleadership.com/loyalty

Fanatical Integrity

Loyalty comes also from fanatical integrity. Let your yes be yes and your no be no. When you commit to pay someone, pay them. Never miss payroll. You'd do better to lay people off if your company is struggling than to have them work there and their checks not clear. Tell the truth in tough times and in good times. Be transparent about how decisions are made and what the team is facing.

Don't cut pay when someone is producing; you will cause them to dislike producing. A company cannot attract and keep quality, talented people when you mistreat them and those around them.

Integrity also means consistency. If you react the same way every time in every similar situation, you don't have to put your company values in a brochure, because your team sees them lived every day. The more predictable you become on matters of principle, values, and culture, the more you grow leaders and team members who you can delegate to. You can delegate to them because they will know what to do by watching your consistency.

If you react the same way every time in every similar situation, you don't have to put your company values in a brochure, because your team sees them lived every day.

Loyalty is born and a quality culture occurs when the EntreLeader follows through in a predictable, positive, and proactive manner on every issue and opportunity.

People only allow themselves to be led when they feel valued and when they are treated with dignity.

Know your team. Know their kids' names, their wives' names, and their dreams. Find out their story—everyone has one. Visit the funeral home, the hospital, and never miss a birth. When you have the power or the connections or the money to help them live their lives better, always do it.

I have reached the point with the size of our company where there is no logistical way I can be that deep in every team member's life. That does not mean it doesn't get done. My leaders at every level need to make really sure they stay in touch with their individual team.

If you think I have gone off the deep end, I have not. I have a goal to get to the end of my life and have one of the great joys be not only winning at business but how I won at business. None of us get to the end of our lives and think we should have done one more deal or made one more dollar; when your life draws to a close you realize what is important: people and how you treated them.

Your team is watching, and just like your children, they would rather see a sermon than hear one anytime.

http://www.entreleadership.com/wounded

Unity

One of the largest, strongest horses in the world is the Belgian draft horse. Competitions are held to see which horse can pull the most, and one Belgian can pull eight thousand pounds. The weird thing is if you put two Belgian horses in the harness who are strangers to each other, together they can pull twenty to twenty-four thousand pounds. Two can pull not twice as much as one but three times as much as one. This example represents the power of synergy. However, if the two horses are raised and trained together they learn to pull and think as one. The trained, and therefore unified, pair can pull not only twenty-four thousand pounds but will hit thirty to thirty-two thousand pounds. The unified pair can pull four times as much as a single horse. They can pull an extra eight thousand pounds simply by being unified. But unity is never simple or easy.

There are numerous examples from the basketball court or the football field of superstars who are jerks and bring disunity to a team due to their self-centeredness. A group of superstars is seldom a dream team in sports. It usually looks more like a large day care, with temper fits and messes. Most sports fans and most athletes yearn to watch and play with the unselfish player. It is amazing how a well-coached team of unified B-level players will often beat the big names, if the big names don't have unity.

In business we often make the same mistake. We can mistakenly believe that if we just hire talented people we will win at business. So some companies gather a group of talented people and among them are several jerks. Because there are some jerks in the bunch no one wants to pull together, and the disunity more than offsets what the talent brings, and together they lose. I would rather have a group of passionate, unified B and C players than have a group of disgruntled superstars. My little band of highly unified folks will win almost every time.

The 1980 "Miracle on Ice" story is proof of the principle of unity. When assembling the 1980 Olympic ice hockey team, Herb Brooks, the coach, turned away some of the most talented ice hockey players of the day. His comment was that he wasn't looking for the best players, he was looking for the *right* players. Herb wanted players who would play with heart, play selflessly, and thereby create tremendous unity. That unity in a band of no-name players pulled off one of the greatest victories in sports that year by winning the gold medal, against all odds.

Building Unity

Unity, like so many other things in this book, is seldom found in companies but is always found in *great* companies. Unity, like so many things, must be intentionally created in your culture. People don't naturally unify; they must be led to do so. To create a culture of unity you have to get your team to buy into a cause bigger than their selfish motives. Unity can be created only when the team not only knows the company cares for them but also cares for each other. Your team will only be unified when they are willing to give up personal glory or gain for the good of each other and

> **People don't naturally unify; they must be led to do so.**

the good of the cause. This phenomenon is so rare that when we find a group that is unified we stand back in awe at the beauty of it.

Five Enemies of Unity

As I have fought to build unity in our team I have discovered, the hard way, what destroys unity. I have found that if we keep these five enemies of unity away from the gate of our company we become increasingly unified. Unity brings us a great work environment where productivity, customer service, creativity, and the resulting profit more naturally occur.

1. Poor Communication

Poor communication causes a lack of unity. This is so important that we spent the whole last chapter on it. To recap, if the right hand doesn't know what the left hand is doing, disunity, anger, and frustration will fill your company. A team is only a team by definition when they are unified, they are on the same page. If you want a fabulously unified team and all the good stuff that brings, you will have to work unbelievably hard to create and maintain high levels of communication.

2. Lack of Shared Purpose

Lack of shared purpose causes a lack of unity. If the team doesn't share the goals of leadership and of each other, there isn't unity. Again, this is so important that I opened the book with dreams that lead into vision, into mission, and into goals. Shared goals create unity. There is no unity where there isn't a common goal, a common mission, a common vision, flowing from a common dream. If you want a fabulously unified team and all the good stuff that brings, you will have to work unbelievably hard to create a common vision and goals.

3. Gossip

I can't stand gossip. I have done it and I have seen people do it, and gossip is gross. In a company culture gossip will destroy all the good things you work so hard to create. There is no possible way you can have unity with a group of gossips. The very nature of gossip is the opposite of unity. Instead of pulling people together, gossip pushes them apart. Everyone knows inherently they can't trust a gossip.

Gossip about the company, or about leadership, is a particularly evil form of disloyalty. And it is suicidal when the person gossiping is hurting and running down the place and the people who pay him so he can feed his family. Why do people want their own company to fail?

I hate gossip so badly that after putting up with it at the start I decided to have a no-gossip policy in our company. You are not allowed to gossip and work for me. If one of my leaders or I catch a team member gossiping we will warn them once, then we will fire them. Yes, I have actually fired people for gossiping, and I will again. Gossip is evil, it is insidious, and it is contagious. Stamp out gossip if you want unity. Proverbs says, "Whoever guards his mouth and tongue keeps his soul from troubles."

People who work on our team will have frustrations. They will have problems, and they will get upset. If they don't have any of these things happening we probably don't need them. Most of our hires are brought in to grow something or fix something, which means problems either way. When they get bumped around or frustrated with leadership or a team member, they need to know how we define gossip so they can avoid it. We know team members are going to have problems. It is how they handle them that matters.

Problems or gripes are fine, but they must be handed up to leadership. Problems or gripes that are handed down or laterally are by definition gossip and run the team member the risk of being fired. We had a man who was constantly struggling with his leader. They clashed and both were talented. He made the mistake of sharing his frustrations with the sales support person in the group. We warned him once, and then he decided to share with two other people, so he doesn't work on our team anymore.

The sales support person can't do anything to help him with his frustrations, so that is gossip. I had a young lady who was processing orders whose computer was trash. IT had done a poor job getting it fixed or replaced, so she had a legitimate gripe. But she made the mistake of sitting with our receptionist and venting for fifteen minutes as to how management didn't care and IT was incompetent and how could Dave let this go on. My receptionist has never fixed a computer or budgeted to replace a computer, so she could do nothing to help this stupid little gossip. If she wants her computer fixed she should try seeing someone who can make that happen.

Hand your negatives up and your positives down. Otherwise it starts to sound a lot like gossip.

Gossips are usually the most small-minded of people anyway. People of greatness don't have time to gossip. As Eleanor Roosevelt once said, "Small minds talk about people, mediocre minds talk about events, and great minds talk about ideas."

The good news is that quality people also hate gossip. Once you have a culture that openly hates gossip and values the awesome environment created by a "gossip-free zone," the whole team will self-police, which is a big help. If a new or errant team member begins to gossip, other team members will remind them they will get fired for that and "none of us do that here." I have had that happen many times in our company and it is really fun to watch people bend to positive peer pressure. If you want a fabulously unified team and all the good stuff that brings, you will have to work unbelievably hard to keep gossip out of your organization.

4. Unresolved Disagreements

When some of your team members have a disagreement it has to be resolved. Unresolved disagreements paralyze people. There are particular levels of maturity and some personality styles who can't stand conflict. Conflict is debilitating to them and must be resolved. Conflicts that remain unresolved grow and grow, and kill unity.

Unresolved disagreements remain unresolved when the Entre-Leader doesn't know they exist. Teach your team to either resolve conflict or openly talk about it with leadership so they can get some help solving the problem. One of the beauties of the high and low points on the weekly reports is conflicts will show up there, giving you the opportunity to help solve the problem.

One week when I was reviewing the team's weekly reports, I saw that one of our sales support ladies had as her low point "I hate it when people talk down to me." My first thought was, *Oh, grow a backbone and get over it.* But then I started to think about what she was really saying. She was really asking for help, so I had her leader check it out.

It turns out that this young lady, who was pregnant, was upset about a comment a fiftysomething coworker, who was having a bad day, had made to her. Let's see . . . a pregnant woman and a lady in her midfifties—no hormones involved there, right? We sat them both down, the older lady apologized, they both cried, and they went on to become great friends, with the older lady even mentoring the new mother for many years. That only happened because leadership stepped in and didn't let an innocent disagreement go unresolved.

I don't require everyone on my team to like each other or be best friends off campus. But I do require they respect each other and agree that while styles may be different we have shared integrity and shared intent. We will sit and talk until we can get to that point.

Sometimes disagreements are unresolved because leadership is chicken or doesn't want to be bothered by the drama. Part of leading a team is helping them grow together, otherwise they will grow apart. EntreLeaders must have the courage to deal with conflict and must bother with the drama. Some days I have felt like I am running a beauty parlor with enough drama for an Academy Award, but it must be dealt with if you want a quality culture that is unity based. If you want a fabulously unified team and all the good stuff that brings, you will have to work unbelievably hard to make sure all disagreements are resolved.

5. Sanctioned Incompetence

John Maxwell says, "Sanctioned incompetence demoralizes." When a team member is incompetent, for whatever reason, and leadership won't act, the good team members become demoralized. *Why should I work hard if he doesn't have to?* becomes the prevailing thought in the whole company. Team members who are motivated will become the exception rather than the rule if you tolerate misbehavior.

Team members will often take their direction from the way you treat other team members. I have struggled between being kind to people, giving them every chance to turn their performance around, and on the other hand letting their lack of performance spread through the whole place.

I had an assistant in the company who was just never going to get to where she needed to be. She just didn't have the mental tool set to rise to where she could perform with excellence in her role. However, she was one of the nicest people I have ever met. Everyone loved her and wanted to see her win. Because she was so well loved and so nice we let her lack of performance go on for a year too long. Finally we started getting the sense that our team was rolling their eyes when her name was put on a project. They really didn't roll their eyes, but there was this sense in the air that everyone knew she was getting a pass.

I finally realized that even in the nicest of circumstances, when we allow someone to stay who isn't excellent we aren't doing anyone any favors. We also didn't have specific clear corrections to give her; it was more this looming black cloud of incompetence.

What happened when we finally gently let her go was amazing. That move sent a message to the whole team that leadership is actually competent. And the message was also sent that while we love you, you still have to perform with excellence.

Like we talked about in chapter 7, the only time our company allows team members to function at a less-than-excellent level is when we are extending grace for them to get through a personal problem. We are so gently tough on performance that if someone is underperforming the rest of the team automatically assumes not that leadership is chicken or incompetent, but instead that we are extending grace for a time of healing.

I think most of us who lead make errors by being too slow to act on issues of incompetence, or too fast and harsh. Finding that balance is tough, but sometimes leadership is more an art than a science. Most leaders have a tendency toward being too slow or too fast to act. Find your tendency and move two steps in the other direction; then you will see your team culture balance out.

If you are too quick to fire someone due to performance issues you can spread a spirit of fear and you will struggle to build loyalty. If you are too slow to fire someone due to performance you become viewed as weak or out of touch with operations. Working this balance to never sanction incompetence and yet give the team member every opportunity to make it is one sign you are becoming a true EntreLeader. When you do this you will see real unity grow along with loyalty. If you want a fabulously unified team and all the good stuff that brings, you will have to work unbelievably hard to avoid sanctioned incompetence.

Fight the Enemies

If you value unity, then fight, and teach your team to fight, these five enemies of unity. These enemies are so strong that any *one* of them can cripple your business and *two* of them can cause you to fail. To the extent any one of them has a foothold in your culture they are stealing your fun as a leader. They are worth fighting to the death.

1. Lack of intention and thoroughness about communication.
2. Lack of intention and thoroughness about goal setting and shared purpose.
3. Gossip.
4. Unresolved disagreements.
5. Sanctioned incompetence.

Unity and Loyalty

So few companies have unity and loyalty that when your company does, it automatically stands out in the marketplace. Great talent stands in line to join your team because the culture becomes the stuff of legend. Great customer service is a natural occurrence in a company that has these values. However, I think most of all, this type of culture is tremendously satisfying to lead. You will not have all perfect days, but you will enjoy a richness of soul in your business that few ever experience.

12

Caught in the Act

*Amplifying the Success of Your Business
Through Recognition and Inspiration*

In an opening scene of the TV show *The Simpsons*, Homer stands among his coworkers ready to receive the "Worker of the Week" award, sure he is going to get it this time because it appears he is the only one in the entire company to have never gotten the award. The boss comes to the balcony overlooking the workers to make the announcement, and as Homer waits expectantly the award is given to "this inanimate carbon rod." Homer then growls, "I'll show him inanimate."

The writers of *The Simpsons* are geniuses and we all know that. But in this scene they really capture the essence of several rules and reasons to give your employees recognition.

- Recognition is important.
- Recognition has no power if diluted by everyone getting the same recognition the same way.
- When people aren't recognized and noticed they become inanimate.
- Where there is no recognition it is very difficult to have passionate, creative, motivated team members.

Jacques Plante, Hall of Fame NHL goalie, said, "How would you like a job where every time you made a mistake a big red light goes on and eighteen thousand people boo?"

The feeling and reality of acceptance gives people the best opportunity to become their best. People yearn for approval. I have a fabulous golden retriever that may be the best dog I have ever owned. This dog will do anything to get approval. Sometimes I think you and I are virtually the same way. People yearn for appreciation. Appreciation can launch even the most educated, sophisticated person into the stratosphere. My wife says women often dress to be appreciated, not only by their husband but even by their friends. In a healthy marriage most men yearn to be appreciated by their wives more than virtually anyone else on the planet. Proof of this is the fact that virtually every ultra-successful man I have met has an appreciative, supportive wife. The old joke is that behind every successful man is a fabulous wife and a surprised mother-in-law.

People yearn for attention. This yearning is so primitive that people will even act out negatively just to be noticed. They often become social morons just to be noticed in a social setting. The push for attention is so strong that it can lead even the most emotionally and spiritually mature person to act contrary to who they really are. Lastly, people yearn for affection. Anyone who has ever taken one semester of psychology has read about the studies of babies who had all their physical needs cared for but were never touched or loved and as a result nearly died.*

We yearn so desperately for affection, even as adults. But affection in the workplace? Eyebrows go up and suddenly running through your mind are visions of sexual harassment lawsuits flying everywhere. Obviously I am not talking about inappropriate workplace affection. However, the bad actors have scared the good people away from ever touching in proper ways. When someone's mom just died of cancer you need to learn how to give a hug, for goodness sakes. The wife of one of my team members recently miscarried in the second trimester. They have three other kids, but the loss of a baby is never easy. We ran into them at lunch on Sunday a week after the loss. Without thinking I walked over and gave her a hug and told her we were hurting with her. That afternoon I got a great e-mail from my team member, her

---

* From a study a hundred years ago when 99 percent of babies in orphanages in the U.S. died from a condition called "marasmus," where lack of touch produces lack of appetite. www.benbenjamin.net/pdfs/Issue2.pdf.

husband, reminding me that the reason he loves working with us is we actually care about people. Don't be afraid to appropriately love people. The PC and lawsuit risk-management police have destroyed real leaders' ability to treat their teams like family. People yearn for acceptance, approval, appreciation, attention, and affection.

So How Do We Do Recognition?

The first rule of recognition is to simply bother to do it. Start making a habit of catching people doing something right. A sincere compliment is so unusual that when you begin giving them you are immediately set apart as a leader and as a human. We have to fight the tendency to only course-correct. "Constructive criticism" is often destructive. Why is it that when my child comes in with all A's and one C on his report card I concentrate on the C? Why do I do that? Why do you do that? It is ridiculous to ignore the C, the area for improvement, but why do I focus on that instead of glorying in the five A's? I guess when we perceive ourselves as "in charge" we somehow think that it becomes our job to correct. Course correction is part of a leader's job, but it's not their *only* job, and some bosses spend all their time finding what is wrong instead of what is right. Also, be careful to recognize activities and character traits you want all through your company. Remember whatever you give recognition for will grow quickly inside your company. I once recognized a guy for being really radical in his reaction to a situation. Guess what? I immediately started getting a ton of radical reactions, most not good, all through my company. Be very intentional to recognize what you want duplicated in scale, because that is what will happen.

Catching people doing something right can be as simple as a nod and a smile expressing approval of the person and/or their actions. When I walk through our building many times I am walking around people on the phone with customers, so I can't really interrupt them. But I often will stand and listen to them serving our customers for a few moments, then nod, smile, and walk on.

I just told my team member they are doing a good job without saying a word. I will admit I have to remind myself to be intentional about recognition.

A compliment has to be real. It cannot be something you fake because you read this chapter and got inspired. As motivating as a real compliment is, cheap flattery is very demotivating. Cheap flattery says to the person you are manipulative and lack integrity, and that will destroy the connection.

Look for opportunities to brag on and give honor to people. Giving one-on-one praise is effective, but giving recognition in front of others is even more powerful. The most effective recognition is given in front of people who the person cares about. With our young team I often get to meet their parents when they visit our offices. Always when I meet Mom and Dad I thank them for "loaning me this one" and tell them "they are special, they are a rock star in our company, and they are really particularly good at . . ." If you give that kind of sincere compliment to someone through their parents, anyone, even the ultra-sophisticated forty-year-old, will stand in front of you beaming. I am smiling just thinking about it.

When you meet a team member's spouse be sure to tell the spouse how special their husband or wife is. One of my leaders even sent flowers to a team member's wife with a card saying how awesome her husband is and how glad we are he works with us. When that guy got home he got a hero's welcome from his wife.

Because of our success and the media I do, I have been blessed to meet many famous and world-class people. A few years ago I met and became friends with the world champion in a particular sport. I was a little worried that he would be arrogant and instead he was gentle, kind, polite, and an amazing athlete. As we talked late one night at my kitchen table he told me of the untold hours and sacrifice his father had gone through to help him train through his teenage years. He humbly attributed his world-champion status to his dad's encouragement and sacrifice.

So without his knowing I researched and found his parents' address. I wrote them a letter telling them what a sterling young man they had raised and that while I was impressed with his athletic ability I was more impressed with the man their son had become. I thanked them for being great parents. Can you possibly imagine the letter I got back? You see, famous, world-class people are complimented on their talent or their looks every day. But just like you and me, seldom are they ever told that they are great in other ways.

Recognize in Writing

One of the EntreLeaders in our company started with us when we were small and very tight on cash. One day he stopped by my office and asked permission to order some embossed stationery. For people in big companies or who have a bunch of money, that might seem like a normal request. But we are blue-collar guys, and embossed stationery sounds, to guys like me, a lot like a frou-frou expense that is borderline crazy. However, he convinced me he would use it to follow up with sales leads, so I grudgingly approved the order. This young EntreLeader is not only a master at sending follow-up notes to prospects, he also sends hundreds of thank-you notes a year. But best of all, he sends hundreds and hundreds of handwritten notes on embossed stationery recognizing people. He recognizes his team, his leaders, their spouses, customers, and even strangers, in writing. It is really hard to do something right within the view of this guy and not get a note of appreciation from him telling you how great you are. He has so inspired people all through our company that there is now a huge amount of embossed personal stationery for our team so we can try to copy him. I even got some, but to be truthful I don't send many handwritten notes because of my handwriting and spelling. Occasionally though, even I venture into that realm, inspired by the power of this simple gesture. Recognize people in writing. They will remember it, and don't be surprised to find your note framed when you visit their office.

Recognize in Front of Peers for Extra Power

As I said earlier, recognition is most powerful when done in front of the people who matter most to the person being recognized. So giving a parenting award to a CPA at a CPA convention might have almost no power, but giving that same award to that guy in front of his whole family at his church could have extreme power.

Because of size we had to change a wonderful tradition we had when our company was small. We had no money and there were just a few of us, so at first our company Christmas party was a home-cooked meal at our home, and later it became a dinner at a decent restaurant's meeting room. At these small gatherings we did not give out lavish gifts, we gave out lavish praise. When it was time for our "program" I would give a short state-of-the-company talk, thank everyone, and then the fun began. I would bring each person up and praise them in detail for their work, their character, and their diligence. Often we would all be crying. You may think I am a big softy, but it is so rare for someone to receive praise or give praise that it can become very emotional. Praise in front of their peers and their spouses and friends was a Christmas gift that was looked forward to every year. Did you know you can get a standing ovation from a group of only twenty people when you do this? Truthfully it isn't you getting the ovation; it is the person being praised. That is truly powerful.

Recognition Doesn't Have to Be Expensive

When I was twenty-two years old I spent three months in a multi-level company. It was amazing how good they were at recognition. In the hyped-up super-enthusiastic weekend meetings, awards were always given. The awards were a T-shirt. Yes, a T-shirt, but I have seen people making over $100,000 a year kill themselves to hit a production mark to earn a T-shirt of a particular color. It was not the T-shirt that mattered, it was the opportunity to be declared a winner in front of peers. Men and women will fight hard for the opportunity to be honored.

Happy Birthday

I have a theory that no one ever becomes too old or too sophisticated to smile when someone says "Happy birthday!" But it is a
little difficult to give someone a "happy birthday" wish when you
don't know it is their birthday. I have a friend who is a world-class
illusionist and magician named Kevin King. Part of Kevin's act is
memorization, and he is the best I have ever seen. He memorizes
the birthday of everyone in his life. In the last ten years every
time my wife or I has had a birthday there has been a voice mail
on our home phone from Kevin with birthday wishes. Without
fail, every time we play the voice mail I look at my wife and she
is smiling like a seven-year-old girl with a new pony. He does an-
niversaries too.

I took a cue from Kevin and decided to have our HR department post every team member's birthday on my personal calendar
so I could send them an e-mail with birthday wishes. I even might
remember to say something when I see that person. This does not
take a lot of effort but it creates a big result. I will come clean and
admit that the humorous birthday e-mail is now even automated,
so I am not really all that thoughtful, but it still has the same effect. Have you ever worked for anyone who sent you a "happy
birthday" e-mail, automated or not?

You might be saying to yourself at this point that if I spoon out
any more sugar you are going to throw up. I get that, but you have
to be smiling reading this and knowing it works to love people
well. If you want to have a different company, a different life, you
have to try to do things differently. Napoleon said, "Leaders are
brokers of hope."

Inspiration

Inspiration touches the emotions and causes activity. When a
book, a sermon, or a person inspired you, they lifted you and
sent you forth. How do you do that in a company or an organization? First, let's look at how you don't do it. You don't give talks
or speeches to hype people up while leaving the entire culture of

the organization in the sewer. Those talks begin to look like a *Saturday Night Live* skit because you are saying one thing while doing another. On the contrary, organizational inspiration is much more complicated than a simple motivational speech. Real inspiration has multiple layers and extreme consistency. If you want to become a real EntreLeader you need to be doing all the team-building steps I have outlined in this book, and the totality of those creates real inspiration. The whole operation must be inspiring, not a simple, single small gesture. Zig Ziglar says, "People say motivation doesn't last, well neither does bathing, that is why we recommend both daily." We intentionally use seven things to make sure the entire environment is inspiring.

1. Vision Casting

Where there is no vision that is understood and repeated to the team, there is no inspiration. There is not much of anything that lifts people more than believing in a dream, vision, and mission bigger than them. I pounded this subject in the first few chapters, but now pause and make sure you see that I am bringing this all together to create an organizational culture where people are fired up.

2. Compensation

I will cover compensation in detail, including how to build it properly, in chapter 14. Ultimately few people who feel underpaid and/or financially taken advantage of are inspired. It is a joke and even insulting to remember someone's birthday when you have taken all the financial incentive out of the equation. If you want an inspired, fired-up team, plan on paying them very well when they earn it. All a good team member wants is a chance to earn when they win.

3. Creating a Crusader Mentality

Crusaders will lay siege to the competition. Crusaders will run into a burning building. Crusaders work while they are at work. Crusaders require strong leaders of huge integrity. Crusaders don't have to be driven like cattle; they run like wild stallions. Crusaders only crusade for something bigger than them. People are lifted up and inspired when they work for something bigger than themselves. I mentioned earlier Tom Peter's old book *In Search of Excellence,* which studied excellent companies. Another of his discoveries was that the excellent companies understand their team has a deep-seated desire to be a part of something larger than themselves. My friend John Rich, of the megastar country group Big and Rich, says, "I play better when I am playing for something bigger than me." The Bible says in Colossians 3:23 to do your work as unto the Lord, heartily, not as unto men. Which again points back to the need to have a higher calling and communicate that to your team. Leo Buscaglia said, "Your talent is God's gift to you. What you do with it is your gift back to God." Don't just be a trim carpenter, be an artisan.

4. Storytelling

We covered the power of telling the story in the chapter 10. You have to tell the story of the history of the company. It is always inspiring. It is like learning that the pioneers went over the mountains in a covered wagon. Our forefathers were tough, independent people. Knowing my heritage is inspiring. The Ramseys fought with William Wallace. Our family coat of arms gives the family motto as *Ora et Labora,* which is Latin for "Pray and Work," which we have always done; that is inspiring to me.

Always keep in mind how powerfully inspiring stories are. The history of the company is just one story, but you should also be continually building the story. One of the things we do in our weekly staff meetings is read mail from customers. I read hate mail aimed at me so we all get a good laugh. I also read e-mails and letters bragging on the team. This predictable, public recognition is unbelievably inspiring to everyone, sends a clear message about our culture and our values, and makes people smile.

Try reading an e-mail in front of the whole company, or even your department, that says, "Just wanted to say thanks and tell you what a great help Jimette has been helping us get our tickets to the live event. She is the best customer service person I have run into in a long time. No wonder your company is successful with people like her, I wish other companies trained like you guys do." Here is what happens: Jimette is obviously red-faced and loving it. Everyone else is inspired to pick up the level of customer service because they might get mentioned someday. Applause breaks out and people are thinking this company really is different. We have just made the statement loud and clear that leadership values high levels of customer service.

Try reading an e-mail in front of the whole company that says, "We wanted to say thanks for our rep Amy. One week before we were to start our classes we were hit by a hurricane and had major damage to our building. All of our class materials were destroyed. We called to tell Amy that our materials and location were destroyed so we would be delaying class. We were not expecting what happened. Without hesitation she replaced all of our materials free of charge!! Wow!! We are now holding the class at another location and wanted to say thanks for having people like Amy on your team." Here is what happens: every team member sits with their chest sticking out in pride over our company, Amy, and how we were all just part of someone doing the right thing. Generosity to the customer, quick thinking, and doing the right thing on autopilot are justly rewarded. Applause breaks out and Amy, who probably hasn't had a perfect life, is set for a great week. She has energy, smiles, and is ready to fight the week ahead. The team is lifted, Amy is lifted, and recognition, unity, loyalty, and communication have occurred.

If you read three e-mails a week to your team you will see mail bragging on your team start stacking up on your desk; they'll be hoping you will read one featuring them. You will even see internal fan mail come to your desk, where one team member is bragging on another. Remember, be careful to recognize what you want duplicated because I can tell you from experience that you will see your culture shift almost immediately.

5. Predictability

Explosive, erratic behavior by leadership does not inspire; on the contrary, not knowing what to expect is one of the greatest causes of organizational paralysis. When people can't predict how you will react, they freeze and do nothing. Assuming you hire motivated, quality people you will see them come to a screeching halt trying to figure out your next unpredictable move. Being predictable in matters of principle is a sign of deep integrity. Amy knew she could be generous and give those class materials away and be praised, not shamed, for doing so because over the years she had seen leadership do the same type of thing over and over. Leadership's predictable response gave her great power to act.

Stated core values and operating principles help communicate how you intend the organization to run. Of course you must live those values on a moment-by-moment, day-by-day basis.

6. Passion

I have discussed that you can't burn out if you were never on fire. Monotones do not inspire. You don't have to yell or be a drama queen, but be aware of the importance of leadership conveying their passion to the team. In the name of sophistication many companies and people have removed, by their words, deeds, and body language, the communication that they care very deeply about the outcome. Show people you care if you want them to care. Be willing to show emotion about issues that matter to the success of the organization. Please don't expect people to be inspired when leadership is asleep.

7. Example

The EntreLeader knows they set the tone, the speed, and the work ethic of the team. I have a friend who had a very successful small business and his profit one year was just over a million dollars. He is an excellent golfer and had always dreamed of making it as a professional golfer. Since his business was booming he decided he could devote three or four days a week to his golf game so he could go pro. He really had the talent to potentially make it too. The next year while he golfed his business's net profit dropped to $300,000. Over coffee he asked me what I thought happened. That was an easy answer. The example left the building to "live his dream." As soon as he quit work, so did his team. As soon as he cared more about something other than the business, so did his team. As soon as he became apparently apathetic, so did his team. I told him his little golf outing was a $700,000 experiment in human behavior and he now had the answer to his question; sell the business to someone who cares about it or go back to work.

One summer in high school my son worked for a family-owned retail business run by a flamboyant character. I am so glad he worked there because in just a few months he was thoroughly taught how not to lead. The owner was a nightmare. He would lie to customers, the employees, and the suppliers. He would come in late and leave early. There are too many stories to recount here, but to show you how important little examples are, we were driving past that business recently and my son commented on how the owner always took the prime parking spot right in front of the business. My son's comment was, "Dad, in all the years I can remember growing up I have never seen you park in the prime spot once at our office; you always reserve those for customers. I thought that was common sense." Well, it is common sense, but common sense isn't very common. When the owner does things like that his actions scream to the rest of the team that the customer doesn't matter. Not to mention his actions say the same thing to the customer.

If you come in late and leave early, please understand what that says to your team about your passion. Your work ethic sets the pace for them. You cannot expect nonowners to care more deeply about the outcome than the actual owner does. Your example in every part and every movement of the organization is huge.

Conclusion

You probably have not read anything in this chapter that has given you a deep revelation or that is so complicated or sophisticated that it is unreachable. Instead it's likely you have been nodding like a bobble-head doll, saying to yourself that this all makes sense. The thing to remember about doing business well is that it isn't complicated, but you do have to pay attention to the details. So it is time for you to do a better job with recognizing and inspiring your team, yourself, and your family.

13

Three Things Successful People Never Skip

Dealing with Contracts, Vendors, and Collections

I was so mad I was spitting nails. I shouldn't admit this, but my eyes were bugging out of my head, my heart was pounding, my fists were doubled up, and I was full-on mad. Pete was on the other end of the phone telling me he was breaking up with me and there was nothing I could do to stop him. "But we have a contract . . . Doesn't that mean anything to you?" I virtually shouted at the guy. I just about exploded when he added insult to injury by laughing at me and saying, "Well, boy, you are just going to have to sue me then."

It was early in my career and I was still so naive that I thought when I had a contract with someone it meant they had to keep their word. A couple of weeks before I had been to a city where Pete owned a radio station; we had done an event there and had made Pete a pile of money. Just a few days later we got notice that he was taking our show off his radio station immediately, in violation of our one-year contract. He had waited until I helped him make money and then messed me over. I was left with two choices: sue him, spending more than I would likely recoup, or grit my teeth and walk away. Sometimes we have to enter lawsuits, and other times it just isn't worth it.

Contracts

Contracts are not protection against a lawsuit. You can have a contract and still get sued, forcing you to defend the contract. Contracts are not a guarantee of people performing or doing what they say. Contracts do not have mystical powers that make people who have no integrity keep their word. Contracts do not have mystical powers to make people competent who aren't. So when you or I utter the words "But I have a contract!" it indicates that you are naive about contracts. You will struggle in business if you try to use words and paper in the form of a contract to create a reality that just isn't there. People who are crooks will crook you even if you have a contract. People who can't sing can't start just because they have a contract. In business, lower your expectations of the power a contract actually has.

Donald Miller says the happiest people are the people with low expectations.* When you wield a contract like it has the power to make people something they aren't you will spend a good deal of time being angry and unhappy in business. Lower your expectations about the power a contract has.

If contracts are useless, why do we use them? I didn't say contracts are useless, I said to have reality-based expectations about what a contract is and isn't. A contract doesn't make a crook straight and it won't turn a cat into a canary. A contract is only as good as the people you are dealing with, so deal only with good people. There are a few occasions where you can spend a pile of money and have a judge force someone to perform, but it is, by and large, an unprofitable process for you; the lawyers love it, but you won't. Sometimes, on principle or to set a marketplace precedent, you have to fight to the legal death regardless of cost—and I have been in a few of those. I will tell you that even after you win you have the nagging feeling that you really lost. Don't deal with crooks or incompetent people thinking your contract will protect you; it won't.

---

* Don's quote refers to this study about Danish people: www.cbsnews.com/stories/ 2008/02/14/60minutes/main3833797.shtml.

Contracts are merely communication on the front end about the points of the deal. Contracts do help people of integrity keep their word in case in the busyness of life they forget what they committed to. I have been ready to leave a deal only to go pull the contract and remind myself what my promise was, so we stayed. Attorneys call this completed and thorough communication "a meeting of the minds." You should do contracts with good people so you and the other party can stick to what was promised, and you should do those contracts in writing. If their handshake isn't good their contract won't be either. But write it down to help communication and to help memory. The old saying is that a verbal contract is worth the paper it is written on. An old attorney friend of mine says, "If it isn't in writing it never happened." Use written contracts only to ensure memory and communication among quality people is executed, but don't expect higher of the contract than you do the people in the deal.

Contract Do's

I am not an attorney and this is not a law book, so seek the counsel of your attorney before following any of my advice. That is not a legal disclaimer, it is a fact. I am not trying to teach law here. As an EntreLeader, however, I do have some basics on contracts I want you to grasp.

Do have your attorney draft the contract if you aren't using a standardized form. The drafting attorney has the advantage of producing a document that pulls the fine points to your favor. Many of those points in your favor are not the items in the contract but the ones left out intentionally. Have you ever heard about George Lucas's original contract with Fox for the first *Star Wars* movie? Lucas's brilliance was that he kept all merchandising rights in the contract. He gave up his director's salary in exchange for 40 percent of the box office sales and all merchandising rights. The studio didn't really care, but Lucas wanted to be able to make shirts and posters to promote the movie himself in case the studio didn't do a good enough marketing job. He owns a piece of *every-*

thing that carries a *Star Wars* logo because of that part of the contract, which has made him an incredible fortune.

Make sure you are dealing with a competent attorney when they draft the core document. It is common practice among many judges to rule for the attorney who did not draft the document on points that are confusing or poorly worded, so make sure you have a good contract lawyer creating your draft.

Plan for the Best Case, Contract for the Best and Worst Case

Do plan your deal for best-case scenarios but contract for all worst-case scenarios as well. Entrepreneurial types are all about putting down on paper what happens when everything works and we all get rich but are notorious for not facing the possible downsides of a deal. We often call the downsides of the deal the "D's" of the deal.

Default

Detail what happens to the deal in the event someone does not do what they are supposed to. What happens in the event one party becomes bankrupt? I actually have in some of my publishing agreements that if the publisher goes into bankruptcy all rights to my books revert to me. One CEO asked me why I would want such a clause. I wanted that clause because I was doing a publishing deal with a publisher and that CEO, not with a bankruptcy trustee running the company until he can sell it out of bankruptcy. I don't want one of my books trapped in a deal gone bad.

Death

What happens to the deal if one party dies? You might be fine working with the widow or family of the party you contracted with, but you really might not want to either. When I am contracted to endorse a company my endorsement would be of very limited value if I died, so that contract would obviously need to end at my death. Consider what would need to happen in a given deal if one of the parties were to die. A lot of our company runs off of me acting as the product. My speaking, or publishing, or radio deals have to address my company's responsibility at my death.

Disability

What happens in the event one of the parties becomes disabled? This can be very important if the contract relies on one or both parties personally. Many entertainers' contracts with their promoters prohibit them from skydiving, scuba diving, or even snow skiing. It would be tough to stand onstage playing a guitar in a full cast because a multimillion-dollar concert obligation has to be met.

Drug Use

What happens if the other party gets involved in bad behaviors that will keep them from doing the deal as agreed? Cocaine makes people absolutely insane, so write up your agreement with a release option should "moral turpitude" occur. Moral turpitude covers a lot of possible misbehavior so it is a good idea to spell it out where needed. Remember, if you are dealing with a known drug user, just don't do a deal; walk away before you bother to draw up a contract.

Divorce

Do you want to be forced to complete the contract with the other party's crazy ex-wife who didn't seem so crazy when you all first met? Contracts can have a value, and the other party's value could be given to a spouse in a divorce proceeding unless you specifically say otherwise in the contract. Another idea here is you can contract with a company only so long as Joe Smith is their CEO, and in the event Joe leaves it will be *your* sole option to stay in the deal. You would only do this if Joe's presence is what makes the deal happen the way you want it to.

Disinterest

Believe it or not, sometimes people just lose interest. You can be stuck in a contract where the other side just doesn't care and wants to walk away. Really what you are doing here is deciding in advance how things will be split and what the concessions or buyout would be in the event one party wants to leave. A college football coach who wants to leave and take a job at another place often has a predetermined buyout clause in his contract. This makes breaking up easier to do.

Destruction

What happens in the event of destruction, hurricanes, famine, war, acts of God? This clause is generally mentioned in most contracts but think about it in light of what it means to the economy in the event the U.S. goes to war. What if you have a supplier in Florida and a hurricane takes them out? This clause gives you the opportunity to define your options should one of these events occur.

Win-Win

Do make sure your contracts are win-win. I suggest only doing deals that cause everyone to win. Don't go into deals where the other party is driven out of business if there is a failure. Only do deals that you will be proud of ten years later.

Copies

Do make sure all parties have fully executed copies. In some states with some types of contracts your contract is not binding unless all parties have fully executed copies. Remember the purpose is to have a meeting of the minds, full communication, which is represented by fully executed copies in everyone's hands.

Read It

Do read every word and have someone explain the parts you don't understand. On unimportant or small deals you balance your time invested versus the risk you take, but on big deals invest the time to know what you are getting into.

Extensions, Renewals, and Options

Do negotiate the right to renew or extend the deal. This right is particularly handy for a real estate lease or a production contract. If you can lock in how much you are paying for your widget you can more accurately predict cash and profits. If you can lock in your location at your option you can stabilize your business.

We originally leased our building for five years with three five-year options at a predetermined price. There was no downside because at the end of five years if the predetermined price was higher than the market price I didn't have to take it and I could renegotiate, but if rents in the area shot up I had locked in a great deal and would simply exercise the option.

Contract Don'ts

We don't use employment contracts at our company. As you read in other chapters we treat our team wonderfully because it is the right thing to do and because it pays dividends in the long run to treat people right. We don't need a contract to make us do those things. We want to do the things we do from a right heart and not from some false compulsion. When it is time for someone to leave our company we want them to leave immediately with as little drama and hassle as possible. We are good to people who quit and who we fire, but never because it is our contractual obligation. We operate in Tennessee, which is an employee-at-will state. Our state, like most states, allows a business to fire someone at any time for any reason other than discrimination. Legally I can decide I don't like you today and fire you for that reason, and you would have no legal recourse. Again, the EntreLeader values his team and never mistreats them, but I am discussing our legal obligation. We don't have, nor will we have, a legal employment obligation arising from a contract. I don't want someone to stay on my team because of their contractual obligation; this would mean they have no passion, have no creativity, and add a lousy element to our culture. Nor do I want to be forced to keep someone when it is time they leave.

Don't try to contract away a law, a statute. For instance, you can't contract away a legal liability. I had a landlord of an office building submit a lease to us stating he had no liability for injury on the property. He can't get rid of his liability. If someone should trip and fall due to faulty sidewalks, the owner of the building would be liable, and no contract can get rid of that liability. The lease could have had my company indemnify (protect) him from liability, but a contract can't remove the fact that he is liable. A contract can't make a criminal act legal. You can have a contract or a lease that says serving alcohol to minors is fine, but it still will get the company in a world of trouble if you do.

Miscellaneous Contract Clauses

Definition time. Take the time to look at some basics so you know what you are getting into when you sign a deal. Learn the definition and meaning of the miscellaneous clauses so you aren't surprised later on.

Severability Clause

Simply stated, a severability clause says that if one clause is invalid the whole contract isn't trash. In some states, and with some judges, without this clause the good parts of the contract are thrown out with the bad.

Entire Agreement Clause

Common sense should tell you that the entire agreement is what's written in the contract, but this clause states that clearly. I am shocked at the number of times over the years someone has proposed that we have a contract, but we don't need to put "that" part in writing. Translation: "that" will never happen. If they aren't willing to put it in writing it won't happen.

State of Venue

The state-of-venue clause says in what state the courts will hear any dispute over this contract. This seems like a small point until you have to buy airline tickets, pay out-of-state lawyers, and then find out the judge plays golf with the guy you are suing. This can be a very expensive mistake. Generally you want the state of venue to be your state unless another state has a particular law on the books in your favor.

I was negotiating a deal for a series pilot with CBS using a rather expensive attorney out of Washington, DC. When the state of venue came up for discussion I said we want it to be my home state of Tennessee, and my attorney quickly corrected me, saying, "No, we want California." He explained to me that because so much of the TV and movie industry is in California, the laws there are the most thorough and in favor of the talent. Since I was contracting to be the "talent" I easily grasped that idea and let CBS choose California as the state of venue. There was never a dispute with them—on the contrary, we had a great relationship—but I still learned something in the contract negotiation.

In Perpetuity

Don't try to do a contract with no end, in perpetuity. In most states most contracts are not valid without an end date.

Don't Sign Personally

If your company is an LLC or is incorporated, then be careful to never sign personally. Always sign as the office you hold on behalf of the company. If one of my team puts a document of importance on my desk to sign as Dave Ramsey it is returned and retyped for me to sign as Dave Ramsey, president of our company. I only sign as an officer of our company to avoid personal liability.

If you aren't careful to do business only as a corporation or an LLC then you can *personally* be held liable for a big mess. Being held personally liable for your company is known as "piercing the corporate veil." So if you just put your name with no title referencing that you are signing on behalf of a company, that vendor can sue you personally as well as your company. So that defeats one of the big reasons for forming a corporation or LLC in the first place.

Personally signing can apply to debt as well. In most every case small-business people will have to sign personally to borrow; that is not what I am talking about here. Remember, though, that

I recommend not taking on debt, so that eliminates any debt liability anyway.

Collections

Collecting money owed to your business can be frustrating and maddening. The main rule of thumb we use for collections is, if you have a collections problem you really have some other problem, like you are selling wrong. Somewhere in the establishment of the relationship the customer got confused about when and how they had to pay. The time to solve a collections problem is long before you have one, as you are selling the customer.

The time to solve a collections problem is long before you have one, as you are selling the customer.

I told you in chapter 9 that the best receivable is one you don't have. If you choose a business model that has you billing your customers you will face collections problems to the extent that your sale isn't made properly. A proper sale is one that is made to a qualified prospect. And while the sense of serving the customer is important, you should not be begging them to be a customer, so don't set up the spirit of the deal so that your customer becomes your boss.

I think my real estate background prepared me to avoid collections problems. Think of your customers as tenants in a rental. You want to market to them to get a tenant, you want them to want the house, but when they move into your property you want them to respect you enough to take care of the house and pay on time.

Serve your customers without becoming subservient. Salespeople who beg instead of serve end up begging for the customer's money because the customer cops an attitude, thinking they have the upper hand. The sale made properly involves qualifying the customer financially and setting the terms and tone of the relationship after the sale. We don't have belligerent or nonpaying customers for long because we fire them as a customer.

When you find a problem area or a category of customer that has constant problems paying, then either change the terms of the deal with them or don't do business with that type. You are better off not making a sale than having people take your goods or services and not pay.

When I first got into real estate I had a lot of lower-income weekly rentals. I found out very quickly that I couldn't give an inch when qualifying or collecting because I would not only lose that rental income, but word would get out that I could be "had." Consequently I had a "renter talk" before they moved in where I was basically insulting to the renter about paying on time and not conducting any criminal activity in the house. If I could make them mad before they moved in, I learned that they were going to be trouble later, but if they planned to pay and didn't plan on criminal activity, then they weren't insulted at all. I started the relationship with fair and firm terms of operation, then if trouble came I had the relational room to give grace to someone who communicated about hard times without appearing weak.

I am not suggesting that you insult your customer, but the spirit of how a relationship is to be conducted is at the core of collections problems. Collections problems are not the problem, they are the symptom.

Procedure

When a client is one day late they get a courtesy call and a kind reminder of the promise of payment they made. After the late payment is made a salesman makes a follow-up call to reset the customer's mind on how payment will work in the future and kindly make sure there is no misunderstanding or lack of service on our part.

If the payment doesn't come in we follow up with another phone call and begin sending notices. In most businesses the accounts that run over ninety days (unless those are the terms) have a very low probability of collection. Accounts at sixty days or later should have delivery or service stopped or be put on a COD (cash on delivery) basis. When you stop doing business with the account you limit your losses, but they will consider you a low priority because they will keep active accounts happy first.

When we have a customer go bad we stop and ask ourselves what we did wrong to get ourselves into this predicament. A small level of loss is acceptable and normal, but even that can creep up on you. In the 1990s when the dot-com boom was happening we had about three dot-coms advertising on our show that went bad. They were large accounts for us and together amounted to over $100,000—which was a big ouch. So we changed our advertising policy. If their company name or primary business model is Internet-based, now they have to prepay to advertise—no billing.

When Receivables Go Bad

When a receivable goes bad you need a process you automatically go through. From experience I will tell you, when you are a small business, the first time or two this happens it is an emotional experience. You will get angry, as if you have been stolen from.

Since you know this emotion and this problem is coming you need to have a collections plan. First go through the gentle steps we outlined above to try to collect. Second, be sure you analyze what mistakes your company made to put you in this place. Third, decide how to handle a completely bad debt.

When a debt goes bad you have only two choices. You can forgive the debt or you can file a lawsuit. You should forgive the debt in two circumstances: one, if your company has screwed up in serving the customer by providing a bad product or service, or two, if the person owing it is flat broke and owns nothing.

> **You should forgive the debt in two circumstances: one, if your company has screwed up in serving the customer by providing a bad product or service, or two, if the person owing it is flat broke and owns nothing.**

Forgiving

In a spiritual discussion there is a difference between forgiveness and reconciliation. If a criminal mugs you and steals your purse, from a spiritual perspective, it is fine to be hurt and angry. It is best to forgive that person, not for their sake, but for yours, because that hurt and anger will eat you alive. However, many people confuse forgiveness with reconciliation. While you should forgive the mugger, it does not mean you should invite them over to dinner or to babysit your kids. If a mean dog bites you, forgive it, but stay away from it; it bites.

Debt owed to you or your company should be viewed the same way. When appropriate you should forgive the debt. However, that does not mean I am suggesting you continue to do business or grant payment terms to that person or company again. There is a difference between forgiveness and reconciliation. That dog bites.

We used to have a saying about complaints and company screwups. I told our team, "If it gets to me it's free." What that means is that my team needs to solve the problem for and with the customer, wowing them so we don't have upset customers in the marketplace. If the problem gets all the way to me and I have to handle the screwups, I am going to give the customer everything in sight, free, and charge it to someone's profit-sharing or commission check. We haven't had company screwups hit my desk except in rare cases in years. Don't try to collect money from someone you didn't serve; that is adding insult to injury. Just forgive the debt and give them some more free stuff to say you are sorry.

You should also forgive a bad debt and walk away when the person or company is broke and owns nothing. It is simple: they can't pay, and you can't get blood out of a rock. You can be angry and hit the rock with a hammer over and over again, but it won't bleed. The broke person hardest to forgive is the one who isn't sorry about not paying. The arrogance of not paying me what is owed me and then not even having the honor to care makes me want to sue them or hit back in some manner. Don't waste your emotional energy or money. You will win the lawsuit and then win a judgment against nothing; suing someone doesn't make them grow money. Save your money and your stress level. Move on to the next deal using the energy you will waste hitting a rock with a hammer.

It is much easier to have mercy on and forgive the debt of the broke person who owes you but can't pay and is deeply distressed about it. One of the dot-coms I mentioned above was run by a great guy who started a website to help people with careers. The site was before its time and didn't make money. No matter how many leads my radio ads sent him, his business model was bad and he was doomed. The poor guy came into my office to meet with me and one of our EVPs owing us about $22,000. We had researched what was going on with the guy and found that his home had been foreclosed on, his wife had left him, and the computers that operated the business were repossessed. He sat at my conference table with tears in his eyes telling us the whole story. Because he was truly broke and because I have been there and because he promised to pay me someday, I reached across the table and wrote "Paid in Full" on his invoice and set him free. He was relieved, and we went on to the next deal with the energy we could have wasted beating this poor guy up. We really needed the $22,000, but that didn't matter; he didn't have it and wasn't going to have it any time soon, and he was man enough to meet in person and have honor.

As a Christian I also reserve the right to forgive a debt if I feel like God is telling me in my prayer time to forgive it. That is weird for some people to try to understand, and in truth it's sometimes hard to know if I am just feeling sorry for someone or if it is God's voice. Some days those two things are one and the same.

Sometimes a debt is owed and unpaid by a broke person, but you still feel like they should pay something, and they really want to. We sold ads to a small insurance firm that went out of business owing us $12,500. The guy demanded that he repay us. We looked at the situation and, knowing we weren't going to collect from this guy any time soon, offered to forgive the debt, but he virtually demanded to pay. He would send in $25 or $10 every month. That was a nice gesture, but mathematically that is all it was, a gesture. It was costing us more in man-hours in accounting to post the payments than we were actually receiving. I remembered a story Larry Burkett once told about letting someone work off their debt at a nonprofit or a ministry. We called this gentleman in and asked him what he did as a service in the community. He explained that when his mother was in a nursing home he observed how many residents had no visitors, so after his mother's death he continued to go to the nursing home at least once a month to read to residents. We offered him the deal of a lifetime: read to nursing home residents and keep a time sheet. We credited him $100 an hour toward his debt and he worked off the whole debt ministering to others. He felt great, nice people in a nursing home got read to, and truthfully—before you think of me as some great guy—we weren't going to see that money anyway.

Suing

The only time I think you should consider suing is when the offending customer has the money and just won't pay. Your company didn't mess up and the jerks just won't pay even though they are perfectly able. Also, the debt must be of great size. You don't want to spend thousands of dollars in attorney fees and court costs to collect $300. I will tell you that most people do not realize what a beehive a lawsuit is. Winnie the Pooh, if you get that hive buzzing you are in for a long fight even if the honey is yours.

I am not afraid of a fight and some fights are worth having. However, enter lawsuits only after you are ready to lay siege and wait years for the outcome. Enter lawsuits only if you have the financial and emotional well deep enough to stay the course until you win. As far as collection lawsuits, I have filed only two as of this writing, and even though the parties were wrong and had the assets, we spent more than was owed and ultimately collected nothing. In the first case they finally went into bankruptcy and in the second they drained the assets from the company. We attempted to pierce that corporate veil, but it didn't work. My conclusion is that lawsuits are almost never profitable. You can win a moral victory, but the cost is high.

Vendors

All businesses outsource. There are the vendors that you work with on a very small basis, basically drive-by vendors. Then there are the vendors that provide you with services or products essential to your operation. These essential vendors become quasi-partners. You develop personal relationships with them and watch them prosper from the business you give them. They often become friends, and at some point you will find that many have been doing business with you longer than much of your team has been on board.

These vendor relationships are so important I am going to spend the balance of this chapter talking about how to properly select and work with vendors. The mistakes made on these basics cost businesses millions of dollars every year. This is the mechanics of how we actually operate our business. If someone wants to be on my leadership team they have to know and practice this material. The bigger or more essential the vendor is to your operation the more important these points are.

A high-quality long-term relationship with an essential vendor can only be established and maintained if the vendor has four key elements.

Integrity

Trust is the basis for any relationship. The depth of the relationship, whether business or personal, is limited to the depth of trust. I have learned the hard way how essential it is for essential vendors to be led by men and women of integrity. You can overcome a lot of bumps in the road working through deals that have gone bad when dealing with quality people. When dealing with your main vendors watch for subtle changes and integrity breakdowns. These signs are your warning lights that the boiler has cracks and may blow at any time.

If an essential vendor or supplier misses a delivery or drops their quality at the wrong time you can be left in a position where you can't serve your customer. Your customer doesn't care about your supplier problems, they just care that they weren't served.

Integrity at the top will allow your relationship to survive the normal bumps and bruises of an imperfect world. In the first chapter I talked about leadership from the top down. I discussed how "the anointing drops from the beard" means that as goes the king, so goes the kingdom.

A few years back we had an essential vendor that was a local small business. We had done business with them for years, with only minor hiccups. However, everything subtly and slowly began to slip. Because it was a business in our area I began hearing rumors that the owner was having an affair. Then the rumors became fact as his wife found out and threw him out of the house. He continued with the girlfriend and moved in with her. It was no surprise with all this drama that their business operations got continually worse. Finally I ended up in his office to discuss our service problems. He shared with me his marital problems and how he was trying to bounce back.

It might seem a little harsh, but I figure if a guy's wife can't trust him, how can I? I explained this to him and put him on final notice that with one more mess-up we would be moving on to another supplier. No, I am not everyone's bedroom police; I certainly don't have time for that. Neither was I trying to punish him because I thought he was out of line, although I did. There is a simple rule here: a man who can't be trusted isn't worthy of trust, so I wasn't going to base my business's future on his delivering the goods. We try to compartmentalize a lot of things in our culture to make our rationalizations comfortable, but we do so at our own peril. I continued to do business with him and was criticized for doing so by friends who were apparently the bedroom police. Sadly, my theory was proven true as his once fine business deteriorated until we couldn't use them. But we were not caught off guard and were ready because we recognize how important integrity at the top, and all through an essential vendor, is. "A good name is to be chosen rather than great riches, loving favor rather than silver and gold" (Proverbs 22:1).

Capacity

You should outsource because a vendor has knowledge you don't have, can do something you can't do, or can do something cheaper than you can. When judging a vendor's capacity you are determining not just if they can do the job but if they can do it at the volume you need and on the schedule you need.

A great price will not save you money if you have nothing to sell because your vendor didn't get your product produced or delivered on time. You can save five cents a minute on your long-distance charges but that does you no good if the phones are down all the time because your vendor is lame. Capacity may be one of the most important considerations when choosing or keeping a vendor.

As your business grows you should know that you will likely outgrow your vendor's capacity, and it is wise to monitor this so it doesn't catch you off guard. When I first self-published the original *Financial Peace* books I had them printed by a local printer who was a friend of mine. He ran the pages from film made from laser-printed originals done in my living room. The cover was done by that same printer and he sent the finished pages with the covers to a local bindery, and voilà, we had a book. My first order was a thousand copies, my second order was four thousand copies, and then I ordered seven thousand copies. When I got ready to place my next order of seven thousand he called me to talk. It seemed my little book was getting big enough that it was overwhelming his capacity. He couldn't get his other clients' printing done because all he was doing was running my books. He suggested, rightly so, that I talk to some printing brokers, and since my volume was up I could cut my hard cost in half. I was so new at managing this kind of thing that I never saw that coming. Thank goodness he did. We are friends to this day and I'm glad our printing career started with him.

http://www.entreleadership.com/capacity

We had pushed the vendor beyond their capacity. Another rule of capacity is to learn your vendors' lead times for production and plan your inventory and orders to fit their schedule. If you are a good customer or a big customer they can, and often will, change their production schedule and normal timeline to super-serve you. But if you do that on a regular basis eventually they will let you down. Learn their normal lead time and set your systems up to match, or change vendors, but don't expect miracles on a regular basis, which is why they are called miracles—they don't happen much.

Price

Price should not be the primary reason to select a vendor. But all things being equal price can be the determining factor. You definitely want to negotiate and get the best deal when working with a vendor, but be aware that your essential vendor will go out of business selling to you at a loss. You want them to make money so you can grow together. Companies who bleed their vendors dry with no consideration of tomorrow usually don't have a long and wonderful life themselves.

Understand we negotiate hard and are very good at getting the best price. But we are also aware that if they are losing twenty cents a watermelon they can't make it up on volume. If you win too big your victory will be short-lived and you will be looking for another essential vendor.

Price Ethics

When taking competitive bids and sharing information you should use the Golden Rule. Treat your vendor how you would want to be treated if you were bidding competitively. Would you want someone to show your competitor all your numbers and specs so your competitor could beat you this time and with other customers as well? I wouldn't, so I don't do that. We pull bids, and if there are two that are close, we tell them that they are one of the last two, so they should sharpen their pencils. At that point, without divulging who the other players are, we will tell them they have to hit a certain price to stay in the running. If I were bidding I would love knowing the range I had to be in to have a shot at winning the business.

When negotiating, use the power of cash. In most cases you are not literally going to pay your bill with cash on delivery, but if you simply clear your payables weekly or biweekly like I taught you in the accounting chapter it is as if you are paying cash. Paying very quickly is so unusual that we expect a further discount for doing that.

If your vendor begins to tell people in brochures or conversations that they do business with you, then they are getting an implied endorsement. In my world people pay for endorsements, so if they are going to mention to other potential customers that they do business with us, that is fine, but I will expect a discount for that service as well. That is a free endorsement, and so there should be some help in pricing.

When negotiating, share your vision for the future with your vendor. Remind them that if you make more money you will be growing your business and as a result they will get more business. Sometimes you can actually work out ways to have them partner with you by providing you some small services for free that will expand both your futures. Never allow your negotiating to be as simple as price per unit; there are always multiple variables.

Quality

Have a reputation in the market for being firm but fair with vendors. Sadly in our culture some companies have become specialists at getting their customers to accept low- or poor-quality goods or services. When dealing with a vendor an unacceptable answer to a quality problem is just that: unacceptable. Don't be mean or tough or a bully, but don't become a vendor pleaser either. As hard as we work at business we still find ourselves pressured to be a nice guy and accept substandard products or services. You can be kind and yet never be willing to accept a wrong answer.

I was having a conversation with a customer who wanted out of a contract early, which would damage our position in the marketplace by hundreds of thousands of dollars. The customer was emotional and declared that I was just unbelievably unreasonable, to which I calmly replied that I could live with being unbelievably unreasonable by holding them to an agreement that had no need to be broken, except for ego on their part. A long discussion ended with my being "unbelievably unreasonable." An unacceptable answer is just that: unacceptable.

We order tens of millions of dollars' of printing every year for our various departments from many different vendors. Printing is not hard to judge. It is either right or it is isn't. There is a color chart and specs to it, so it either is or isn't what was ordered, and yet we spend a lot of time in conversations with new vendors telling them we don't accept substandard work. We help when we can, but if we put out junk it makes us look bad, so we don't do it.

My radio show shares a glass wall with our front lobby so I can observe what is happening in our lobby while I am behind soundproof glass. Recently I watched the body language and hand motions of a conversation that was so clear it reminded me of a silent movie. An EntreLeader who has been with me for years had ordered a small run of a new printed product to test-market it. The color charting and specs on the product were very clear. The new vendor brought the small volume of product in and met my EntreLeader. I watched as my EntreLeader's head cocked to one side while inspecting the product. He pulled out the color chart, prototype, and specs and began shaking his head. The vendor tensed up, stood up straighter, and began flapping his arms, gesturing more and more wildly. My EntreLeader smiled, nodded, listened, and then shook his head no again. The vendor became more agitated and the scene repeated. The scene finally ended with a red-faced vendor leaving with his substandard product. It was very interesting to watch all this happen, not hearing a single word and yet knowing exactly what had transpired. My team has learned these lessons well.

Conclusion

This chapter is very hands-on and mechanical. The EntreLeader understands that running a business successfully is very hands-on and mechanical. Sometimes the handling of areas of the business like contracts, vendors, and collections can make or break your success. Maybe these areas are not deal killers in your organization, but how you handle these operational functions reveals clearly who you are as a leader. Be intentional about the statement you are making to your team, your competitors, your customers, and the community through your actions in these areas. Entre-Leaders are always considering the unintended consequences of how day-to-day activities are handled.

14

Show Me the Money!

Compensation Plans That Fire People Up

C lose your eyes and picture your best, most loyal, and favorite team member's face. Now picture their spouse's face, their children's faces, and even the face of their dog. In your mind walk in their shoes as they come to work with you each day, as they are passionate about helping you win. If that person has been with you for a decade and is an integral part of your success, they are virtually a partner of yours. Are they compensated like a valued partner or like a unit of production that can be tossed to the curb like last week's garbage? If you have team members like I am describing and you make a net profit of $10 million this year, would you be okay with paying them $1 million?

Your team with varying degrees of tenure and varying degrees of maturity and varying degrees of talent and varying degrees of contribution are all having a Jerry Maguire moment every payday. They are shouting inside their spirits, "Show me the money!" Some of them have an unrealistic view of what contribution they have brought to the table and some of them deserve for you to be more generous. Treat your team like you would want to be treated if you were in their shoes. Pay them.

Jesus said, "Your treasure is where your heart is." What you spend money on says what is important to you. A company's compensation system is a clear reflection of its corporate values and culture. No leader wants a building filled with mindless clock-punchers. Instead, EntreLeaders take pay structures seriously, identifying ways to encourage overall productivity and incentivize excellent performance. From profit sharing to commissions, bonuses to benefits, creativity is key when considering compensation.

Again, what an organization spends money on is what they value. I once was visiting a church board meeting, as a guest, to give advice about their budget. This particular church was a wonderful place, with very warm, loving people. However, they were facing some difficult budget decisions, and it was a multimillion-dollar budget. To impress himself, or the others around him, one of the leaders gave a five-minute speech about how important the youth and children of the church were and how this church really valued the children. I am not very good at being in those settings—I don't like serving on boards or even advising them—so I was being unusually quiet. After his little speech I decided maybe a dose of reality was in order, so I spoke up. I addressed the pastor and the leaders, telling them all the things they were doing right, then said, "However, you do not really think the children are important." As you might guess that was not a popular thing to say. I pointed out to them that the children's and youth directors were the lowest-paid team members and that less than 1.5 percent of their multimillion-dollar budget was allocated to people under eighteen years old. They could say they love and value children all day long, but when they don't put their money where their mouth is, they simply aren't telling the truth.

If you value your team, they will know it in a lot of ways, and one of the ways is that they'll be paid and paid well. Paying them well does not mean overpaying based on contribution. Your team can tell what the money looks like and how it is flowing around them; they are not fooled. This chapter is about creatively compensating your deserving team. I have had plenty of team members over the years who thought they were more deserving than they were—that is a matter for the hiring and firing chapter—but the great ones should be rewarded with money.

I have an acquaintance whose company, at its high point, had gross sales over $50 million a year. This owner's personal income was several million dollars a year. The owner had started in his garage ten years before and his key leaders had been with him from the start—and were a lot of the reason for his success. He had about 120 employees and not a single employee, including leaders who had been there from the start, made over $100,000. That may sound smart to some of you, but it is raw greed. Have you already figured out the end of the story? You guessed it: the unappreciated, talented leaders (virtual partners) got really tired of hearing how important they were and not seeing it in their checks. The company began to unravel as the talent left the building.

You can follow everything I've said about team-building and still fail at it if you don't say thank you in the paycheck. Recognition, unity, loyalty, and communication all start to have muted effects and even appear hypocritical if they aren't combined with generous pay.

I love incentives that allow people to share in the win. If you work on my team and get up, leave the cave, kill something, and drag it in, I will share it with you. I would put the receptionist on straight commission if I could figure out a way. I want everyone to have a self-employed mentality, a sense of ownership, so they fight for the win. I am very happy to have commissioned people getting rich, and I am just as comfortable if they starve out due to their lack of work or effectiveness. Given my love for sharing with the team members who cause us to win, we have a complicated compensation program—probably too complicated, but it conveys the message that winning is rewarded and losing isn't.

Be Intentional

Be intentional about what you value. Compensation plans are like recognition: be careful to reward the activities you want duplicated. The team's activity will gravitate quickly toward how they get paid, so make sure to pay only for the things you want done.

There are many ways to pay people. Take a look at a few of them and see how you can use these different methods to pay your team.

Salary

There are very few examples of salary-only positions that motivate and inspire people to win. Eventually, even the most content person will get tired of seeing people all around them prospering while they work just as hard. There are many positions in a company where a salary is the only logical way to pay people, but you have to work hard at creatively adding to that package. We don't have a single person on our team who is on salary only. Everyone participates in some way with the winnings.

Profit Sharing

Sharing your profits is a great way to say thank you or "we appreciate you." However, this is very dangerous if done poorly. If done poorly the employee can start to take the profit sharing for granted or start to see that money as a "right," or worse yet, not even "count" that money (see below). We have had all these things happen so we have worked really hard to defeat these problems.

When we first started sharing our profits we thought everyone would be thrilled. Cash was tight, so we set aside some of the profits for the team, quarterly, and called it "the quarterly bonus." There were several problems with this method that we missed. Many years ago we started uncovering how ineffective this bonus system was when one of my VPs' awesome assistant turned in her two weeks' notice. She was a great assistant so my VP asked her why she was leaving. She replied that another company was paying her more. Really? Her new employer was paying her a $38,000 salary. We were paying her $35,000 and her quarterly bonus was $7,000 the year before, for a total of $42,000. She took a pay cut! When asked why she didn't take into consideration the $7,000, her response was that she couldn't "count" that money since it wasn't guaranteed. *What?* If you aren't going to "count" it, I will keep it, and I'll "count" it!

Once I got up off the floor I found a few similar instances around the company and realized we were wasting hundreds of thousands of dollars. Our plan had always been to pay slightly less than market for the salary, but by sharing in the profits the team would be some of the best-paid in our area. But they emotionally weren't "counting" it! This is what is known as a failed program.

New Animals

I formed a brainstorming group of some of our support people, assistants, IT people, and any other salaried position. About fifteen of us spent days in my conference room discussing this issue. I listened and listened and finally began to understand that we had people in that room who were wired completely different than me. To oversimplify it, we had two types of animals in our company. Those like me were straight-commission, entrepreneurial types. The type who loves to walk the wire with no net. We are so confident in our ability that we are willing to take the chance of having no income in order to have the shot at a great income. Whatever you do, don't put a lid on this type of animal. We call this type of animal a tiger. They roar and run through the jungle taking what they want; they will not be denied.

In those meetings I started to realize, for the first time, that our company was not all tigers. I was making assumptions and designing comp plans as if everyone was a tiger. I loved and appreciated our team members in administrative or support roles and thought we had hired tigers into those positions because they were all excellent team members. I was wrong; they weren't tigers at all and they were, frankly, a little disgusted at being treated like tigers.

One lady did a great job getting me to this revelation. She said, "As an assistant I kind of feel like a snooty waiter at a super-expensive restaurant. I will serve you, but I really feel like I am better than you. I get great dignity and the thrill of accomplishment from helping you perform at a level you would never reach if I wasn't here. I don't need to leave the cave to kill something; making the company and you better in spite of yourself is my win." As I started understanding this different kind of animal I felt even more respect for them. We named them koala bears because they may look cute and cuddly but they have the ability to kill when you least expect it.

My goal for meeting with this group was to learn how to share money with them and for them to "count" it. I don't want to pay out money and have someone not emotionally "count" that money. In those discussions I learned that recognition is huge with koala bears and that payment monthly would help them "count" it more than quarterly. I also learned that with everyone we have to talk about the DNA of our profit sharing so it doesn't become *entitlement*. The purpose of sharing profits is to get everyone feeling like a self-employed entrepreneurial partner.

So we dramatically changed our profit sharing. First, we kicked out all the high-earning, commission team members and leaders who were already getting great incomes from other comp methods tied to production. The smaller pool made more money available to the administrative and noncommission positions. We took some of the profit sharing away and applied it through the whole company, raising koala bear salaries to slightly above market. Then we transformed the "Quarterly Bonus" into a monthly "Profit Sharing" plan. The team does not know the percentage of profit we allocate because we may raise or lower the percentage year to year in order to accomplish our motivational goals.

We developed and went through, in great detail, a formula, figuring out how to allocate the money to everyone. We are all execution- and performance-driven people, so we thought "time on the job" or "seniority" sounded corporate. But as we talked through the formula and ran several trial runs, we discovered something about ourselves. We discovered that if someone is a lousy employee they don't get to stay, so we don't have people who have been with us for years unless they are excellent. We also figured out that our culture honors the pioneers in our company, so the longer they have been with us the more we feel we owe them, since they have helped us get where we are. Consequently, and to our surprise, the formula that we came up with gives years on the job 50 percent of the weight in determining the team member's profit sharing. Thirty-three percent of the weight goes to a personal score given for effort and attitude, and the other 17 percent is based on the profitability of the department the person works in. You will need to determine what you want to reward and what weight you give it, but I will tell you to invest the time to get it right, otherwise you might as well keep your money.

The last thing we changed is how we give the profit sharing money. Each month in staff meeting, before the checks come out, I stand before my staff and go through a very silly and elementary reminder. First I remind them that profit sharing means I am "sharing" some of my . . ."profits" (I wait and make them finish the sentence in unison). I do this because I want to break off any sense of entitlement to this money; it does not need to become automatic. Then we continue the routine where I remind them that profits happen when revenues go "up" (said in unison) and expenses go "down" (ditto). Then I announce that our profits were up or down over last month and up or down over the same month last year, explaining further that their checks will be up or down over last month and up or down over the same time last year. We do this to remind everyone that ultimately we are all self-employed, so anyone who keeps expenses down is to be celebrated as much as anyone who brings revenue up, because it affects everyone's check, including mine.

This sounds like a lot of trouble and a little juvenile, but we no longer have confusion about where profit comes from and what role everyone plays in making money together. We pay out millions of dollars in profit sharing every year, and I am thrilled to share it with my team that has caused us to win. I am thrilled to share because they "count" it, they are grateful, and the formula rewards the things we value. That is bang for your buck. I would love it if we had a secretary somewhere in our company who was getting two or three times what other companies pay that position because our profit sharing rewards the number of years of excellence they have brought to us. And keep in mind that when profits are down it really stings and gets everyone's attention, as it should.

Commission

Commission is easy because it is all about incentive. There are several types of commission programs.

Straight Commission

Straight commission is simple: you make a sale and collect the money, then you get your percentage. This means no sale, no money. Being from a real estate background this is how my mind works. However, I have learned that often quality people need a little more support when they start with me to get their pipeline full and start making money.

Salary Plus

One way to deal with the issue of start-up time is to have a small salary plus commission, at a lower commission rate. The small salary can cover basic eating money so the rep can eat as they get started or if they have a down month. Keep the salary just over starvation level; the last thing you want is a rep who isn't money motivated.

Draw Plus

A draw plus commission is my personal favorite. The draw is like a salary that gives the rep a base to get started or cover a down month. The commission is at a good high rate but isn't paid until the draw is repaid each month. So if there is a $2,000 monthly draw, until there is $2,000 in commissions earned, there will be no extra pay that month.

If you are letting the unpaid draw balance roll over month to month be careful not to let the draw balance grow too large. If it grows large you may need to release a rep, or if they've been selling a new, unproven product line, you might need to wipe the balance clean and start them over. A draw that the rep can't see themselves earning through becomes demotivating.

We launched a new product and the rep's draw balance reached almost $30,000. The rep started feeling like she was in debt. The large draw balance was not only mathematically demotivating, it also seemed to say to her every morning that she was a failure. If it was a proven product line with ten other reps winning we would not have let the balance get that high; we would have cut her loose earlier. But we had a great rep and we were working the kinks out of this new offering. So we decided to wipe the slate clean and let her make some money. The relief on her face was awesome and she has gone on to make all of us a lot of money, proof that she's a good one.

Some companies make a rep sign a note for the draw balance, which truly is debt. I am not a believer in that method. I think I should be willing to invest in the rep and the product line as the owner of the company.

Some of our departments let the draw drop off and go to straight commission after enough time has passed and the rep has accounts to eat from. The length of time you allow the draw to run should be in line with the type of product or service you are selling. A rep for a lower-price-point product can usually fill their pipeline in ninety days; we call those rabbit hunters. The rep for elephants—products at higher price points—or products that are ordered less often may need a draw for 180 days. You should be sensitive to find the balance between starvation and incentive. It will require some trial and error but the thing to remember is that broke salespeople smell bad. They tend to pressure customers and take your brand places you don't want to go.

For "on commission" reps you should never put a cap on what they can make. Many companies are so shallow that they will cap reps so they don't out-earn an executive salary. That is short-sighted and stupid. Don't shoot the producer in the wallet and expect them to stay.

Profit and Loss Bonus

The profit and loss bonus plan is the scariest and most ingenious compensation plan we use. This plan is for EntreLeaders who run a major department or division for us. We set up each major area with its own P & L. The VP or EVP of that area is running their own company within our company. They receive a lousy salary and a percentage of the net profits paid the fifteenth of the month following the month being calculated. So they will get their percentage of net check for March on April 15th. Every single person on this plan is making more money than they have ever made in their lives.

This plan is scary because you really have to be emotionally prepared for one of them to grow their business to the point they are paid millions of dollars. Wow. The best part of that happening, of course, is that for them to be paid millions you would have to be paid millions and millions and millions. Still, this tests your philosophy on sharing with your producers.

This plan is ingenious because the comp method causes them to run and view their department as their own business. They fight to manage cash flow, keep revenues up and expenses down, keep good people, fire bad people, and have a vision for the future. If you put the right people in this seat on your bus, and you don't get greedy, you will have fabulous results; I have. These team members are not stockholders in the company. They have no stock options, but they have the potential to make fabulous incomes as if they were partners.

Vesting

The last type of comp plan that we invented is for key leaders who don't run a P & L department. I want my CFO, my COO, and some of the key leaders to participate in the ups and downs of our revenues, and for that matter to have a large portion of their great incomes be based on business performance metrics. Always, in an effort to share and to incentivize, we have developed guidelines to vest certain key team leaders. This vesting gives them their salary *plus* an undisclosed percentage of gross revenues for the whole company or just from their division. We are very clear with them that this obligation is limited to profitability and subject to change as we need to make the numbers work. However, we almost never change it, because again it is intended to pump people up about participating in the wins and losses, so if I mess with it all the time they lose the feeling that they have some say over the destiny of their income.

Changing Compensation

Raises are easy and fun to give. Always give raises with a praise sandwich. Praise the person and their actions, give the raise, and then praise the person. Always involve all leaders around the person so they know the raise is unanimous; this avoids some leader saying they fought someone else for the employee. Present a unified front. The immediate supervisor should do all the talking, with the other "big" leaders being quiet. The immediate supervisor is doing the day-to-day leading, so give them the influence gained by letting them give the raise; in a sense they are taking the credit. The other couple of leaders are there just to present a unified front.

Never cut pay unless there is poor performance or you had an experimental comp plan that you reserved the right to adjust. We almost never cut pay due to poor performance; we either get the performance up or let them go. I am not trying to get a great deal on a mediocre player; I would rather pay top dollar for a superstar.

When you are designing a new comp plan or a comp plan for a new, unproven area, always reserve the right to adjust the plan after a period of time. If you don't reserve that right, and you get squeezed by the margins, you can end up losing money to keep your word.

When we first started I hired a guy to get us on the radio in more cities. We agreed I would pay him $5,000 for stations in the top one hundred cities. I don't make money immediately when a station carries our show. Over time, from ad sales and things like book sales, we make money, but it takes a while. My new rep went out and got four cities in a couple of months. I owed him $20,000 and had no money coming in. This was a disastrous comp plan. I was not smart enough to reserve the right to change the plan if it didn't work, but thank goodness he caught on quick that he was in a no-win situation. We sat down and reworked his plan so we could both profit. But that taught me a lesson to always give myself room to reset the plan if it turns out to be a bad one.

Benefits

Most small businesses don't have the cash to provide much in the way of benefits like the big companies do. I used to feel like I was at a competitive disadvantage when trying to hire people. You really don't have a disadvantage. The type of employee who takes a job for the insurance and the 401(k) match as their primary motivation isn't the type I want on my team. I want people with a self-employed EntreLeader mentality. I want people who value the family atmosphere and fabulous culture that we have built— which very few companies have. So the huge companies with big benefits packages aren't really competing with me for talent because I offer a completely different world. They might not want the type of person I want, and the type of person I want won't work for them.

The first benefits we offered were free products of ours. Later we were able to barter with different advertisers and we would share free meals at a restaurant with our team members. We just didn't have the money to offer traditional benefits.

Health Insurance

We finally got enough team members that the premiums for our little group insurance plan were less than an individual policy, so we put a health insurance plan in place. But the team members had to pay 100 percent of their insurance. Then we agreed to pay

$25 a month toward their insurance one year, then $50, then $75. And every year or two as we grew, and grew more profitable, we paid a little more, until we were paying hundreds per month. We made the decision to never pay 100 percent of health insurance. The premiums with a small company go up dramatically every year, and we want our team to always have that self-employed feel, that dose of reality. If you pay 100 percent, that is nice, but your cost can double in a single year and your team won't care. One year we increased what we pay by $50 a month, but the premiums went up by $75 per month. So we announced the $75 increase and let that sting for a few minutes before we announced that we were increasing our benefit by $50. That created gratitude rather than entitlement. I know health care is a touchy subject and you can do whatever you want with your company; this is what I do with mine.

Disability Insurance

Look into disability insurance. It is the only insurance we pay 100 percent of. We do this because most people go underinsured in this category and frankly because it doesn't cost much. Group rates on disability insurance are still very good.

Cool and Creative

Do weird things for your team that promote things you value. About a third of our team runs the local Country Music Marathon or half marathon every year. We refund their registration fee if they wear a company marathon T-shirt and finish the race. We can usually get the T-shirts donated, with some sponsor logos, which make them look cool and make them free.

We pay for warehouse club membership cards and gym memberships. We got a great deal with an online legal website, so we furnish a free will for every team member. We did the same thing with ID theft protection, so we furnish it free. We rent out the local movie theater for private showings just for our team and their families every so often.

We started organizing the occasional company-wide potluck lunch during the workweek. The relationship-building created such synergies that we started catering a free lunch once a month. As of this writing we furnish lunch once a week. Every month we announce birthdays in staff meeting and have cake and ice cream afterward. We buy season tickets to our local NFL and NHL teams and give them away in a drawing every week.

We do a lot of really cool stuff, but when we started we didn't do anything; we didn't have the money. We had to get creative to say thanks, and as profits increased we allocated a percentage to human resources programs that we constantly try to dream up.

Ministry Week

A huge home-run benefit was the decision to give team members an extra week of time off if they used it working for a certified nonprofit. So we have people working in orphanages in Haiti, programming websites for homeless shelters or domestic violence shelters, translating for missionaries, building Habitat for Humanity homes, and any other possible ministry you can think of locally or around the world. They qualify for this extra week after they have been with us a year and after submitting the activity for approval. We had to define it because some people wanted to count ministering to their bulldog while sitting on the couch.

Retirement Accounts

Again, when we started we offered no retirement plan. As we grew we started a SIMPLE 401(k), which costs almost nothing for administrative expense, but we are required to match the first 3 percent the team member contributes. As we got larger we put in the traditional 401(k) with Roth options and started matching 4 percent once team members have been with us a year.

Education

John Maxwell says, "You will either invest in your team to learn, and they might leave with your free education, or you don't invest in them to learn and they will remain dumb and stay." When the web was in its early, primitive years Thomas, an assistant, came to me and asked if he could build one of these new things called a website. He promised to do it in the evenings and not take up valuable work time because he knew we had no idea what he was talking about. He built our first little site, put it up, and it actually made some money. Who would have thought? He began spending more and more time on it and finally he showed up in my office and told me we should invest in his taking a class. He wanted me to pay $4,500 for a class, plus airfare and hotel, for him to go to Oklahoma City to a weeklong ColdFusion class. I didn't know what ColdFusion was—still don't—and we thought $4,500 was a huge sum of money, but the World Wide Web was starting to look like it might be a big deal. So we sprung for Thomas to become a ColdFusion expert.

Three weeks after he got home he had revamped everything. He was an on-fire programmer. Then one day I looked up and he was standing in front of my desk with this weird look on his face. "Dave, I have a huge problem," he said. It seems a dot-com company had just offered our little ColdFusion expert $90,000 a year and we were paying him less than $30,000. He was a good man, so he felt conflicted about leaving mere weeks after we paid for his training. But I always take a deep breath and do for my team what I would want someone to do for me. He had two small children and I couldn't pay him that kind of money, so I smiled and helped him pack his desk, blessed him, and wished him well. Ouch.

Sometimes you pay for education and they leave with your training, but the alternative is to not pay for education and have them stay, and stay dumb. If your organization wants to place a premium on personal growth and knowledge, then put your money where your mouth is.

Our first education program paid for a team member to take classes if the class had something to do with their job. Now we have expanded to say we value education and growing people so much we will pay up to a certain amount every year for any classes they pass. The weird thing is people with stimulated minds make better, more creative, and more passionate team members.

We have spent tens of thousands of dollars sending team members through the Dale Carnegie classes. They are great classes for people skills, confidence, and of course public speaking. This has been a great investment and we continue to do it.

We have also expanded our education program to give a couple of scholarships to graduating high school seniors who are our team members' children. My goal is to someday be profitable enough to pay for every team member's kids' college to a certain level. Do you think that would attract some talent? Wow.

Social Gatherings

In addition to renting a movie theater and serving lunch weekly, we try to do other social gatherings. I remember the first time we were big enough and had enough money to buy out a place for the night. We all went to a spaghetti joint and then next door to play laser tag. These were private functions just for us, so we thought we were a big deal.

One time we rented an ice rink for the night for the team and their families, with open skate on one sheet of ice and pickup hockey on the other sheet, and hot dogs and pizza catered in. We have big summer picnics at the water park or at a private camp with tons of fun stuff for the little kids. One year at the summer picnic we gave away five cars. We brought the owners of the fifteen worst cars (which at our place is a badge of honor) up onstage and played Deal or No Deal for two envelopes. One envelope had $1,000 or $2,000 in it, and the other had the name of a car.

Our Christmas parties are the stuff of legend. When other companies are scaling back because times are tough, we've ratcheted up the Christmas party a few more notches. We give generous Christmas bonuses, gift cards to restaurants, movie tickets, and then try to create some kind of wow experience. One year just as everyone thought the five-star dining experience and fellowship was enough, the back doors opened and VPs came walking through pushing two-wheelers with flat-screen TVs, laptops, iPod Touches, Xboxes, Wiis, and GPS devices, a total electronics extravaganza. The best image of the night was all of our team members waiting for the valets on the curb with rows of TVs and other electronics waiting to be put into trunks. Everyone who sees or hears about stuff like this knows we are a different kind of company. When you love on your team it is not hard to attract talent.

Keep in mind, though, our first Christmas party was at my house and was a potluck. We gave away country hams we had traded radio ads for. Our first summer picnic was at a campground at the lake and I pulled people skiing behind a boat. Start where you are, but be aiming higher all the time.

HR Fund

We allocate a percentage of profits to reinvest into the team. This fund pays for education, 401(k)s, benefits, and things like marriage counseling that I mentioned earlier. We use this fund to send flowers to funerals or buy airline tickets for family emergencies. We use this fund to do all the things I have just discussed in this chapter and much more. We have an HR fund and a profit sharing fund to invest in and love on our team that are both calculated as a percentage of profits. This is how you put your treasure where your heart is.

Conclusion

Develop a generous spirit toward your team in general. Not a spirit that tolerates or overpays underperforming people, but be generous to the people who cause you to win. Realize your team is your secret weapon. Bad companies become so worried about Q1 profit that they squeeze their secret weapon and kill the culture that brings profit. When in doubt, be generous. You will live with fewer regrets and you will profit more by attracting and keeping extremely talented and passionate people.

15

Mastering "the Rope"

Delegation: The Best Way to Build a
Business Bigger Than You

When my oldest daughter was about to be our first child to leave home and head to college, it was a time of reflection and an emotional time. The first time as parents we were going to set one free. The mom and dad eagle were pushing one out of the nest and looking on with sadness and pride as she spread her wings and flew with more majesty than we realized she had.

As our children were growing up and starting to make those first teen decisions on their own, we talked to them a lot about trust. Humpty Dumpty is hard to put back together, and so is trust. As young Ramseys they were told clearly not to bust the trust—if you say you are going somewhere, that better be where you are. If you say you are doing something, that better be what you are doing. As Dad I am all-knowing and wise, and you will be discovered if you lie. At least we convinced them of that idea as if it were fact.

We explained to the kids that the more they kept their word and the more we observed them making great decisions, the more freedom they would have. Visualize that I have a rope attached to you, and the more worthy of trust you have proven yourself the more I will lengthen the rope. If you lie or exhibit bad peer-based decision making, the rope will be shortened. Every teen yearns more than anything on the planet "to be treated like an adult." So if you want more rope, more freedom, then act more and more like an adult. So if someone comes in later than promised, the rope is shortened, and the next time there is an event the answer might be no. Parents who let teens run around with unearned adult freedoms are naive and stupid. They grow children with no boundaries who generally end up with serious problems. Parents who use a very short rope or a straitjacket, preventing teens from ever developing the emotional skill of wise decision making, are controlling. They raise children who go crazy the first semester at college because they don't know how to make wise decisions.

That week we were packing the car for the first one to fly away to college, I had a great idea. I stopped by the local drapery store and bought some beautiful rope. I coiled the rope and tied it with ribbons. One purple ribbon for her spiritual walk, a red one for academics, a white one for sexual purity, a yellow one because she could feel safe that home was waiting, and an orange one because she was going to the University of Tennessee. We gathered the whole family in the rec room and presented her with her rope. I told her that we were very proud of the mature young woman of God she had grown into. I reminded her that because of her life she had earned our trust; she was trustworthy. I told her she was moving several hundred miles away and now she would be making her own decisions about every area of her life. We were sure she was capable of doing that. We told her that we were standing behind her now, not over her. This event was a rite of passage. We all cried. It was wonderful.

Two months later we visited her dorm room and there, on her bedpost, was the rope. Wow. I thought that corny deal would be in the bottom of a box. No, instead the rope had become legendary in that dorm. As the story spread, girls she hardly knew would drop by her room and ask to hear the story and see the rope. Powerful.

Teams and Teens

The art of delegating to your team is somewhat like lengthening the rope for your teens. I realize you are dealing with adults, or you should be, and so there are differences, but at its core, delegation is the lengthening of the rope.

Last, Not First

This chapter on delegation is the last chapter in this book, not the first. I have covered up until now how to properly build a company and a team. Until you have done the things I have covered so far in this book, your organization is not ready to be delegated to properly.

Beginning leaders always ask me about how they can properly delegate. As a young owner I wanted to hire people quickly and have them carry out tasks and goals that I didn't want to fool with. I wanted people to read my mind and do things I didn't like doing. Delegation may be the most misunderstood and abused subject area of leadership. When you delegate to someone improperly you will make a huge mess and add more drama to your life than you can stand. But when you properly prepare your organization's culture, hire and keep only the right people, build unity and loyalty, recognize achievement, and creatively compensate, then delegation will become the joy of your life. As a fully developed EntreLeader you will get great joy from your organization as it runs smoothly, makes a profit, and has a richness to its soul.

Talent Is Not Enough

Delegating to broken people in a broken culture simply won't work, no matter how talented they are. In chapter 11 I discussed the failure of companies in America as they attempt to hire talent when that person with talent doesn't play well with others. We have made the mistake of thinking that talent qualifies a person to be delegated to; it doesn't.

Leaders can only delegate to someone to the extent the leader is mature and the team member is mature. Emotional, relational maturing is needed in a team for a team culture to be formed. If there isn't a quality team culture you will struggle to actually accomplish real and satisfying delegation.

Work on Your Business

Michael E. Gerber wrote a wonderful book titled *The E-Myth*. The thesis of the book is that you should learn to work "on" your business rather than just "in" your business. He outlines a start-up, growing small business that makes pies. At first the owner is the pie maker, but if she stays only at that level she merely owns her job. Your goal needs to be that you grow enough personally as an EntreLeader so you can delegate. Your first experience working *on* your business instead of merely *in* your business is when you emotionally and structurally learn to delegate. The first time you look up and realize you are at that level, it feels like the first time you actually balanced and pedaled learning to ride a bike. It is exciting and you feel a new level of freedom you have never felt before.

Build the Culture and the Team

The process of building a team and a culture in which delegation can be seamless is lengthy but rewarding. Delegation with little negative result takes a tremendous investment. In our microwave culture companies hire a talented team member and have the ridiculous idea that they can add water and have an instant leader ready for delegation. For real delegation to grow you must have first prepared the field, and it still takes time and sweat to grow and harvest the crop.

If you have a great culture, have a great hiring process, and are an accomplished EntreLeader, it still takes time to teach the new talent the core values and operating principles. We hired a very high-quality leader from another company to come into our company and lead a troubled area. He is talented and very bright. However, we did not toss him the keys and walk away saying good luck. His leader and I were involved in every decision at first. The more he proved himself—not his talent, but that he understood our mission and core values—the more we lengthened the rope. He is a thoroughbred, so we had to pull the reins a few times and have teachable moments on concepts. But the more he was able to finish our sentences the more rope, freedom, he was given.

The Magic Formula

You were looking for the magic formula for how to delegate; here it is. Are you ready? In order for an EntreLeader to successfully delegate, they must come to trust the team members' *integrity* and *competency*. Wise people trust other people with big important things only to the extent they have spent time with them. The more important the delegation, the more time you will need to spend making sure the person gets it. "Important" can be relative; what is important for one company might not be important for another. When we were first starting and had no money, what we paid for copier paper was important relative to staying open. Now if someone screwed up and paid double for our paper it wouldn't close the company. Not to say we don't watch details, but I used to order the paper and now I really do not stress about who orders the paper or what we pay for it.

If you run a small-to-medium-size business and you turn over all the financial decisions and accounting duties to someone you don't have a long track record with, you are a candidate for embezzlement. Before someone works with your money, know them a long time. Their reference from the last job is not enough.

When I said earlier that the building of a team and an organizational culture in which delegation flows is a lengthy process, it's because it takes time to trust in people's integrity and competency. Other than spending large blocks of raw time to create a relationship that fosters enough trust for you to be able to delegate, you also use follow-up and reporting systems. We could hire a new payables clerk and allow them to write our checks the first week. We could do that not because we have come to completely trust them with our checkbook in a week, but instead because they are not on an island, meaning we have tons of systems and supervision.

Integrity

You can only delegate important, complicated tasks to someone to the degree you trust their integrity. That is why I will spend zero time trying to redeem a team member who steals; I just fire them instantly. Once they steal I can't trust them with anything. That is why I will instantly fire a team member who has an extramarital affair. If their spouse can't trust them, there is no way I can. Trust for the purpose of culture and delegation is essential.

I can only delegate to someone to the extent that I trust their integrity.

Integrity is more than simply telling the truth and not stealing, although those are foundational. My friend Dr. Henry Cloud has written an entire book giving us a view of what integrity is all about, entitled *Integrity*. In his book he explains that the word "integrity" comes from the root word "integer." An integer is a mathematic term from grade school; an integer is any whole number. A number that has no fraction is a whole number. A life that has no fraction to it is a whole life. Integrity, Henry explains, is truly a life lived in wholeness, completeness. If you or I act differently with some people than with other people, it is hypocritical. If we are not generally the same all the time we are fractured, split, not whole, or lacking in integrity. When people observe that your actions are inconsistent in different settings they don't trust anything about you. The preacher who is holy and sweet with the congregation and a terror at home loses all his influence with his children. They can't even spell "hypocrite" and yet they completely understand what one is. The employee who is one person at work and a completely different person in a social setting isn't functioning in wholeness and will give you trouble.

This concept of wholeness equaling integrity is another great reason we do the spousal interview I wrote about in the hiring and firing chapter. When we all relax at the table eating a nice meal, people let their guard down and reveal more of who they really are than was revealed in an interview. The more conversations and interviews you have with someone in different settings, the more you will see the real person. It is a pleasant experience to find confident people so comfortable in their own skin that no matter how much time you spend with them they are always the same.

I have a friend who owns a small company, and when he is hiring a potential leader he always has the potential hire and their spouse over to his home and asks them to bring their children to dinner. How that potential leader treats and interacts with his or her kids is a great indication of how they are going to lead. Unruly and rude kids misbehaving all over my friend's house is a great indicator that they are really not a leader. Freaked-out over-disciplined little robots with no personality in them indicate he has a control freak or a tyrant on his hands. If the kids are confident, well-behaved, and comfortable with adults, it indicates he may have found a quality leader.

Hiring for wholeness is hiring for integrity. The longer you work with someone and observe consistency in their life and their work, the more you can delegate to them. To the extent you give big tasks to unproven people, you will have drama and problems. Don't delegate too quickly.

Just because someone hits one home run doesn't mean you hand them the keys to the kingdom. The one-hit wonder often becomes the new favorite of everyone around, but that doesn't really mean they are proven in wholeness. Being competent or talented in one area of life is not necessarily an indication of wholeness. Most of us have been guilty of crediting someone with wholeness, integrity, because they are very talented in one area. When we make this mistake we are always let down.

An example of this is when someone becomes famous for a particular talent, like a professional athlete, or a music star, or an actor. We become fans of their world-class performance and mistakenly credit them with a wholeness they don't possess. It turns out just because someone can play a guitar doesn't mean she will make a great wife. It turns out just because someone can catch a football doesn't mean he won't end up bankrupt after making millions of dollars a year. It turns out that just because someone is a great big-screen actor who brings tears to your eyes, it doesn't mean they don't spend most of their life in and out of rehab. The public whines and says, "How could you do that?

You are supposed to be a role model!" The football player looks back at the cameras with a curious look and says, "Role model? I thought I played football." I am not saying people in the public eye shouldn't endeavor to behave, but I am saying that they did not earn their fame by their character and wholeness, they earned it by their particular talent, so it is our fault for crediting them with something that is not their platform.

Athletes, actors, and music artists should have their talent respected, and when they prove themselves to be men or women of character, we respect them for their character. That is only fair to them. Billy Graham is respected and known throughout the world for his character, and rightly so, as *character* is what has made him known, not playing the piano. I have had the pleasure to meet and get to know Tony Dungy, a world-class coach, formerly of the Colts. He was known and respected for his ability to coach football at a world-class level. Over the years, through his influence, he has gradually extended in the public eye as a great man and a great leader. Tony is an example of the public rightly crediting someone with qualities in addition to their talent. But you can coach at that level and not be a great man; I have met those guys too. So don't delegate the right for someone to be your role model unless they demonstrate over time the integrity, the wholeness, of their lives.

> So don't delegate the right for someone to be your role model unless they demonstrate over time the integrity, the wholeness, of their lives.

Competency

When our teens were learning to drive we had some interesting discussions with some of their friends' parents. Other parents would say things like "Aren't you just scared to death when your child is out driving on their own?" or "The first time they left the driveway and I saw those brake lights as they hit the street I was just terrified, weren't you?" No, I wasn't scared to death, nor was I terrified. If I hadn't developed trust in my teens' competency they would not have left the driveway. Until I had spent hour after hour being jerked around in the passenger seat and felt they were competent, I was not going to let them drive by themselves. So when my teen left the driveway I wasn't freaked out, because we had discussed and seen examples of what "stupid behind the wheel" looks like. And over an extended period of time my teens had a proven level of competency, or they wouldn't have been leaving.

You can't delegate to someone until you trust their competency. And there is no better way to trust their competency than to walk with them as they display their knowledge and abilities. We have brought talented, proven people on board with us several times and we don't toss them the keys the first day. For someone on your team to be competent they have to have the ability not only to do the task, but to do the task within your culture. An NFL team can recruit a world-class wide receiver whose ability to catch a football is masterful, but his competency will be limited until he learns that team's playbook and gets a rhythm with that quarterback. There will be days and days spent studying the playbook and working out with the quarterback before anything good will happen consistently.

Don't think because you hired talent that they are competent. Competency is more than just the simple ability to accomplish the task. Competency involves *how* the task was accomplished. How did all the people involved feel? Were all the problems handled right? Were all the downsides considered? Were the financial considerations of cash flow and profit accounted for and handled? If we do a live event in an arena with twelve thousand people and the attendees have a wonderful experience, it is only a part of competency for my live event coordinator. If the arena staff were all mistreated and cussed at, we will have a hard time contracting for another date there. If problems with the fire marshal were not addressed properly and the parking issues weren't taken care of, we will struggle next time we return. If we didn't make a profit because expenses weren't kept in check or we can't pay the arena bill on time because we didn't plan to have enough cash, well, then the event was not a success. Competency is about much more than whether the task is accomplished; it is also about *how* the task is accomplished.

As an EntreLeader you never expect what you don't inspect. You never throw the whole rope at a team member or even a leader. You are always holding the end of the rope, watching and measuring integrity and competency. The larger the delegation, the more your inspection methods change, but you never surrender 100 percent of the oversight. That type of surrender is leadership laziness and will cause your organization to stray from its vision. An EntreLeader who has been on my team for fifteen years and leads hundreds of people within a division that generates tens of millions of dollars will require only concept and problem inspection. The EntreLeaders like that on my team have extreme amounts of freedom that match the years of competency and integrity they've displayed. I mainly watch the accounting reports for profitability and sales, to look for signs of problems at that level. On the other hand someone who's just started with us has a much shorter rope to work with until they have proven they understand our culture. I want to raise EntreLeaders who can finish my sentences, meaning they know automatically what the next move is.

Levels of Delegation

Dr. Stephen Covey, in his book *Principle-Centered Leadership*, discusses several levels or layers of delegation. To further grasp proper delegation, let's look at just two of those, one on each end of the spectrum. Systems and processes can only do so much verification of integrity and competency. You must ensure that your team is continually taught the "why" of your organization and let the "how" flow from that.

Gofers

The most basic level of delegation is gofer-level delegation. Gofer-level delegation is typically seen in entry-level or temp positions that are assigned simple tasks that are easily verified. If you made the copy, delivered the box, or drove the nail, you are competent. People who are told to "go for this" or "go for that" are in a gofer position.

If you start your business as a one-person operation then you are either doing or outsourcing 100 percent of the tasks. Usually your first hire is a gofer position. This is a good hire because it is practical and easy to lead. You don't have to have years of quality culture built to guide the gofer, you just show them what you want done in detail and then check every bit of their work. You are learning to inspect, to delegate, to communicate, to establish key result areas (KRAs), and to begin the building of a full-on EntreLeader culture.

Management

Covey discusses many levels and layers of delegation, but at the complete other end of the spectrum from gofers is management-level delegation. At this level of delegation you are not delegating tasks; you are delegating concepts that imply tasks, maybe thousands of tasks.

A few years back we built a custom home. The builder was excellent and we became friends through the process. Once we had agreed on the budget, the plans, and the schedule, I had officially delegated to the builder the concept of building our home. That concept involved a million details, hundreds of people, and many months of production. I inspected what I expected by meeting once a week to review the schedule, review the budget, and make minor course corrections. Because I was excited I visited the job site several times a week. However, I never pulled a subcontractor aside and corrected problems. I simply made notes and e-mailed the builder that night when I got home so he could make the adjustments. Custom-home clients are the world's worst for delegating and then interfering. When the customer corrects the sub, the whole spirit on the job site changes, because they have trashed the builder's authority. I am convinced that the reason the house came in almost two months ahead of schedule and within 2 percent of budget was proper delegation and leadership. The builder continually proved his competency and integrity throughout the process. The project was inspected physically and on paper weekly to make minor course corrections before they became a major mess. The result was a great home, on budget, on schedule, and a new friendship. Transpose that result with most people who build a custom home and almost divorce their spouse and end up suing their builder. When you delegate a concept you imply thousands of details, but you lead the concept and inspect the concept. It is your team's job to watch the details.

Micromanaging

Micromanagers are leaders who never delegate well. They are, at best, bad bosses. A micromanager is the person who does not have enough self-confidence to release tasks or concepts when integrity and competency have been proven repeatedly. Micromanagers are either control freaks or they have very low emotional maturity. The micromanager is the interfering mother-in-law still instructing "helpfully" after the couple has been married ten years.

If you catch yourself micromanaging every nuance and every detail you will never grow your company into one that you work *on* instead of merely *in*. As a micromanager you will have a very difficult time attracting and keeping high-quality people because they won't put up with that trash.

The Bad Time to Micromanage

There is one good time to micromanage and two bad times. Let's start with the bad. If your micromanaging is the result of your personal lack of confidence or emotional immaturity, chapter 1 is for you. You are the limiting factor on your business and you can grow and change that.

If your micromanaging is the result of your team's inability to prove competency or integrity, then the problem is a team problem. A couple of years ago I had a young guy who stayed with me only about ninety days. His work was inconsistent, he was a drama queen, and he thought more highly of his abilities than he should. He came by my office the day he quit, to teach me about my problem. He said, "The reason I am leaving is that with my talent and my education you still couldn't stop micromanaging me. A guy like me with an MBA should be left alone to get the job done." Seems that in his MBA curriculum they didn't do a good job of helping him understand the basics of delegation. In his immaturity he felt micromanaged, when in reality he hadn't been with us long enough for us to trust him yet. We had toilet paper that had been in the building longer than him and yet he wanted me to toss the keys to the kingdom to him.

If you find yourself unable to stop micromanaging, ask yourself if your team has a problem. You may have to reorganize or bring in some more talented people who have the capacity to earn the right to be delegated to. If your team continually drops the ball you are right to micromanage until they don't drop the ball or you get some new team members.

The Good Time to Micromanage

I used to think as a young leader that I was wrong to micromanage when a quality person joined my team. As I have become very good at delegating I have realized that when someone first joins my team, until they prove their integrity and competency, it is not micromanaging at all but should be called training. You should watch every detail and push every button until you see that they can do the job. Competency can be proven very quickly on more basic things, allowing you to begin the gradual release, lengthen the rope. More complicated things will take more training and more of your involvement before you develop that trust. This training is not micromanaging, although it can feel like it. This training is an EntreLeader serving a team member. This training can be the gradual process of mentoring a diamond in the rough into a big-time EntreLeader on your team over five years.

Authority

If you want to completely destroy the EntreLeader culture of your organization there is one simple rule you can violate. The rule is, never give someone responsibility without the authority to perform. When someone first starts on the team they likely won't have a ton of authority, but neither will I hold them responsible.

If I am holding someone accountable, responsible, for the cost of a widget produced by their department, but I micromanage their vendor selection, they will become demoralized. I have to step outside my comfort zone and release the power to make the decision to someone who I am holding accountable for the results.

Titles don't make leaders, and if you give someone the title and hold them to the results you must also give them the authority to act. Responsibility without authority is an explosive shell of a position. Until the late eighties the branch manager of a local bank often had lending authority of $50,000 to $100,000. What that means is that a branch manager could loan that much money as his or her sole decision without checking with a committee or even their boss. The bank manager of those olden days was well respected in the community and often a pillar of that community. Those branch managers were typically people of wisdom, not just academic learning, and they looked at multiple variables when lending.

There are very few of those positions or people left in banking. If you find one it is most often at a community bank. The megabanks have centralized all decision making to the point the typical branch manager can't make a $3,000 decision without approval. Today's megabank branch managers have become little more than glorified tellers. They are given the responsibility for loan production but not the authority to produce loans based on wisdom. The result is a dumbed-down industry that in most cases has lost its soul.

When an organization or its leaders begin to dish out responsibility without authority, it is a sign they have people whose integrity or competency they don't trust. That is a symptom of a company having outgrown the quality of its team, and that is the beginning of the end for them.

Ronald Reagan said, "Surround yourself with the best people you can find, delegate authority, and don't interfere."

Conclusion

This is a different kind of business and leadership book. The pages have spanned high-level leadership philosophy all the way to the daily mechanics of starting a business in your living room. That wide reach has sometimes made it difficult to message and brand this book properly. Is this a really great leadership book that any-one aspiring to lead well should read? Yes, I hope so. Is this a handbook for someone wanting to know how to start and run a small business? Yes, I hope so.

From the time we started this project until I typed these final words, my goal has been to share with you our playbook, what has caused our company to be successful beyond my wildest dreams by any measure. To share our playbook with transparency and ac-curacy required that the subject matter cover a wide range of top-ics. We have covered those topics in an effort to serve you as you grow your organization and/or grow within your organization.

I challenge you to become more of an EntreLeader every day from this day forth. I am sure that quality leadership skills are always valuable in our marketplace. I am sure that the passion of the entrepreneur is a skill that is always valuable in the market-place. I am sure that we have become so successful because God has chosen to bless us as we have worked really hard to become not just leaders, and not just entrepreneurs, but EntreLeaders. I am also sure that God will bless you on that same journey. Go make a difference in the way business is conducted!

EntreLeadership Bonus Online Resources

I had a lot more to say about building and running your business, but my editor told me to stop coming up with new great ideas—she cut me off! So just to spite her, we're going to keep adding to the conversation by putting a ton of great bonus resources online, including a few more full-length, exclusive chapters! These are available to download now, so come check us out online at www.entreleadership.com.

Bonus Chapters

- Money Doesn't Grow On Trees, It Grows Online: Designing a Web Strategy That Works

- Ad Nauseam: Curing Your Love-Hate Relationship with Advertising

- Reading the Numbers: Accounting Tells the Story of Your Business

Additional Worksheets and Information

- How to Develop a Mission Statement

- Sample Key Results Area (KRA) Document